Teacher Morale, Job Satisfaction
and Motivation

Linda Evans was a primary schoolteacher before her appointment as lecturer in education at Warwick University's Institute of Education. She is co-director of the institute's Teacher Development Research and Dissemination Unit. She has researched and published widely in the fields of teachers' attitudes to their work, school-based and school-centred initial teacher training, and teaching and learning in higher education.

Teacher Morale, Job Satisfaction and Motivation

LINDA EVANS

P·C·P

Paul Chapman
Publishing Ltd

Paul Chapman Publishing Ltd
A SAGE Publications Company
6 Bonhill Street
London EC2A 4PU

SAGE Publications Inc.
2455 Teller Road
Thousand Oaks, California 91320

SAGE Publications India Pvt Ltd
32, M-Block Market
Greater Kailash-I
New Delhi 110 048

British Cataloguing in Publication Data

Evans, Linda, 1945–
    Teacher morale, job satisfaction and motivation
    1. Teacher morale – Great Britain.   2. Teachers – Job
    satisfaction – Great Britain   I. Title
    372.1'1'00941

    ISBN 1 85396 418 2
    ISBN 1 85396 389 5 (pbk)

Typeset by Dorwyn Ltd, Rowlands Castle, Hampshire
Printed and bound in Great Britain by Athenaeum Press

A B C D E F   3 2 1 0 9 8

Contents

Introduction

Ask anyone in the street how to raise teacher morale and, almost certainly, s/he will suggest increasing pay. Ask what factors might have created dissatisfaction amongst teachers, and the answers from those who read newspapers or watch the television news will probably include references to discipline problems created by unruly pupils, class sizes, the introduction of the National Curriculum, lowered professional status and, most recently, changes to pension regulations. In fact, in January 1997, *The Times Educational Supplement* gave extensive coverage to teacher morale, motivation and satisfaction, which began with publication of a survey of teachers' attitudes it had conducted in 1996 revealing, it was reported, that 'Morale in Britain's staffrooms has hit rock bottom' (Sutcliffe, 1997, p. 1). This was attributed, in the main, to government reforms and conditions of service: 'Teachers are feeling disillusioned, demoralised and angry at being forced to carry out unpopular Government policies, while being constantly blamed for society's ills. They are fed up with having to teach children in ever larger classes, working in schools which are dilapidated, underfunded and overstretched' (*ibid.*). Yet, as someone who has spent many years as a primary schoolteacher and who has continued to work closely with teachers, I have long felt that factors such as these, whilst they reflect common-sense reasoning and are those identified by the media, by teachers' unions and, sometimes, by politicians, are not necessarily the most significant causes of negative attitudes amongst teachers.

It was my doubts that teacher morale, motivation and job satisfaction are as uncomplicated as these kinds of assumptions suggest that prompted me to undertake research in this area. This book presents, analyses and examines the management and policy implications of the findings of that research – a five-year composite study of attitudes towards their work of 19 primary schoolteachers in the UK.

Consistent with other work in the field (which, very broadly, is that of applied social psychology), my collective categorisation of morale, job satisfaction and motivation is as attitudes, or more specifically in the context of my research, as job-related attitudes. Yet, as concepts these specific attitudes are, in this field of study, unclearly defined. Referring to his own experiences as a researcher in this field, Vroom (1964, p. 277) outlines the difficulties this has posed:

> There are some advantages to be gained by the use of a relatively simple and basic set of concepts to describe and analyze the complex phenomena of inter-est to the applied psychologist. Applied psychologists have rarely been precise or systematic in their language. It is not uncommon to find almost as many terms for a referent as there are investigators concerned with it. These terms are usually borrowed from 'everyday' language and are seldom adequately de-fined or systematically applied to other concepts. As a result, the relationship between the work of different investigators is often obscured and the lines of progress are difficult to discern.

In this book I have attempted to tackle the conceptual problems of work-ing in this area by examining the concepts of, and defining, job satisfac-tion, morale and motivation. These conceptual analyses are presented in the first three chapters which, together with Chapter 4's outline of the design of the research upon which the book is based, constitute Part I: 'Concepts and contexts'.

Part II of the book focuses on my research findings. Throughout six chapters it unfolds the natures of teacher morale, motivation and job satisfaction by revealing evidence of what influences them. These chap-ters draw upon comments made by teachers during research interviews and incorporate illustrative quotes that help to convey the realities of their working lives and, in particular, the effects of specific circumstances, situations and events upon their job-related attitudes. To preserve ano-nymity, fictitious names are used throughout. Chapter 5 presents a case study of what was reputed to be a 'low morale' primary school, and includes examination of how and to what extent its teachers were affected by prevailing circumstances and situations. Chapters 6, 7 and 8 each focus upon the cases of three teachers who shared professional-related charac-teristics or similar experiences which influenced their job-related atti-tudes. These chapters are predominantly descriptive rather than analytical. Analysis occurs later. This is because to incorporate analysis into these three chapters would involve making comparisons, which would necessitate drawing on material included in later chapters and pre-empting the discussion in them.

Chapter 9 examines the importance of school leadership as a determi-nant of teachers' attitudes and identifies key attitudes-influencing leader-ship features. Chapter 10 draws together all the research evidence examined in earlier chapters to develop an overall understanding of what it is that determines whether or not teachers are happy at work. This chapter elucidates the nature of teacher morale, motivation and job satisfaction.

At the end of each of the chapters in Part II is a section, 'A management perspective: issues for consideration'. These sections are intended for use by school managers or those involved in management training provision. It is important to emphasise, however, that although this book incorporates a management perspective, its focus throughout is on presenting the perceptions, views and attitudes of the 'managed'. In this respect it represents a very valuable but much neglected perspective in work in the field of school management: an 'other side of the coin' view. In my research, headteachers' views and attitudes were not sought and they are not presented here. The reasoning and motives of headteachers are not scrutinised, since it is not within the remit of this book to try to understand why they did things. My concern is with teachers' perceptions, which include those of characteristics of their headteachers and of those aspects and features of schools' leadership which were important to them. Attitudes are based upon subjective interpretations of reality.

The two chapters in Part III relate to the policy implications of my findings. Chapter 11 focuses on school-level policy and presents ideas for approaches to school management and supportive organisational structures that are intended to foster and sustain high levels of staff morale, job satisfaction and motivation. In Chapter 12 wider policy implications and issues are examined, including those relating to headteacher accountability and to teachers' professional culture.

Transcending the specificity of the individual cases I present and analyse are important issues with wider applicability. These issues are relevant both to the study of, and to policy-making which relates to, areas such as teachers' working lives, schools as workplaces, teacher development, organisational behaviour and institutional staff management. Such areas are clearly not UK-specific, nor are they necessarily education-specific nor, within education contexts, subject or phase-specific. This book contributes much, at home and abroad, to work in these fields.

Acknowledgements

I would like to thank my colleague, Ann Lewis, for her very helpful comments on earlier drafts of some of the material in this book.

Thanks also to my husband, Glyn, for his help in putting the manuscript together.

Part I

Concepts and contexts

1

Job satisfaction

Introduction

Since it was pioneered in the 1930s, the study of employees' attitudes to their work and, more specifically, of job satisfaction, has contributed a substantial body of knowledge about what makes people happy or unhappy with their jobs. Locke (1969), for example, estimates that, as of 1955, over 2,000 articles on the subject of job satisfaction had been published and that, by 1969, the total may have exceeded 4,000. Whilst much of the work in this field has focused on employees in general, some has been related to specific occupations, and a small proportion of this to teachers (see, for example, Galloway *et al.*, 1985; Lowther *et al.*, 1985; Farrugia, 1986; Shreeve *et al.*, 1986; Poppleton, 1988; Nias, 1980; 1989). Opinions differ on the width of the applicability of research findings and theories relating to job satisfaction. In particular, teaching has sometimes been regarded as atypical when compared with occupations of similar professional status, and Herzberg's (1968) dual factor theory on job satisfaction, which was generated from research on US engineers and accountants, has been tested in education contexts (Nias, 1981; Young and Davis, 1983; Farrugia, 1986).

There are, however, conceptual problems related to researching teachers' job satisfaction. These emanate from a lack both of clarity and of consensus about what is meant by 'job satisfaction'. Nias (1989, p. 83) refers to these problems, and attributes them, in part, to neglect of the study of teachers' job satisfaction. This explanation lacks plausibility though, because – although teacher-specific job satisfaction may be under-researched – job satisfaction as a general issue has not been. And whilst a case may be made for influential factors being job or profession specific, the universal applicability of the concept of job satisfaction precludes dependence upon job-specific research for conceptual analyses and clarification.

This chapter addresses the conceptual problems associated with the study of job satisfaction. It examines the concept by critical review of pertinent literature and by analysis of the findings of my own research, and it outlines research findings that have identified determinants of job satisfaction. Analysis of my research data reveals a perspective on, and informs a conceptualisation of, job satisfaction on which previous work has evidently failed to focus sufficiently sharply. In this chapter I highlight methodological issues arising out of problems of construct validity which are revealed by the analysis and reconceptualisation of job satisfaction, and I present a model of the job fulfilment process.

Identifying the problems

The essential, underlying conceptual problem associated with researching job satisfaction is that there is no agreed definition of the term. A range of definitions is evident, and the disparity amongst these relates both to the depths of analyses of the concept and to interpretation of it. Moreover, not all of what are passed off as definitions *are* actual definitions. Some are merely descriptions of possible consequences of job satisfaction, or lists of its characteristics. Mumford (1972, p. 4), commenting that 'job satisfaction is a nebulous concept', expresses the nature of the difficulties facing researchers in this field. Drawing on the example of Vroom's definition, which, she suggests, is inadequate because it provides no information about the components of job satisfaction, she continues (Mumford, 1972, pp. 4, 67):

> The literature on job satisfaction is of equally small help in providing us with an understanding of the concept. There appear to be no all-embracing theories of job satisfaction and work on the subject has been focussed on certain factors thought to be related to feelings of satisfaction or dissatisfaction at work. Few studies take a wide and simultaneous survey of a large number of related variables. Job dissatisfaction has been found easier to identify and measure than job satisfaction. . . .
>
> Two points emerge clearly from the work that has been done up to date. One is the elusiveness of the concept of job satisfaction. What does it mean? . . . The second is the complexity of the whole subject.

Over 25 years after Mumford made these observations, there has been little change. Indeed, a general neglect of concern for conceptual clarity seems to have pervaded more recent work in this field, prompting Nias to comment in 1989 (p. 83): 'I encountered several difficulties . . . The first was a conceptual one. As a topic for enquiry, teachers' job satisfaction has been largely ignored. Partly in consequence, it lacks clarity of definition.' In order to appreciate the points that both Nias and Mumford make, and in order to attempt to uncover what job satisfaction is, it is worth comparing a few of the definitions and interpretations that are available.

What is job satisfaction?

Schaffer's (1953, p. 3) interpretation of job satisfaction is one of individuals' needs fulfilment: 'Overall job satisfaction will vary directly with the extent to which those needs of an individual which can be satisfied in a job are actually satisfied; the stronger the need, the more closely will job satisfaction depend on its fulfilment.' Sergiovanni (1968) also supports the personal needs fulfilment interpretation and draws attention to the evident link between Herzberg's (1968) motivation-hygiene theory, which I examine below, and Maslow's (1954) theory of human motivation (see Chapter 3), based upon a hierarchy of human needs.

Lawler (1973) focuses on expectations rather than needs: 'Overall job satisfaction is determined by the difference between all those things a person feels he *should* receive from his job and all those things he actually *does* receive.' Locke (1969), however, dismisses both needs and expectations in favour of values. He defines job satisfaction (*ibid.*, p. 316) as 'the pleasurable emotional state resulting from the appraisal of one's job as achieving or facilitating the achievement of one's job values', whilst Nias (1989) accepts Lortie's (1975) interpretation of job satisfaction as a summary of the total rewards experienced (in teaching).

Kalleberg (1977, p. 126) identifies both job rewards and job values as determinants of job satisfaction, which he defines as 'an overall affective orientation on the part of individuals toward work roles which they are presently occupying'. Katzell (1964, p. 348) adopts the all-encompassing term 'frame of reference', to include 'values', 'goals', 'desires' or 'interests'. He refers to 'job features which a person perceives as attractive or repellent, desirable or undesirable', and interprets job satisfaction as 'a response to the activities, events and conditions which compose the job'. Similarly, Rosen and Rosen (1955, p. 305) use the rather generic term 'desires'.

Clearly, then, there is no real consensus about what job satisfaction is. The source of much of the lack of agreement lies with the hierarchical positions, as determinants of job satisfaction, of what Katzell (1964) identifies as the different 'frames of reference'. It arises over whether, for example, needs determine values or values determine needs. The repercussions of this, however, are far-reaching since they have a potential impact upon any study that aims to investigate what influences job satisfaction.

Threats to construct validity

The second problem associated with researching job satisfaction is a methodological problem which stems from the fundamental conceptual one. This is the problem of construct validity. Construct validity involves consensual acceptance and understanding of specific terms. It is threatened when researchers and subjects do not share the same interpretation and understanding of key constructs such as, in this context, job satisfaction. Locke (1969) argues the need to understand and define job satisfaction in order to be able to measure and study it yet, despite the plethora of studies in this field, there have been relatively few definitions or attempts at conceptualisation. Even Herzberg, whose two-factor theory (1968) is generally regarded as a seminal study which has prompted and influenced much work in this field, does not provide a definition of job satisfaction.

Because there is lack of agreement over what is meant by job satisfaction, problems of construct validity potentially arise when researchers fail to provide a clear indication of what they mean by the term, or when they fail to clarify how research subjects interpret the concept. However, research in this field is subject to an additional threat to construct validity, arising out of the ambiguity of the concept of job satisfaction.

The ambiguity of job satisfaction: a need for reconceptualisation

Essentially, the conceptual problem arising out of the ambiguity of the term 'job satisfaction' stems from the application of the word 'satisfaction' to something which results from circumstances which are satisfactory or/ and from circumstances which are satisfying. There is a clear distinction between things which are satisfactory and those which are satisfying, which can be illustrated by contrasting the meaning attached to customer satisfaction, for example, with the satisfaction of having conquered Everest. Yet nowhere in reports and analyses of work on job satisfaction have I found explicit reference to this distinction.

The distinction is implicit in Herzberg's (1968) motivation-hygiene or two-factor theory. Grounded in research into the job satisfaction of accountants and engineers in Pittsburgh, Herzberg's theory distinguishes between two sets of factors: motivation factors and hygiene factors. Five specific motivation factors are identified: achievement, recognition (for achievement), responsibility, advancement and the work itself. These, Herzberg argues, are the factors that have the potential to provide job satisfaction. Their absence does not create dissatisfaction but a state of 'no satisfaction'. The other set of factors, which Herzberg calls hygiene factors, and which include salary, supervision and interpersonal relations, are capable of creating dissatisfaction but are not capable of satisfying – except, as Herzberg (*ibid.*, pp. 75–6) points out, in the cases of a minority of individuals who are 'hygiene seekers' –

> In summary, two essential findings were derived from this study. First, the factors involved in producing job satisfaction were separate and distinct from the factors that led to job dissatisfaction. Since separate factors needed to be considered, depending on whether job satisfaction or job dissatisfaction was involved, if followed that these two feelings were not the obverse of each other. Thus, the opposite of job satisfaction would not be job dissatisfaction, but rather *no* job satisfaction; similarly, the opposite of job dissatisfaction is *no* job dissatisfaction, not satisfaction with one's job. The fact that job satisfaction is made up of two unipolar traits is not unique, but it remains a difficult concept to grasp.

Herzberg's hygiene factors are those which would generally influence how satisfactory a job is considered, whereas motivation factors relate more to the extent to which work is satisfying. There is no evidence that Herzberg acknowledges this. Indeed, his theory emphasises what has often been regarded as a revelation; that the opposite of satisfaction is not dissatisfaction but 'no satisfaction', and that the opposite of dissatisfaction is not satisfaction but 'no dissatisfaction'. The issue is, I believe, much more simple and straightforward. Since one category relates to factors which are capable only of making things satisfactory, and the other to factors which are capable of satisfying, then, clearly, they *are* distinct and separate. But realisation of this should not form the basis of a theory; it merely follows on from awareness that there are separate but related components of what has tended to be regarded as a single concept.

The distinction is similarly implicit where there are identified other categories of job satisfaction factors than those which Herzberg uses. Farrugia (1986), for example, uses Herzberg's categories of 'extrinsic' and 'intrinsic' factors, and adds a third, 'interjacent' factors. Nias (1981) refers to 'satisfiers', 'dissatisfies' and 'negative satisfiers', and Lortie (1975, p. 101) identifies 'psychic', 'ancillary' and 'extrinsic' rewards. However, since in all cases all the categories are identified as components of job satisfaction, which, as a result, becomes an umbrella term, there is no evidence that the basis of the distinction is recognised.

While some writers evidently interpret job satisfaction as encompassing both what is satisfying and what is satisfactory, there are those whose interpretation of the term is apparently narrower and concerned only with what is satisfying. There is, in fact, evidence that Herzberg (1968) falls into this category, since his theory emphasises that dissatisfaction is not the same as no satisfaction. This suggests that he considers 'dissatisfaction' to mean 'unsatisfactory', which does not fall within the parameters of what he relates to job satisfaction, and that he considers 'no satisfaction' to mean 'lacking the capacity to be satisfying'.

In some cases, interpretations of job satisfaction as being concerned only with what is satisfying, and excluding that which is satisfactory only, are evident in the selections of specific job satisfaction factors identified. Chapman (1983), for example, identifies 'recognition by administration and supervision' and 'achievement in learning new things' as significant influential factors. Sergiovanni (1968, p. 264) similarly identifies 'opportunities for success', 'achievement' and 'responsibility' as 'the really potent factors . . . the real determiners of job satisfaction'.

There is, of course, a danger in drawing inferences about interpretations of job satisfaction by examining the influential factors identified. The danger lies in the unreliability of making assumptions about what is either satisfying or satisfactory to others. Nevertheless, it is not unreasonable to assume that writers who identify job satisfaction factors such as 'feeling competent', 'being able to meet a challenge' or 'feeling that I've "reached" a child' hold an interpretation of job satisfaction which is different from, and narrower than, that of writers who include factors such as 'physical setting' or 'long holidays'.

One problem with much work on teachers' job satisfaction is that, by referring to satisfaction without defining the term, it fails to make clear whether what is reported are satisfying or satisfactory elements of work. Another problem is that, since the simple ambiguity of the word 'satisfaction' is overlooked when interpretations or definitions of job satisfaction are offered, they fail to incorporate recognition of its duality and there is a danger that the research process of data collection, analysis and presentation is, throughout, inconsistent with the definition used.

Whilst it has made an invaluable contribution to the study of teachers' job satisfaction, the work of Jennifer Nias (1981; 1989) is an example of work which is flawed in this way. Nias (1989, p. 84) reports how, through interviews, she sought information from teachers about their job satisfaction: 'In the first [set of interviews] I simply enquired: What do you like about your job? What plans do you have for the future, and why? In the second, I used these questions, but also asked those who said they liked their jobs to tell me half a dozen things they enjoyed doing and to give their reasons.'

Threats to construct validity arise out of the inconsistency between how Nias defines job satisfaction (*ibid.*, p. 83) and how she asks interviewees about their job satisfaction. Each involves different terminology. Her definition focuses on the 'rewards of teaching'. Indeed, she interprets teachers' self-reports of personally rewarding aspects of their work as being synonymous with chief sources of job satisfaction (*ibid.*). Her interview questions, however, focus on 'enjoyable' and 'likeable' aspects of teaching and the implication of her own report of her interviewing is that she did not use the terms 'rewards' or 'rewarding'. Yet Nias's interviewees may not have shared her interpretation that 'likeable' or 'enjoyable' are synonymous with 'rewarding'. Her claim (*ibid.*, p. 84) that the questions used in her interviews were consistent with what she identifies as her 'loose definition' of job satisfaction is highly questionable.

Nias's (1981; 1989) reports of how she applied Herzberg's (1968) two-factor theory to her own research provide a further illustration of the problems arising out of the lack of recognition of the ambiguity of the term 'job satisfaction'. She identifies (1989, pp. 88–9) as 'satisfiers' factors which may be considered to be intrinsic to the job, which are concerned with the work itself and with opportunities for personal achievement, recognition and growth. These findings, she suggests, corroborate Herzberg's findings. She then presents findings which, she suggests (*ibid.*, p. 89), are inconsistent with Herzberg's theory:

> However, nearly a quarter of these teachers also derived satisfaction from extrinsic factors. Ten liked the hours and the holidays, two thought they did not

have to work very hard, one enjoyed the physical setting provided by his new open-plan building. Twelve (all women) enjoyed the comradeship they found in staffrooms.

What is more likely than Nias's findings failing to corroborate Herzberg's, though, is that her and Herzberg's interpretations of the concept of job satisfaction differ, and that those of Nias's teachers who reported deriving satisfaction from extrinsic factors were actually satisfied *with* them, rather than *by* them.

Since Herzberg fails to make explicit his interpretation of job satisfaction it is only possible to make assumptions. I have already suggested that he interprets it narrowly, confining job satisfaction to involving satisfying elements of work. His exclusion of extrinsic factors, such as salary and working conditions, as satisfiers is consistent with this assumption. Those specific extrinsic factors which Nias (1989, p. 89) identifies as satisfiers would have been excluded by Herzberg because they fall outside the parameters of what, to him, job satisfaction is all about. They may be satisfactory (or unsatisfactory) to teachers but they are unlikely to be capable of satisfying. Nias's interpretation of job satisfaction is evidently wider, though, and incorporates both satisfactory and satisfying elements. The extrinsic factors which she identifies as satisfiers lie within the parameters of her interpretation of the concept. Thus, what are interpreted as, and presented by, one researcher as research findings which fail to corroborate those of another researcher may, in fact, be nothing of the sort. Herzberg's theory is challenged and its applicability to education settings questioned when, all the time, the lack of agreement is much more likely to be conceptual. If this is, indeed, the case, then the misconception has its origins first in the failure (on Herzberg's part) to define the key concept under study and, secondly, in failure to recognise the ambiguity associated with the concept.

Testing the ambiguity issue
It was in the course of the research upon which this book focuses that I was able to test the potential implications of the ambiguity issue. My research design, which is described in Chapter 4, involved interviews with 19 English teachers employed in four different primary schools. These interviews were carried out in batches, as four separate studies.

In the first batch of interviews, in which I asked teachers to identify those aspects of their work which were sources of satisfaction, some responses focused exclusively on the kinds of factors which fall into Herzberg's (1968) 'intrinsic' category: working with children and watching them progress, organising in-service training days for colleagues, feeling that individual children's learning needs were being accommodated. Some also included references to 'hygiene' (*ibid.*)

factors, such as internal decor of the school, room size, resources and proximity of the school to home.

By the time of the second batch of interviews, over a year later, I had analysed the first set of data, given extensive consideration to the possible reasons why some of my findings were inconsistent with those of Herzberg (*ibid.*), and was in a position to be able to test what had emerged as a possible explanation for the discrepancy, not only between Herzberg's findings and mine but also between those of other researchers. In order to test the ambiguity issue, I altered the key terminology used in my questioning and asked interviewees two separate questions relating to satisfaction. I first asked them to identify sources of fulfilment and, secondly, to identify aspects of their work which could not be categorised as fulfilling, but which were satisfactory. I summed up this second question by saying: 'Tell me about the things that you are satisfied *with* but not satisfied *by*.' Finally, I asked teachers to focus on unfulfilling and unsatisfactory aspects of their work.

Without exception, this resulted in the identification of two separate, distinct categories of factors, broadly consistent with Herzberg's (*ibid.*) two factors, but which some teachers in the first batch of interviews had indiscriminately identified as sources of satisfaction.

The second batch of interviews related to the second of my four studies, described in Chapter 4, and used a different sample from that upon which the first interviews focused. However, of greater significance with respect to the implications of the ambiguity issue are data collected during follow-up interviews with the same sample of teachers as was used in the first study. These follow-up interviews, with the teachers of Rockville County Primary School, and which incorporated the revised form of questioning, resulted in specific teachers distinguishing between factors which they identified as fulfilling and those which they identified as satisfactory, but which, in their initial interviews, had all been reported indiscriminately as sources of satisfaction.

Addressing the problems

Evidence from my own research indicates that what is needed is either a definition of job satisfaction which incorporates and clarifies the ambiguity of the term, or a bifurcation of both terminology and definition.

Reconceptualising and redefining

My findings, presented in later chapters throughout this book, revealed heterogeneity amongst teachers with respect to what they found satisfying and/or satisfactory, but the key distinguishing constituent, common to all, was whether or not a sense of personal achievement was associated with the factors. Thus, good staff relations may be satisfactory to some teachers but would only be satisfying to individuals who felt they had contributed towards achieving them.

To clarify the distinction between factors from which individuals may or may not derive a sense of achievement, I suggest two distinct terms: *job comfort* and *job fulfilment*.

Job comfort relates to the extent to which the individual feels comfortable in his/her job. More specifically, it is about the extent to which the individual is satisfied with, but not by, the conditions and circumstances of his/her job. In his ethnographic study of the working life of Ed Bell, an American school principal, Wolcott (1973, p. 293) includes, in what he identifies as topics which 'represent recurring themes whenever . . . teachers discussed their school', reference to 'a "comfortable" school':

> I have been real comfortable at this school in that I've been allowed to do as I wanted . . .
> One of Ed's real strong points is making almost anyone who comes in here feel comfortable and feel relaxed and feel wanted and needed.
> I had a real comfortable feeling here last year, even though it was my beginning year. The cooperation was extremely high. I think it's probably even more so this year.
>
> *(Ibid.)*

It is factors such as these, identified by Wolcott's teachers, and other factors that constitute what I identify as job comfort factors.

Job fulfilment, on the other hand, involves the individual's assessing how well s/he performs her/his job. This self-assessment may be influenced by the assessments of others, such as, in the case of teachers, headteachers, colleagues and parents but, essentially, it is a 'return' on job performance. In this sense, job fulfilment is a reciprocation. It is dependent upon the perception of having achieved something which is considered sufficiently worth while to enhance job-related, achievement-related, self-esteem. I define job fulfilment as *'a state of mind encompassing all the feelings determined by the extent of the sense of personal achievement which the individual attributes to his/her performance of those components of his/her job which s/he values'*.

I suggest that re-examination of Herzberg's (1968) two-factor theory reveals that all his motivation factors are tributaries of what he includes as one of his motivation factors: achievement. Some, such as 'the work itself', are contributory and some, such as 'recognition (for achievement)', are reinforcers, but the essential point is that they may all be reduced to one single factor which is the key constituent of what I refer to as job fulfilment and what Herzberg (*ibid.*) labels 'job satisfaction'. To be more accurate, job fulfilment is ultimately about individuals' self-perceptions of achievement, rather than more objective evaluations of whether or not achievement has occurred.

Both job comfort and job fulfilment are determined by the individual's evaluation of the diverse conditions and circumstances into which her/his job may be compartmentalised. Where these conditions and circumstances are not perceived by the individual as the results of his/her achievement, job comfort applies and, depending upon how satisfactory individual conditions and circumstances are perceived to be, it ranges from high to low. However, where the individual perceives him/herself to have influenced, or effected, specific job-related conditions and circumstances which s/he values and perceives as important, job fulfilment applies. As with job comfort, job fulfilment may range from high to low.

Both job comfort and job fulfilment are components of job satisfaction, which I interpret as *'a state of mind encompassing all those feelings determined by the extent to which the individual perceives her/his job-related needs to be being met'*. Moreover, I share Sergiovanni's (1968) view that there appears to be a link between Maslow's (1954) theory of human motivation (see Chapter 3), which distinguishes between lower-order and higher-order needs, and Herzberg's (1968) theory. This link requires further exploration and testing but a tentative suggestion, and one which incorporates my own reappraisal of Herzberg's theory, is that what I identify as 'job comfort' concerns the extent of individuals' lower-order, job-related needs fulfilment and that 'job fulfilment', as I interpret it, relates to the extent of individuals' higher-order, job-related needs fulfilment.

It is not enough, though, for researchers to clarify their own conceptualisations of key concepts being examined; in this case, job satisfaction. If construct validity is to be achieved in the research certain measures need to be applied, and in Chapter 4 I outline ways of incorporating this into data collection and analysis.

The rationale for studying job satisfaction is that it is intended to shed light on what influences how people feel about their work, so that positive job-related attitudes may be cultivated. In order to achieve this, it is important to understand and to clarify what job satisfaction is, and the first part of this chapter has been directed towards this. However, even greater elucidation is provided through examining not only the conceptual parameters, and the principles underlying application, of job satisfaction but also the *process* involved in attaining it. Informed by analyses of the findings both of my research into primary schoolteachers' job satisfaction, which is the focus of this book, and of my research into the job satisfaction of university tutors (see Evans and Abbott, 1998), I have developed a model of the process whereby individuals attain job fulfilment. Relating it to teachers, I present and explain this model below.

The job fulfilment process

The process whereby job fulfilment is achieved by individuals is represented in my model, illustrated in Figure 1.1. Eight stages are identified. According to my interpretation of job fulfilment, all eight stages are essential components of the process. These stages reflect the subjectivity of the individual experiencing job fulfilment and relate to her/his actions without necessarily reflecting general consensus and without necessarily incorporating objectivity. Below, I explain the job fulfilment process, stage by stage, as represented by my model.

Explaining the process

Stage 1
The first stage is the individual's awareness of an imperfect situation in relation to his/her job. The imperfection reflects the individual's perception, which may not necessarily be shared by others. Perceived imperfections may range in magnitude, from being tiny to being enormous, but it is likely that their perceived magnitude will, under certain circumstances, correlate with the magnitude of the job fulfilment experienced at the end of the process.

As a basic component of the job fulfilment process, individuals' perceived job-related imperfections need not and, indeed, often do not, represent obvious deficiencies. My interpretation of an imperfect situation, in the context of its being a catalyst for the job fulfilment process, is simply a situation in relation to which some measure of improvement, no matter how small, is desirable. Such imperfections may be so slight that they would scarcely be identified as sources of dissatisfaction. Often they will reflect individuals' perfectionism, or self-imposed high standards for themselves. The teacher who feels that it is essential, for example, to hear every pupil read at least once a week will identify as an imperfection any situation or circumstance that prevents her/him from doing so. Most commonly, though, the imperfections which are the basis of the job fulfilment process are more general and pervasive, and are taken for granted since they represent constituents of the work itself, provide its justification and determine its nature. Teaching, for example, has as its rationale the 'imperfections' reflected by pupils' inadequate knowledge, understanding and skills. In this sense, all work represents a response to an unsatisfactory situation.

Imperfect situations may be within, or outside, the individual's control, but it is only those upon which the individual may exercise some degree of control which may spark off the job fulfilment process.

Stage 2
Stage 2 involves the individual's formulating a strategy for removing or reducing the perceived imperfection, in order to bring about an

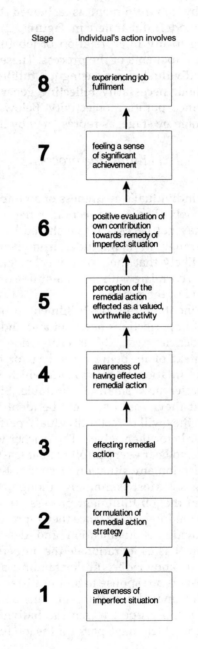

Figure 1.1   Model of the job fulfilment process in individuals

improvement in his/her job-related situation. Strategies, as I interpret the term in this context, may range in magnitude from, for example, a passing thought which leads to an idea for a slight change to a way of working, to a carefully constructed school improvement plan, or a personal career development plan. This stage does not involve putting the remedial strategy into effect; it merely involves formulating it. It is a conceptual stage. It involves nothing more than recognition of what would remove, or reduce, the imperfections in a specific job-related situation. Remedial strategies need not reflect the individual's own, original, ideas nor represent her/his own creative input, but creativity and originality at this stage greatly influence the extent to which job fulfilment is experienced.

Stage 3
This stage involves effecting the remedial strategy, without which job fulfilment in relation to it will not occur.

A successfully implemented remedial strategy points the individual towards the path which leads to job fulfilment. It is important to re-emphasise, however, the taken-for-granted element in the job fulfilment process, to which I have referred in my explanation of stage 1. The implications of this are that the formulation and the putting into effect of what I refer to as remedial action, or a remedial strategy, need not necessarily be, and often are not, anything other than what is accepted and carried out as part of the work itself. Clearly, if imperfect situations constitute the rationale and the very need for the work, then, by the same token, the work itself *is* in this sense the remedial action. If, for example, pupils' inadequate knowledge is the pervasive imperfect situation which is the underlying rationale for schooling, then the job of teaching them is, in its entirety, the remedial action strategy. Thus, every time teachers teach they are effecting, in a taken-for-granted way, remedial action in response to a prevailing imperfect situation, and their formulation of a remedial strategy, which precedes their effecting it, is their choice of teaching methods and classroom organisational strategies.

Stage 4
Stage 4 is the individual's awareness of having effected remedial action. This awareness is essential to the job fulfilment process, yet it is by no means automatic that individuals who have formulated and effected a strategy for remedying an imperfect job-related situation will be aware of having done so. Since much of this occurs in the taken-for-granted way I have described, by teachers simply carrying out their day-to-day work which, in itself, constitutes remedial action, it may often go unrecognised by them. Teachers may not always be aware of the extent to which they have helped children, nor of the influence which they may

have had upon their lives. Pupils' responses to learning activities may be deceptive or misleading, resulting in even experienced teachers not only overestimating but also underestimating their success. Unless there is an awareness of having successfully effected remedial action, job fulfilment, in relation to the remedial action in question, will not occur. One cannot experience fulfilment from something unless one is aware that it has happened.

Stage 5
This is a key stage in the process. It involves the individual's perceiving the remedial action which has been effected as a valued, worthwhile activity. Without this perception job fulfilment, as I interpret it, will not occur. This perception is the key distinction between job fulfilment and job comfort. The extent to which a specific activity has the potential to fulfil, rather than merely to be considered satisfactory, is determined by the status, significance and value attached to it by the individual. The subjectivity of the value judgement gives rise to a diversity which is reflected by differences in individuals' sources of job fulfilment. The higher the status and value afforded by an individual to an activity, the greater will be its potential as a source of job fulfilment. Individuals will not be able to derive job fulfilment from an activity or task or component of their work to which they afford little value. Differentiation in relation to teachers' task-valuing may, for example, result in some teachers deriving fulfilment from participation in curriculum development, policy- and decision-making, while others rate class teaching much higher.

The reasons underlying individuals' differential, hierarchical, ranking of the values attached to the components of their work are complex. Perceptions of value may be influenced by many factors, such as professional cultural norms and attitudes, prevailing and changing trends, the views of respected colleagues and institutional ethos. They are also influenced by biographical factors and individuals' experiences, which may serve to reaffirm or to alter preconceptions or/and long-held attitudes. The value afforded by individuals to specific tasks, or components of work, clearly does not remain static but is liable to fluctuate in response to individuals' changed, and changing, circumstances and situations in their lives. In this sense, the status of a particular activity or task is somewhat precarious since this relativity aspect leaves it susceptible to displacement or alteration. This is particularly likely to occur alongside individuals' professional development and career progression. The dynamism of the hierarchical task- or work component-ranking process is influenced by the changing perceptions and reprioritisation which are an inevitable consequence of personal and professional growth and by the extent to which goals are achieved and ambitions fulfilled. Thwarted ambitions in one area may focus attention more narrowly on other areas of the work and elevate their status. Conversely, career progression may bring increased responsibilities and wider experiences, in relation to which what was once perceived as a valued, worthwhile activity may be relegated to the status of a routine chore. Thus, for example, the managerial responsibilities of a deputy headship may displace the value formerly afforded co-ordination of the school's mathematics teaching. Similarly, individuals' non-work lives are also influential on this dynamic process. Insights as parents may, for example, change perceptions of task values (see Sikes, 1997).

Stage 6

Stage 6 involves the individual attributing some measure of success in remedying the imperfect situation in question to the contribution s/he has made. Without this attribution of success job fulfilment cannot occur. It is important to emphasize that the degree of success attributed may be wide ranging, and that job fulfilment is not necessarily dependent upon perceptions of total success. Depending upon factors such as the standards set for her/himself by the individual (that is, the extent of her/his propensity for perfectionism and the circumstances surrounding each case), the job fulfilment process may be unimpeded even if only a small measure of success is recognised at this stage. In cases of particularly challenging situations, for example where much imperfection was acknowledged at stage 1, what is perceived as partially effective remedial action may lead to job fulfilment, particularly if the remedial action is considered to be part of a repetitive process of erosion or as a contribution towards a larger, cohesive team effort.

Individuals' positive evaluations of their contributions towards remedying imperfect situations may be influenced by, or based entirely upon, the views of others whom they recognise as competent assessors of their performance, such as headteachers, colleagues or LEA advisers. Recognition of this kind serves as an important reinforcer of positive self-assessment. It is, however, important to emphasise that, whilst the views of others may be influential, they are not essential to individuals' self-assessments. Consistent with the focus on individuals' subjectivity which is reflected in all stages of the job fulfilment process outlined in my model, stage 6 represents the individual's own, subjective, positive evaluation of her/his contribution towards the remedy of what s/he perceives as an imperfect situation. Precisely how this positive evaluation is formulated is unimportant. In many cases it will reflect a consensual view, and it is likely to be strengthened if the individual knows it to be supported by others but, essentially, it reflects the individual's view only even if this may be generally considered to be misguided. In the job fulfilment process, misperceptions at stage 6 are as valid as what may be considered to be more objectively accurate perceptions. The teacher who holds firm to the view that s/he is the best teacher in the school remains well on track for experiencing job fulfilment even though colleagues, parents and pupils consider her/him to be the worst teacher they have ever encountered.

Stage 7

In most cases, stage 7 is an inevitable stage which occurs automatically as a result of the previous six stages having been achieved. In some cases, however, the job fulfilment process is arrested once stage 6 has been reached, because there are some circumstances which prevent the individual feeling a sense of significant achievement, despite the awareness of having made an effective contribution in relation to a valued component of his/her job.

One of the factors underlying individuals' failure to feel a sense of significant achievement in their work is the relativity factor, which concerns the relative consideration the individual affords to his/her work or to aspects of it alongside other, competing priorities. Essentially, what this means is that, although it may be valued by the individual within the sphere of his/her *working* life, the job component to which s/he considers her/himself to have made an effective contribution is not valued *enough*, because work itself, in relation to other aspects of the individual's life, is not ranked sufficiently highly.

Stage 8

Stage 8 is the final stage in the process – that involving the individual experiencing job fulfilment as I define it earlier in this chapter. As my definition makes clear, individuals' job fulfilment does not necessarily apply to their work in its entirety, but may be specific to certain components of it or even, within these job components, to specific activities and/or tasks. Overall job fulfilment depends upon what is effectively an unconsciously applied equation or calculation which balances fulfilling activities against those which are not fulfilling, at any one point of time, and which incorporates consideration of other, non-work-related circumstances and situations, bringing in the relativity factor.

What influences job satisfaction?

The problems involved in researching in this field, resulting from the general neglect of conceptual clarity, make it very difficult to make meaningful examinations of what have been found to be determinants of job satisfaction. In cases where researchers do not make explicit how they define, or even interpret, job satisfaction, or where insufficient information is provided on the methods of data collection and, in particular, on the terminology employed, there is no certainty whether the investigation focused on job fulfilment or job comfort, or both.

Allowing for these limitations, it is nevertheless possible to identify five levels of elucidation in understanding what affects teachers' job satisfaction – even if it is not always possible to apply distinctions that allow job comfort and job fulfilment factors to be categorised separately.

The first level has, as its basis, conventional wisdom and common-sense, but oversimplistic, reasoning. It is exemplified by arguments that are typically promulgated by the media, such as those which equate job satisfaction with centrally initiated policy and conditions of service, including pay. Such arguments evidently assume much homogeneity amongst teachers and are, therefore, highly generalisable.

The second level is based upon empirical research, but its underlying analysis is inadequately developed. It moves partly away from an homogeneity basis towards typologies and trends, exemplified by studies which reveal teachers' seniority, or headteachers' leadership styles, or schools' organisational climates to be key determinants of job satisfaction or morale. Lowther *et al.*'s (1985, p. 520) study of the influence on job satisfaction of age is illustrative of this level, and is summarised as follows: 'The following results are presented: (1) job satisfaction increases with age, (2) job values remain constant with age, (3) job rewards increase with age, and (4) the major determinants of job satisfaction are intrinsic to teaching for younger teachers and extrinsic for older teachers.'

The third level is a subtly enhanced variant of the second, incorporating greater depth and sophistication in its analysis, and focusing on narrower, more specific typologies which have emerged from empirical data. This level moves towards awareness of the significance both of teachers' heterogeneity and of match or mismatch between teachers and the contexts in which they work. It is exemplified by studies such as that of Vancouver and Schmitt (1991, p. 348), which supports the 'contention that organizational goals are an important point of comparison between individuals and the organizations in which they find themselves', and which 'confirms the idea that person–organization fit relates to positive employee attitudes and intentions' (*ibid.*, p. 350). Other examples of this level of analysis and understanding are Galloway *et al.*'s study (1985), which makes comparisons between groups of teachers, and Shreeve *et al.*'s (1986) study revealing recognition to be an important influence on job satisfaction.

At the fourth level are studies such as those of Schaffer (1953), Sergiovanni (1968), Locke (1969), Lawler (1973) and Kalleberg (1977), which are not necessarily education specific. This is a level of in-depth analysis and recognition of the need for conceptual clarity and precision. This level of understanding, recognising the inaccuracies associated with crude generalisation which ignores individualism, focuses upon the lowest common factor in relation to determinants of job satisfaction amongst individuals. Analysis at this level seeks commonalties and generalisation, but it seeks commonalties and generalisation which are accurate, because they are free from contextual specificity. This level has contributed much to elucidation not only of what job satisfaction and morale are but also of what, fundamentally, are their determinants. At this level, suggested determinants of job satisfaction are, typically, individuals' needs fulfilment, expectations fulfilment or values congruence.

For practical purposes, however, despite its analytical and conceptual sophistication, the elucidation provided by level four has, on its own, limited value. If we accept that the rationale for undertaking any piece of research must not simply be to develop theory but also to apply that developed theory to policy and practice, then information that, for example, teachers' job satisfaction is dependent upon their job-related needs or expectations being met is useful, but needs supplementing if it is to be applied meaningfully. A fifth level, which this book exemplifies, is needed in order to provide that supplementary information. The analysis upon which this level of understanding is based applies the lowest common factor analysis of level four to teaching-specific exemplars, which are illustrated in colourful detail through the chapters in Part II of the book. By drawing out both the diversity and the consensus, the research findings presented highlight the intricacies and complexities involved in understanding not only teachers' job satisfaction but also morale and motivation, in a way which has clear potential for application to policy and practice.

2

Morale

Introduction

Traditionally, and typically, any concern over how members of the teaching profession feel about their work is interpreted as a morale issue. Anticipated and actual responses on the part of teachers to imposed change, reactions to pay rises or freezes, as well as challenges to popular perceptions of their status as a profession, or of what their work entails, are all categorised, from outside and inside the profession alike, as manifestations of morale. Impressions that teachers are generally content with their lot are identified as an indication of high morale. Evidence of much disaffection, and of widespread malaise, is described as low morale.

Reflecting this tendency to attribute the pervasive mood of the profession as a whole to it, teacher morale has, understandably, been the focus of considerable attention in the UK over the last decade. Factors such as teachers' low salaries and low status, changes effected by the Education Reform Act 1988, threatened deprofessionalisation resulting from school-based teacher training, growing class sizes and, most recently, changes to teachers' pensions regulations, have all been attributed as underlying causes of what has been interpreted as endemic low morale within the profession. Widespread job-related stress, a steady exodus, teacher shortages and problems of recruitment have all been reported as prevalent in recent years (see, for example, Garner, 1985; Andain, 1990; Blackbourne, 1990; Gold, 1990; Hofkins, 1990; Rafferty and Dore, 1993), and have been collectively identified as symptoms of demoralisation.

In relation to teachers' attitudes to their jobs then, it is 'morale' which is the most frequently used term. Indeed, it is widely used word in general; one which is often applied to contexts related to work and productivity, community spirit, teamwork, institutional ethos and military activity. In everyday parlance it is a term with which everyone is familiar, with whose use they are comfortable and whose meaning is apparently clear and uncomplicated.

Amongst those whose work involves the study of morale, however, the concept is far from clear and uncomplicated. Within the research and academic community in particular, those who take conceptual analysis and definition seriously accept that morale is a very nebulous, ill-defined concept whose meaning is generally inadequately explored. Indeed, the kinds of conceptual problems related to the study of job satisfaction, identified in Chapter 1, are similarly prevalent in the study of morale.

This chapter represents an attempt to address some of the conceptual issues involved in studying morale and to contribute towards clarifying what, precisely, morale is. It examines some of the definitions and inter-pretations that are available. It presents my own interpretation and defi-nition of morale, which were developed and formulated in the light of analyses of the research findings upon which this book is based. It also illustrates the nature of the relationship between morale and job satisfaction.

Identifying the problems

There is a general perception that the morale of teachers in the UK is currently quite low. This is attributed to those factors identified above. Teachers' morale is low, it is claimed, because the changes to education that have been effected over the last decade have, in various ways, im-poverished their working lives.

Such claims are largely impressionistic and, of necessity, based upon common-sense reasoning since there is a shortage, particularly in Britain, of up-to-date research into teacher morale and those factors which influ-ence it. What is particularly interesting, though, is the implicit homo-geneity which these claims ascribe to teachers.

To some extent the paucity of appropriate research evidence encour-ages generalisation, but it is also the case that what research and literature there is has tended to focus on a characteristic ascribed to morale which may best be described as its communality. A result of this has been school-based research into factors influencing staff morale yielding inter-pretations based upon the premise that prevailing working conditions and circumstances affect all members of staff similarly.

The most effective way of challenging such interpretations is through research, yet this presents problems. Effective research is clearly depend-ent upon investigating what it purports to investigate but, since morale is notoriously difficult to define, it is the subject of multi-interpretation. What is required before any meaningful discussion about what influences morale can occur, is greater understanding of the concept.

What is morale?

Anyone who makes a serious attempt to get to grips with the complexity of the issues surrounding teacher morale becomes aware of the concep-tual difficulties which have confounded others. Guion (1958) refers to the 'definitional limb' on which writers about morale find themselves and indeed, as Smith (1976) points out, use of the term is often avoided in order to eliminate the problems of defining it. Williams and Lane (1975), employing a chameleon analogy, emphasise the elusiveness of the concept. Redefer (1959a, p. 59) describes it as a 'complex and complicated area of investigation' and one which lacks a succinct definition, while Williams (1986, p. 2) writes that 'the attempts at defining and measuring morale in the literature seem like a quagmire'.

Over 30 years ago Baehr and Renck (1959, p. 188) observed that 'literature on morale yields definitions which are as varied as they are numerous'. Clearly, definitions reflect perceptions of morale's various conceptual constituents. In an attempt to present my own interpretation, which is grounded in qualitative research evidence, I focus on three conceptual areas: morale as a group or an individual phenomenon; the dimensionality of morale; and the relationship between morale and satisfaction.

Morale: a group or an individual phenomenon?
There is a lack of agreement over whether or not morale may be applied to individuals. Many writers focus exclusively on group morale and employ definitions incorporating phrases such as 'shared purpose' (Smith, 1976), 'group goals' and 'feelings of togetherness' (Guba, 1958). The notion of individual morale, or morale in isolation, is eschewed and morale is determined only in relation to common objectives:

> Morale can be defined as a prevailing temper or spirit in the individuals forming a group.
>
> (Bohrer and Ebenrett, in Smith, *c.* 1988)

> A confident, resolute, willing, often self-sacrificing and courageous attitude of an individual to the function or tasks demanded or expected of him by a group of which he is part.
>
> (McLaine, in Smith, *c.* 1988)

Indeed, such perspectives typically interpret deviant attitudes as symptomatic of *low* morale (Stagner, 1958). Research, too, has often been directed towards eliciting group rather than individual attitudes, typified by questionnaires inviting respondents to estimate the attitudes of their colleagues. In current parlance morale is represented as a group attitude and reference made, for example, to the morale of a whole school staff, a particular category of teachers or even to the entire profession.

Those who see morale as a group phenomenon relate it to group goals and estimate individuals' morale in terms of assimilation with the group, as demonstrated by acceptance of its aims. My own research, by contrast, as I illustrate in the chapters in Part II of this book, has revealed very little evidence of such group cohesiveness amongst my sample. The 19 teachers upon whom my studies focused demonstrated individuality to the extent that I seriously question the notion of group goals as a baseline against which morale may be measured. What are often presented as group goals may be simply the leader's individual aspirations, which may or may not coincide with the other members' aspirations. Group goals may, of course, constitute a uniformity or a consensus of individual goals, but the essential point is that individuals come to groups with hidden agendas.

I interpret morale as primarily an attribute of the individual, which is determined in relation to *individual* goals. Individual goals may be explicit as, for example, a clear set of ambitions, but in many cases they are implicit in individuals' reactions to situations which arise and responses to choices offered. Central to this is the individual's perception of self, which will incorporate an image of the 'ideal self' and the 'real self', where the ideal self is that to which the individual aspires and the real self is that which is perceived as reality. Both 'selves', of course, are suscept- ible to continual fluctuation and modification which, as a result of certain circumstances, may be quite intense. Turner (1968, referred to in Ball, 1972), labels these the self-conception (the ideal) and the self-image (the perceived 'real' self):

> The self-conception is the result of the accretion of a life-time of self-images, gradually building up a biographical self for the person. And as these images contribute to the more basic self-conception, the latter forms a baseline for comparison and evaluation of momentary images. These are judged as true or false, desirable or undesirable as they contrast or complement the actor's con- ception of himself as a self . . . Images too dissonant for incorporating in exist- ing conceptions exert pressure toward change. Such change may, of course, be readily accepted or actively fought depending on the valence of the emotional freight it bears.
>
> (Ball, 1972, p. 180)

For teachers, self-conception must include a professional sense of self, even if this area of their lives is given low priority. The professional element of their self-*image* is related to, and formed within, the context(s) in which they work and, more specifically, is influenced by the overall prevailing professional ethos within that context. Nias (1984, p. 268), adopting Ball's terminology, writes of the effects on teachers of the degree of congruence between their 'substantive selves', comprising the 'most salient and most valued views of and attitude to self' and their 'situa- tional selves'. The extent to which such congruence exists is a key deter- minant of individual morale.

The process by which the individual attempts to realise his/her self- conception of substantial self is reflected by his/her implicit and explicit set of goals which, in turn, is influenced by values held. It seems feasible that the greater the proximity between substantial self and the situational self, or between self-conception and self-image, the greater the satisfac- tion. The ideal would be a perfect match, rendering a state of content- ment, though, in reality, this would never occur since the self-conception would constantly change and thus retain its elusiveness.

Pollard (1982) points out that teachers are both enabled and constrained by the institutional bias which prevails in their schools. I interpret this as the individual's perception of the extent of realisation of his/her self-conception or substantial self. This is demonstrated very clearly by the cases, presented in later chapters, of teachers who participated in my research. Some of these teachers felt constrained by the professional climates that prevailed in their schools, and which were, to varying degrees, at odds with their own educational ideologies and professional values. Their generally 'extended' professionality (see Hoyle, 1975; Evans, 1986) was out of place amid the intuitively, rather than rationally-based climates that determined norms in relation to policy, structure and organisation, and practice within their schools (see, in particular, Chapter 6; also, Evans, 1997).

Other teachers, on the other hand, manifested self-conceptions which more evenly encompassed non-professional aspects of their lives, so that teaching was regarded as more of a job than a vocation (see Chapter 8). These teachers did not experience the professionality-influenced feelings of being constrained by irrational decision-making. Their self-conceptions were quite distinct, in form, from those of the 'extended' professionals.

One's ideal self or self-conception will incorporate biographical factors and personality traits, such as tolerance, ambition, patience and sensitivity, which determine individual boundaries of acceptability. For one teacher, being permitted to practise within her own classroom in a style which satisfies her may be enough, whereas another may not be content unless the entire professional ethos of the school is compatible with her ideal.

These two 'types' of teachers represent a polarisation of attitudes towards their jobs, but the rest of my sample also demonstrated individuality to the extent that I believe it is the pursuit of one's self-conception, or one's substantial self, which is the fundamental goal of each individual.

Guion (1958) appreciates the significance of individuals' goals in determining morale. His definition of morale, also adopted by Coughlan (1970, pp. 221–2), is close to my own interpretation of the concept: 'Morale is the extent to which an individual's needs are satisfied and the extent to which the individual perceives that satisfaction as stemming from his total job situation.' Yet it falls short, I feel, in that it fails to distinguish between morale and job satisfaction.

How is morale related to job satisfaction?

Smith (1976) criticises American studies for confusing morale with satisfaction, or at least for failing to distinguish between them. He makes the distinction (1966, p. 144) that 'high morale may exist in a situation where many job dissatisfactions exist and are being overcome'. Guba (1958), on the other hand, sees high morale as dependent upon achievement of a high level of satisfaction. Satisfying acts require less expenditure of energy than do unsatisfying acts, he argues, and so satisfaction is necessary to avoid expending the requisite energy for morale.

My interpretation is centred around Smith's distinction that job satisfaction is a static, shallow concept, whereas morale is dynamic and forward-looking. The basis of the distinction is that of temporal orientation – the one being present oriented and the other future oriented. Both are states of mind, but I perceive satisfaction to be a *response* to a situation whereas morale is *anticipatory*. This is best illustrated by reference to one of the teachers involved in my study. Brenda, whose case is presented in Chapter 8, was much happier in her job after reducing to part-time status since she then had the time to pursue non-work activities that she valued, but for which she had been too busy when she was employed full time. She may, therefore, be deemed to have high morale since reducing to part-time status. My interpretation identifies Brenda's response to her reduction of teaching hours as job satisfaction – more specifically, job comfort, as I explain it in Chapter 1. However, her anticipation that, in the future, working part time will continue to provide high job satisfaction I interpret as morale. In this way job satisfaction and morale (each of which may range from high to low) continually interact and, by this process, may present the illusion of being one. Morale, though, as I interpret it, is an extension of job satisfaction.

Morale involves anticipation of continued or sustained job satisfaction in the form of job comfort, as in the example of Brenda's case, or/and of job fulfilment. There are, therefore, two possible routes to morale: the job comfort route and the job fulfilment route. Following on from my analysis of job satisfaction in Chapter 1, and building on my model of the job fulfilment process, the process involved in achieving job fulfilment-based high morale is illustrated in Figure 2.1.

The dimensions of morale
There appears to be widespread acceptance of the multidimensionality of morale, but a lack of agreement on the application of the term. Guion (1958) does not make explicit his interpretation of 'dimension' but interchanges it with 'component', 'factor' and, later, 'variable': 'morale is not a single dimension . . . it has many components or factors.'

Richardson and Blocker's (1963) and Coughlan's (1970) interpretations appear to differ only in degree of specificity. They both use 'factor' and 'dimension' interchangeably and apply the terms to mean categories of satisfaction and dissatisfaction, rather like Child's (1941) 'variables' and Herzberg's (1968) motivation and hygiene 'factors'.

However, those writers who are influenced by the work of Cattel and Stice (1960), such as Williams and Lane (1975), Smith (1976) and Williams (1986), interpret the multidimensionality of morale as the various facets or categories of morale itself rather than the actual causes. For them, the

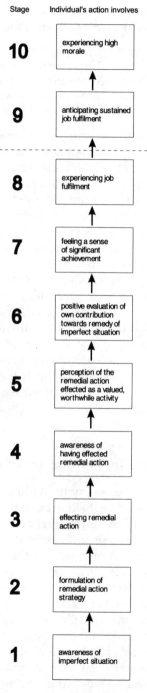

Stage   Individual's action involves

10   experiencing high morale

9   anticipating sustained job fulfilment

8   experiencing job fulfilment

7   feeling a sense of significant achievement

6   positive evaluation of own contribution towards remedy of imperfect situation

5   perception of the remedial action effected as a valued, worthwhile activity

4   awareness of having effected remedial action

3   effecting remedial action

2   formulation of remedial action strategy

1   awareness of imperfect situation

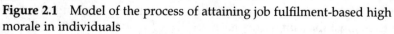

Figure 2.1   Model of the process of attaining job fulfilment-based high morale in individuals

dimensions of morale represent *responses* to different sources of satisfaction or dissatisfaction. Williams (1986, p. 2) cites Cattel and Stice (1960):

> By our hypothesis we should not expect morale to be a single dimension, but several, each contributing certain characteristics toward the general area of behaviour connected by such notions as resistance of the group against dispersion, tenacity in pursuing goals, and such non-syntality, personnel profile measures as confident attitudes in individuals about the future of the group.

If my understanding is correct, adherents to this interpretation would, in effect, acknowledge several different 'morales'. Cattell and Stice (*ibid.*) propose five dimensions: morale of leadership synergy, morale of tenacity and fortitude, morale of group cohesion, morale of adventurous striving and morale of personal reward. In 1966 Smith proposed a model for investigating teacher morale, based upon these five dimensions. By 1976 he had reduced them to three: leadership synergy, cohesive pride and personal challenge. His realisation that questionnaire items intended to reveal five dimensions could, in fact, be categorised into three was assisted by revelations of Williams and Lane (1975) whom Smith (1976), retaining their chameleon analogy, credits with having given us a very well focused and useful coloured photograph of the whole fascinating creature.

However, I have found that attempts to measure teachers' morale with respect to three dimensions show morale to be unidimensional. Fundamentally, morale is related to the individual's pursuit of goals requisite for the realisation of self-concept. Indeed, this is the only frame of reference that ultimately matters, in so far as what have been identified as specific dimensions of morale can all be cancelled down even further to this single dimension.

An individual interpretation of morale

Morale is essentially about the extent of individuals' goal-oriented needs fulfilment and, since needs relate to the pursuit of self-conception or substantial self, they relate to the individual as a whole rather than to disparate constituents. For this reason I prefer to consider morale to be *situation*-specific, rather than *job* or *school*-specific. The term 'situation-specific' is intended to convey the idea of the individual's entire work-related circumstances, which are not confined to events occurring at the workplace but are elements of what the individual may identify as 'the situation I am in at the moment'. Countless constituents of an individual's situation – which is constantly reshaping itself – are what I would identify as the 'intricacies' of morale, and it is to their amalgamated whole that morale relates. An individual's morale level may be determined by a kind of unconscious summing up process whereby, at any one point in time, the anticipated dissatisfying constituents are balanced against the satisfying ones.

Redefer (1959b, p. 136) attempts to convey this idea by means of an equation, formulated as a result of research into teacher morale at New York University:

The morale status of a faculty may be expressed by the equation, $M = f(P_I, P_c, P_A, P_H)$. In other words the morale status of the individuals who compose a staff is a function of P_I (the person's feelings about his position and the acceptance and possibility of achieving his objectives), P_c (the person in relation to his professional community – school neighborhood, parents, fellow teachers, and students), P_A (the person in his relation to administrators, supervisors, and administrative relationships), and P_H (the person in relation to himself and his profession). These are variables of the morale status of the teacher.

Guion (1958) however, refers simply to the individual's 'total job situation', whilst Baehr and Renck (1959, p. 160) suggest that 'Levels of motivation and morale are a result of the total work situation and of its many overlapping dynamic interrelations which involve both the individual and the smaller groups in a larger social field'.

The notion of an all-encompassing situation which extends far beyond the confines of a single school has not always been appreciated by researchers, with the result that questionnaire items aimed at revealing a dynamic and multidimensional morale have been unable to do more than simply identify sources of satisfaction and dissatisfaction. The inadequacies of this are succinctly expressed by Baehr and Renck's (1959, pp. 161–2) reference to Moore (1954), 'who states that the employee does not generally view his environment in the way in which a questionnaire or survey usually presents his views, i.e., as a set of distinct and separate opinions'. I interpret morale as a state of mind which is determined by reference to anticipated future events; by the anticipated form they will take and their anticipated effect upon satisfaction. It is dependent upon, and guided by, past events in so far as past experiences provide a basis upon which to anticipate. However, this alone is inadequate as a description of morale since it may equally apply to the optimism/pessimism continuum. In some contexts the two concepts overlap yet, clearly, they are by no means synonymous. The distinction, I believe, is twofold.

First, much depends upon how significant the individual perceives events to be in terms of their contribution towards the pursuit of self-conception, although this will almost certainly be represented by an intuitive, unconscious ranking. Other issues will tend to be trivialised in comparison and, whilst they may give rise to optimism or pessimism, do not affect morale although, under certain circumstances, they may escalate into morale issues. The individual will formulate a hierarchy of goals which will be modified in accordance with the changes and fluctuations of his/her self-conception. At any one time the pursuit of an individual goal will affect morale in relation to its rank in the goal hierarchy at that time. As the individual's priorities change, so too will the factors which affect morale, and what was a morale issue last week may be relegated to being a minor irritant this week.

Secondly, the *reaction* of the individual distinguishes morale from optimism/pessimism. Optimism/pessimism is a passive state of mind which may even coexist with complacency since it pertains to that which is trivialised. Morale, on the other hand, predisposes towards a goal-focused reaction. High morale may motivate, stimulate, encourage or energise, whilst low morale may do the opposite. This interpretation is compatible with my interpretation of morale as an anticipatory, rather than a responsive, state of mind, for I see morale as the facilitator or stimulus of a response rather than the response itself. Definitions of morale such as that of Chase (1955), adopted by and cited in Guba (1958, p. 198) 'morale is a predisposition on the part of persons engaged in an enterprise to put forth extra effort in the achievement of group goals or objectives' and, to some extent, that of Smith (1966, p. 143): 'A forward looking and confident state of mind relevant to a shared and vital purpose' describe possible consequences of, or response to morale, rather than define the concept itself. Moreover, they describe responses to *high* morale and fail to incorporate the notion that morale may range from high to low. Another failing is that the responses described are not exclusive to morale; fear, intimidation or competitiveness, for example, may equally well give rise to a predisposition to put forth extra effort.

My definition of morale modifies that of Guion (1958) to accommodate my own interpretation of the concept: '*morale is a state of mind encompassing all the feelings determined by the individual's anticipation of the extent of satisfaction of those needs which s/he perceives as significantly affecting his/her total work situation.*' Work on morale has generally been weakened by misinterpretation, misapplication and misconception. Too frequently specific forms of individual group behaviour have been misinterpreted as manifestations of particular morale levels, leading to the inaccurate assumptions about morale's causal factors. There is agreement that morale is essentially a state of mind, yet in spite of the fact that a state of mind is fundamentally an attribute of the individual, individual attitudes have evidently been neglected in the pursuit of the notion of group mentality. The result has been a predominance of research yielding generalisations which have obscured the intricacies of morale. The concept has remained elusive and what has been presented as morale has often been group cohesiveness or job satisfaction.

Researchers should focus, first and foremost, on individuals and only then search for commonalties and emerging patterns which may yield generalisation.

In Britain, educationalists now recognise the importance of the individuality of the pupil in the teaching–learning situation. Individual needs are the main focus of what is, within education circles, currently respected pedagogy, and the caring teacher works to help the child fulfil those needs. Similarly, those concerned with raising the level of teachers' morale must now recognise its assimilation with the individual's conception of self. As Goodson (1991) points out, teachers' work should be examined in the context of their lives if we are to find out what their priorities are. The key to understanding what influences teachers' morale is to uncover those personal priorities. By uncovering, in the chapters in Part II, the personal priorities of those teachers who were involved in my research, this book makes a significant contribution towards understanding the complexities and intricacies that underpin teacher morale.

3

Motivation

Introduction

Of the three concepts examined in Part I of this book, motivation is probably the one for which the fewest definitions are available. Much has been written about what motivates or demotivates but conceptual analyses are very thin on the ground.

What motivates, on the other hand, is not underexamined. The plethora of literature that began to emerge, principally from the USA, from the 1930s onwards, and which was aimed at informing the industrial world how it might best increase output and efficiency by improving workers' performance, has been the medium for the dissemination and critical analysis of several motivation theories. Indeed, it is possible that the attention directed at investigation of what motivates may be another reason for the underexamination of the concept of motivation in so far as the interest in developing motivation theories created a bandwagon, in relation to areas of inquiry, which detracted from analysis of the concept itself.

This chapter incorporates consideration both of the concept and of the theories of motivation. It presents my own definition of motivation, which I apply to the work reported in this book. It examines in outline the key features of a number of motivation theories, and it examines work on employees' motivation that may have implications for understanding what motivates teachers.

What is motivation?

It is certainly the case, as Steers *et al.* (1996, p. 9) point out, that 'the concept of motivation has received considerable attention over the course of this century', but this attention has, for the most part, focused on clarification of what motivation encompasses and on identifying its features. This has resulted in descriptions, or interpretations, of motivation rather than definitions. Some of the major studies of motivation fail to incorporate conceptual definitions. Neither Maslow (1954) nor Herzberg (1968), for example, whose work is generally considered seminal, provide an explicit definition of motivation. The closest that Maslow (1954, pp. 6–7) comes to defining motivation is to make the observation:

Current conceptions of motivation seem to proceed on the assumption that a motivational state is a special, peculiar state, sharply marked off from the other happenings in the organism. Sound motivational theory should, on the contrary, assume that motivation is constant, never ending, fluctuating, and complex, and that it is an almost universal characteristic of practically every organismic state of affairs.

The outcome has been, without doubt and with a few exceptions, the provision of valuable elucidation of what motivation may look like and how it may be recognised, but not of what, precisely, it is.

Steers *et al.* (1996, p. 8) suggest: 'What is needed is a description which sufficiently covers the various components and processes associated with how human behavior is activated.' They present what they describe as an illustrative selection of definitions of motivation:

> the contemporary (immediate) influence on the direction, vigor and persistence of action.
>
> (Atkinson, 1964, cited in Steers *et al.*, 1996, p. 8)

> how behavior gets started, is energised, is sustained, is directed, is stopped, and what kind of subjective reaction is present in the organism while all this is going on.
>
> (Jones, 1955, cited in Steers *et al.*, 1996, p. 8)

> a process governing choice made by persons or lower organisms among alternative forms of voluntary activity.
>
> (Vroom, 1964, cited in Steers *et al.*, 1996, p. 8)

> motivation has to do with a set of independent/dependent variable relationships that explain the direction, amplitude, and persistence of an individual's behavior, holding constant the effects of aptitude, skill, and understanding of the task, and the constraints operating in the environment.
>
> (Campbell and Pritchard, 1976, cited in Steers *et al.*, 1996, p. 8)

What these selected definitions highlight is the different applications of the term 'motivation'. We may consider the term in the sense of its being causal; that is, the factor that influences whether or not, and to what extent, we feel an inclination to do something. We may say, for example, that teachers' motivation to apply *en masse* for early retirement was changes to pensions regulations. We may also consider motivation in the sense of its being attitudinal; that is, as a state of mind or attitude. We may, for example, refer to a teacher's motivation being high. Thirdly, motivation may be considered in the sense of its being an activity, directed at an object, illustrated by the example of referring to teachers' motivation of their pupils. The basis of the distinctions between these three applications is probably less conceptual than semantic. Nevertheless, consideration of these distinctions, whatever their basis, should be incorporated into definitions of motivation. Definitions should be sufficiently narrow to preclude their application to anything other than the concept in question, while yet being sufficiently wide to encompass all applications of the concept unless each application is to be defined separately.

Of the definitions presented above, as cited in Steers *et al.* (1996), none meets all these criteria. That of Jones is not actually a definition but a description, since the word 'how', employed in this context, provides sufficient width for application other than to the concept of motivation. Jones's description applies to all three applications or interpretations of motivation I identify above, but it could also apply to, for example, 'understanding' or 'confidence'. Similarly, Campbell and Pritchard use the terms 'has to do with' and 'explain' which preclude exclusivity of application, despite reference to the constancy of specific effects. The word 'motivation' in their description could be replaced with, for example, 'ruthlessness' or 'ambition'.

Atkinson's and Vroom's definitions, as cited by Steers *et al.* (*ibid.*), are succinct, focused and sufficiently exclusive in relation to applicability. However, they fail to encompass applicability to what I have identified as the attitudinal interpretation of motivation; that which represents motivation in the sense of its being a state of mind or attitude. In the case of Vroom's definition, it is the use of the word 'process' that narrows its applicability in this way, and, in the case of Atkinson's, the use of the word 'influence'.

My own definition of motivation, which I apply to my research and to the analyses throughout this book, is '*motivation is a condition, or the creation of a condition, that encompasses all those factors that determine the degree of inclination towards engagement in an activity*'. This incorporates recognition that motivation does not necessarily determine whether or not activity occurs, it need only determine the extent to which individuals feel inclined towards activity. It is, of course, possible to be motivated to do something without actually doing it.

In my references throughout this book to teachers' motivation I also employ the terms 'motivator' and 'demotivator'. I define these as follows:

- A motivator is the impetus that creates inclination towards an activity.
- A demotivator is the impetus for disinclination towards an activity.

The essential purpose in examining motivation in the context of this book is to identify the motivators and demotivators that have been found to apply to teachers. The next stage in this identification process is to examine some of the motivation theories that have been developed.

Theories of motivation

In this section I briefly outline some key theories of work motivation and evaluate them in the light of evidence from my own research. It is important to emphasise that these evaluations are nothing more than unsystematically applied observations, based on a somewhat impressionistic application of empirical evidence which was not gathered with the intention of testing any specific motivation theories. As a result, research data collection was not designed to incorporate reliable procedures for theory testing. It was, as I explain in the next chapter, qualitative and, more specifically, open-endedly investigative. Many of the theories outlined below have been tested by appropriately designed replication studies which tend, for the most part, to employ quantitative data collection. My research does not fall into this category. Nevertheless, it provides some interesting evaluative insights into the wider applicability of some theories.

An outline of key theories

Maslow's needs hierarchy (Maslow, 1954) is one of the best known and most influential motivation theories. It is founded on the premise that goals or needs underpin motivation by being the fundamental source of all desires:

> deeper analysis . . . will always lead ultimately to certain goals or needs behind which we cannot go, that is, to certain need satisfactions that seem to be ends in themselves and seem not to need any further justification or demonstration. These needs have the particular quality in the average person of not being seen directly very often but of being more often a kind of conceptual derivation from the multiplicity of specific conscious desires. In other words, then, the study of motivation must be in part the study of the ultimate human goals or desire or needs.

> If only by the process of logical exclusion alone we are finally left with the largely unconscious fundamental goals or needs as the only sound foundations for classification in motivation theory.

> *(Ibid.,* pp. 5, 9)

Maslow's theory recognises a hierarchy of needs. He distinguishes between lower-order and higher-order needs, identifying specific categories: physiological needs, safety needs, belongingness and love needs, esteem needs and the self-actualising need. Satisfaction of needs is sought incrementally so that, for example, the lowest-level needs, physiological, usually must be satisfied before satisfaction of the next level, safety, is sought. The low-level needs (physiological, safety, and belongingness and love) are also categorised as deficiency needs since their remaining unsatisfied constitutes a deficiency. These are distinct from the other two needs, esteem and self-actualising, which are higher-order needs, and which Maslow calls growth needs, since their satisfaction influences personal growth. The needs hierarchy theory is predicated on the belief that complete and permanent satisfaction is elusive, since the satisfaction of one need merely presents other needs to be satisfied, and it is the unremitting succession of unsatisfied needs that motivates activity directed at seeking satisfaction:

man is a perpetually wanting animal. Ordinarily the satisfaction of these wants is not altogether mutually exclusive but only tends to be. The average member of our society is most often partially satisfied and partially unsatisfied in all of his wants. The hierarchy principle is usually empirically observed in terms of increasing percentages of non-satisfaction as we go up the hierarchy.

(Maslow, 1970, p. 40)

Aldefer (1972, cited in Steers *et al.*, 1996, p. 16) has developed a theory based on Maslow's needs hierarchy. Aldefer's theory is more specific to organisational settings than is Maslow's, and its categorisation of needs is different. Three, more general, categories are identified: existence needs, relatedness needs and growth needs. Existence needs parallel Maslow's physiological, and some of his safety, needs. Relatedness needs are those concerned with interpersonal relationships at work, and are comparable to Maslow's belongingness and love needs and to some of his safety and esteem needs. Growth needs concern personal and professional develop-ment and correlate with Maslow's esteem and self-actualisation needs.

Aldefer's model is, like Maslow's, hierarchical in the sense that it posits that the tendency is to progress from existence, to relatedness, to growth needs. However, it accepts that satisfaction of more than one category of need may be sought simultaneously. It also incorporates acknowledge-ment of, alongside the satisfaction–progression process, a frustration–regression sequence, which involves individuals' regressing towards seeking 'lower-level' needs satisfaction as a response to repeated frustra-tion of 'higher-level' needs satisfaction.

Herzberg's (1968) motivation-hygiene, or two-factor, theory is gener-ally accepted as a key motivation theory, even though it is contentious. This theory, more than any of the others outlined in this chapter, incorp-orates overlapping concern with job satisfaction and, on this basis, I have afforded it considerable attention in Chapter 1. The two-factor theory is developed from research findings and is specific to work contexts. Essen-tially, it identifies five factors: achievement, recognition, responsibility, advancement and the work itself, which were found to influence job satisfaction and which are categorised as motivators. These, Herzberg (*ibid.*, p. 73) argues, are the factors capable of motivating in the work context: 'The "satisfier" factors were named the motivators, since other findings of the study suggest that they are effective in motivating the individual to superior performance and effort.' Other specific job-related factors, such as salary and supervision, are incapable of creating job satis-faction. These are referred to as hygiene factors. Hygiene factors may create dissatisfaction, but no matter how they are modified will never be able to satisfy and, as such, do not motivate. Herzberg (*ibid.*, p. 77) ex-plains what underlies the distinction between the two sets of factors:

> It is clear why the hygiene factors fail to provide for positive satisfactions: they do not possess the characteristics necessary for giving an individual a sense of growth. To feel that one has grown depends on achievement in tasks that have

meaning to the individual, and since the hygiene factors do not relate to the task, they are powerless to give such meaning to the individual. Growth is dependent on some achievements, but achievement requires a task. The motivators are task factors and thus are necessary for growth; they provide the psychological stimulation by which the individual can be activated toward his self-realization needs.

McClelland's learned needs theory (McClelland, 1961; 1962; 1971; cited in Steers *et al.*, 1996, pp. 18–20) identifies four specific needs: the need for achievement, the need for power, the need for affiliation and the need for autonomy, which are derived from the learning that stems from individuals' life experiences and, particularly, from their early lives. These needs, McClelland contends, become personal predispositions that influence individuals' perspectives on, and attitudes towards, work and, in doing so, orientate them towards certain goals.

McClelland's studies revealed four characteristics of individuals whose need for achievement was prominent: a strong desire to assume personal responsibility for finding solutions to a problem or for performing a task; a tendency towards setting moderately difficult achievement goals and towards risk-taking; a strong desire for concrete performance feedback on tasks; and single-mindedness in relation to task accomplishment (Steers *et al.*, 1996, p. 19).

The need for power involves needing to exert control and influence and manifests itself through two main characteristics: a desire to direct and control someone else, and a concern for maintaining leader–follower relations (*ibid.*). The need for affiliation incorporates a wish to establish, and maintain, good interpersonal relationships. Three characteristics are associated with it: a strong desire for approval and reassurance; a tendency to conform to the wishes and norms of those whose friendship is valued; and a sincere interest in others' feelings (*ibid.*). The need for autonomy stems from a desire for independence and is characterised by non-conformity, a preference for working alone and a lack of corporate allegiance and collegial feeling (*ibid.*).

Vroom's expectancy theory is predicated on a 'view of behavior as subjectively rational and as directed toward the attainment of desired outcomes and away from aversive outcomes' (Vroom, 1964, p. 276). Using the term 'valence' to refer to 'affective orientations toward particular outcomes' (*ibid.*, p. 15) or, more simply, preferences, Vroom contends that individuals' motivation is determined by a combination of valence and expectancies; essentially, that choices of behaviour result from consideration of both preference for a particular activity and its expected outcome.

Research evidence of the applicability of motivation theories

My research yielded findings that, to varying degrees, may be considered to manifest consistencies with all the motivation theories outlined above.

The needs hierarchy theories of Maslow and Aldefer seemed to be borne out by the disparity amongst my sample in relation to what was valued in the work context. Some teachers implied that social interaction within the staff peer group, good interpersonal relations and a positive and supportive collegial climate were, for them, the greatest attraction and the most important aspect of the job. Those who rated these factors higher than any other job-related factors were all what I categorise as more 'restricted' professionals – whose concern was mainly focused on practical issues, whose educational ideologies were less developed than those of many of their colleagues, and who adopted an intuitive and relatively unreflective approach to teaching (see Chapter 6 for a more detailed explanation of professionality, and of the 'restricted–extended' continuum). The evidence suggests that these comparatively underdeveloped teachers were situated at the love and belongingness, or relatedness, level of the needs hierarchy.

Most teachers, however, seemed, to varying degrees of intensity, to have needs that were located at the higher level of the hierarchy: growth or esteem. These teachers were, variously, 'extended' professionals. What they evidently valued most about the job were the opportunities it presented in diverse ways to feel a sense of achievement. Yet most of these teachers also seemed quite clearly to have love and belongingness, or relatedness, needs since they greatly valued collegial interaction and friendships. This suggests that Aldefer's refinement of Maslow's needs hierarchy, in recognising that individuals may, simultaneously, seek satisfaction of needs from more than one category, is more accurate.

Consistent with Herzberg's theory, as I explain in more detail in my conceptually based critique of it in Chapter 1, my teachers seemed, for the most part, to be motivated by the opportunity of being satisfied *by* those factors Herzberg identifies as motivators, and to be potentially satisfied *with*, but not generally motivated by, what he categorises as hygiene factors.

McClelland's learned needs theory appears to be partially borne out by evidence from my research. Several teachers manifested characteristics of individuals with a high need for achievement, and many teachers manifested characteristics of individuals with a high need for affiliation. None of my sample demonstrated a high need for power, though it is not unreasonable to assume that teachers who do have this need may wish to conceal it, believing it to be incompatible with teachers' professional culture. However, my observation in schools, which constituted one of my data collection methods (see Chapter 4), revealed one headteacher whose behaviour was consistent with the characteristics of individuals with a high need for power, and interview-generated data from teachers who were her subordinates corroborated this finding. None of my teachers manifested characteristics of individuals with a high need for autonomy, though one reason for this may be that such individuals are generally not attracted to the teaching profession and are more likely to be found in jobs where they may exercise more autonomy than teaching allows. Furthermore, it seemed that many of my teachers did not fit exclusively into one need-oriented category. Many manifested behaviour that combined the characteristics of individuals with a high need for achievement and a high need for affiliation.

Of the motivation theories outlined in this chapter, Vroom's expectancy theory is the most difficult to apply to my research evidence since my data collection seldom revealed insight into the thought processes underlying teachers' activity-oriented choices which was of sufficient depth to test Vroom's theory. Steers *et al.*, (1996, pp. 22–3) identify what has been found to be a similar problem with testing the theory, and one which overlaps with the difficulty I have identified:

> the expectancy approach contains the implicit assumption that motivation is a conscious rational choice process. That is, individuals are assumed consciously to calculate the pleasure or pain that they expect to attain or avoid when making a choice. However, it is generally accepted that individuals are not always conscious of their motives, expectancies, and perceptual processes. Yet expectancy theory tends to ignore habitual behavior and subconscious motivation.

Nevertheless, with limitations, some research evidence did emerge that seems to be consistent with the expectancy theory's basic premises. For example, among my sample were some teachers whose motivation to either change schools or to remain in their current post was influenced by their calculating anticipated outcomes of their options and off-setting these against their valence. One such teacher was Kay, whose case is examined in Chapter 7. She wanted to advance to a deputy headship, but applied very serious consideration to every deputy headship post in which she was interested, calculating whether the advantages it offered seemed to be potentially greater or fewer than those of remaining in her current post.

Finding the common factor

What becomes apparent on deeper analysis is that all the motivation theories outlined in this chapter share an underlying common factor. Underpinning all of them, at the lowest level of reduction, is the premise that motivation involves needs fulfilment. Maslow's (1954, p. 5) observation, presented earlier in this chapter, that motivation ultimately hinges on the pursuit of needs satisfaction and that this is the deepest level of analysis that can be attained, is accurate. Many motivation theories incorporate recognition of this that is explicit in the terminology they employ. In other theories the needs fulfilment factor is implicit and may require the deeper analysis, to which Maslow refers, to uncover it.

Herzberg's theory, for example, identifies five specific motivators which may be cancelled down, not only to a level which recognises all five as needs: the need for recognition, the need for responsibility, the need to be engaged in the kinds of activities that constitute the work itself, etc., but (ignoring consideration of my refinement, and reduction, of Herzberg's motivation factors, presented in Chapter 1, since it is irrelevant to the issue being discussed here) to a level beyond this. Underpinning the need for satisfaction, which in a work context is specifically job satisfaction, the lowest common factor is the need for individuals to approach the realisation of their conception of their ideal self. In a work context this ideal self will be work specific – the ideal-self-at-work. This ideal-self conception determines goals and, wherever possible, activity is aimed at these, although both the determination and the pursuit of goals may often be unconscious. The underlying need is to achieve these ideal-oriented goals and all the motivation theories presented above incorporate this lowest common factor.

The link between job satisfaction, morale and motivation becomes apparent through this deeper analysis. Job satisfaction, as I define it in Chapter 1, is a state of mind encompassing all the feelings determined by the extent to which the individual perceives her/his job-related needs to be being met. Morale, as I define it in Chapter 2, is a state of mind encompassing all the feelings determined by the individual's anticipation of the extent of satisfaction of those needs which s/he perceives as significantly affecting his/her total work situation. Thus, as I point out in Chapter 2, morale is linked to job satisfaction by its being determined by the anticipation of job satisfaction. Motivation is concerned with the degree of inclination towards an activity, but that degree of inclination is determined by the pursuit of goals which will satisfy needs. What motivates, therefore, in a work context is the desire for job satisfaction; individuals are motivated to participate in activities that appear to them to be oriented towards job satisfaction. Morale levels are determined by expectancy of continued job satisfaction, and high morale, resulting from high expectations, motivates individuals towards goal-focused activity which is expected to sustain, and increase, job satisfaction, which, in turn, raises morale. Figure 3.1 illustrates the relationship between motivation, job satisfaction and morale.

What motivates teachers?

At the level of practical application though, understanding that teachers are motivated by the need to achieve ideal-oriented goals is of no real use. For practical purposes, much more specificity is required and attention needs to be directed at *what*, precisely, motivates rather than at *why* it motivates.

Outside the academic community there seems to be a commonly held assumption that motivation is pay-related. In relation to teachers in the

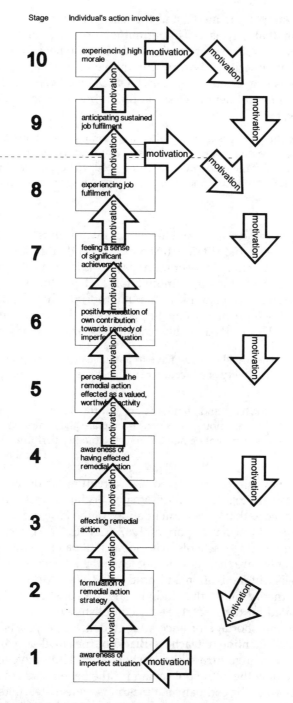

Figure 3.1 Model of the interaction of the motivation process with the processes of individuals' attainment of job satisfaction and high morale

UK, for example, the media and the teachers' unions have promulgated the notion that pay is an important determinant of three aspects of motivation: recruitment, retention and improvement. In response to the report of the interim Advisory Committee on teachers' pay and conditions, it was suggested in *The Times Educational Supplement* that, in relation first to recruitment and, secondly, to improvement, pay could be a key motivator:

> If our teaching force is to be recruited from among the brightest and best of our graduates, the money must come first. Then there is every chance that quality will follow. But the graduate in question needs to be attracted by a competitive starting salary, and confident of a career progression that will reward ability and application.
>
> (Anon, 1991, p. 23)

Pay is also assumed to be an effective motivator in relation to improving job performance. Indeed, it is this assumption that underlies the practice of performance-related pay or merit pay. This is predicated on acceptance of the expectancy theory of motivation and productivity, which posits that individuals are more likely to put effort into their work if there is an anticipated reward they value. Supporters of this view contend that the ultimate goal, improved quality, can only be achieved at a price:

> this government will one day have to pay its teaching force sufficiently highly to achieve the quality of education to which it has so far merely paid lip service.
>
> (Andain, 1990)

> Teachers work hard and standards are improving in some aspects of school work. But they are not good enough, nor are they improving fast enough, because teachers are not being paid for high quality performance.
>
> (Tomlinson, 1990, p. 11)

Similarly, pay is often perceived as a retention factor. For example, the allowances paid to schools in designated Social Priority Areas in the UK, in accordance with the recommendations of the Plowden Committee published in the Plowden Report of 1967 (CACE, 1967), were intended to retain staff in these schools. The idea that paying employees enough money will ensure that they do not leave the job stems, in part, from the equity theory of motivation and productivity (see Mowday, 1996, pp. 53–71). This theory holds that individuals are satisfied if they feel justly compensated for their efforts and accomplishments.

There is no shortage of anecdotal evidence that pay is an important factor in the retention of teachers. Blackbourne (1990, p. A4), for example, reported on a huge turnout of teachers at an alternative jobs fair: 'And who can blame them? A spokesman for the Bacteriostatic Water Systems stall said two of the company's top earners were ex-teachers with salaries per month – not per year – of more than £25,000.' However, such evidence tends to identify pay as a demotivator, rather than a motivator. It is important to recognise that the factors that demotivate may not necessarily be those that motivate; indeed, Herzberg's (1968) two-factor theory, outlined above and examined in greater detail in Chapter 1, makes a clear distinction between the two. It is not only Herzberg's work which provides evidence that pay is not a motivator. Research into the effectiveness of merit pay, or performance-related pay, has revealed the practice generally to be flawed. Johnson (1986) highlights the failure of a number of merit pay schemes introduced in the USA during this century and points out that some were even found to demotivate. Chandler's (1959) research in the USA compared morale levels in schools where merit pay policies were operational and schools where they were not. His findings revealed no significant difference in morale levels. Mathis' (1959) research findings corroborate Chandler's. Mayston (1992), moreover, concludes that performance-related pay is an oversimplistic approach to tackling problems of teacher motivation, that its potential for success is questionable and that it may even demotivate.

Research evidence generally supports Herzberg's contention that pay is a hygiene factor and, as such, is incapable of motivating. It is not enough, however, to know what does *not* motivate; what is more important is knowing what *does* motivate.

Evidence of what motivates teachers is, for the most part, confined to more general studies of employee motivation or, reflecting the neglect in recent years of conceptual rigour which might distinguish between morale, motivation and job satisfaction, to studies of teachers' overall attitudes to their work. The research evidence that does provide elucidation though, again, tends broadly to corroborate Herzberg's findings. Chapman's (1983) study, which focused on 437 college graduates who had entered the teaching profession and were still teaching, revealed recognition and approval to be key motivational factors. Chapman and Hutcheson (1982) found a distinction, in relation to the kinds of factors that motivated them, between teachers and ex-teachers. Those who had left teaching were more extrinsically motivated than those remaining in it:

> Those who left teaching indicated salary, job autonomy, and, in the case of those leaving elementary teaching, the chance to contribute to important decisions, to be most important . . . Individuals remaining in teaching were more oriented toward interpersonal rewards: the approval and recognition of supervisors, family and friends.
>
> (*Ibid.*, p. 104)

Similarly, of Kasten's (1984, p. 4) sample of 138 American elementary classroom teachers, the 64% whose responses to a questionnaire item indicated that they would choose teaching as a career again 'overwhelmingly focused on the delights and satisfactions of working with children. Other reasons given were the importance of the job, personal rewards, variety in the work, and a feeling of competence'.

Intrinsic rewards were identified as important retainers in a qualitative study of the motivation of American secondary schoolteachers (Bredeson *et al.*, 1983, p. 57):

> The most powerful motivational forces which attract, maintain, and keep successful teachers in the classroom are a complex of intrinsic rewards which come together in the ideal occupational combination of working with students, seeing students learn and succeed, believing one's job in service to others is valuable, and being able to grow personally and professionally.

McLaughlin *et al.*'s (1986, pp. 420–1) study of teachers' incentives, rewards and working environment revealed similar motivators:

> We found . . . that the dominant motivation and source of reward for teachers lies in promoting students' growth and development. The thing that makes teaching meaningful and worthwhile is watching students learn and 'working with wonder'. 'If it weren't for the natural responsiveness of children', one teacher said, 'I would have walked away a long time ago, sold stockings at Macey's, and made the same amount of money.'

Galloway *et al.* (1985), Farrugia (1986) and Nias (1981; 1989) all make explicit reference to a broad consistency between their research findings and Herzberg's two-factor theory. More specifically, Nias (1989) identifies 'affective' and 'competence-related' rewards, both of which she relates to working with children. Furthermore, the importance of leadership and collegial support as motivators, which has been emphasised in several studies (see, for example, Nias, 1980; ILEA, 1986; Johnson, 1986; Nias *et al.*, 1989) is also evidence of the applicability to education contexts of Herzberg's theory, since it is partly the recognition and approbation of leaders and colleagues that motivates teachers, as Nias's (1989, p. 146) interviewees demonstrate:

> 'The head's a tremendous force in the school . . . she can be a real demon and sometimes the tension gets you down because you know she's watching you all the time, but you really feel pleased if she pats you on the back.'
> 'The head says he's pleased with what I've done so far and that's given me confidence that I'm on the right track.'
> 'We have a new head and she's made us all feel much better about things because she takes a real interest in what we're doing – comes round and has a look, talks to the children about their work, asks us before she buys equipment, all that sort of thing.'

On the other hand, research findings have revealed leadership to be potentially an equally potent demotivator. Of Nias's sample of 99 graduate primary schoolteachers, nearly 25% reported a need for their motivation to be sustained by effective leadership (*ibid.*, p. 263):

> 'After three years I decided to leave. The head never appeared in the classroom, never kept a check on anything we did. I was getting too good at papering over things, and he didn't notice', or, 'By Christmas I needed to be told to put things

right, and wasn't strong enough to do it on my own. I'd got into very bad habits and really would have appreciated it if the head had come and told me so.'

'In this school, you feel as if your efforts were wasted because the head is so uninterested, and it rubs off on the staff. She couldn't really care less any more about teaching. We never see her in the classrooms; in fact we don't see much of her in the school. She often comes late, gets her hair done in school time, and when she is in, sits in her office learning her part for her amateur dramatics. She can't be doing requisitions all the time . . . If I can't move, I think I'll leave and have a baby. It gets so disheartening when you work hard yourself and there's no back-up.'

'She's very nice, but a 9-to-4 head and never available to discuss anything. You have no incentive to improve when no-one cares what you do'.

My own research findings revealed my sample of teachers to be moti-vated by recognition of their efforts or their talents and, in many cases, to be demotivated by insufficient recognition. Yet, reflecting differences in the professional climates of the schools involved in my study, as well as differences amongst the headteachers and the teachers themselves, spe-cific sources and forms of recognition varied within the sample as a whole. The nature of these differences and the effects they had on motivation are examined throughout the chapters in Part II.

4

The research design

Introduction

The research upon which this book is based originated, as I explain in the Introduction, from a wish to investigate what I had long believed to be a generally misunderstood subject: that of teachers' attitudes to their work and, in particular, what influences these attitudes. Based upon my own experiences from an earlier career as a primary schoolteacher, as well as those of my teacher colleagues, I felt that misunderstandings about what motivates teachers, what affects their morale and what influences their job satisfaction emanate from two factors: uninformed conventional wisdom and inappropriately designed research.

Conventional wisdom makes simplistic assumptions and connections, and research which is inappropriately designed perpetuates these assumptions and connections, mainly though not exclusively through its data collection. Such research will often produce findings that support conventional wisdom because research subjects' choices of responses are limited to exclude anything else, or because researchers do not probe sufficiently deeply to reveal anything else. This process represents the first and second levels of understanding or elucidation of factors affecting teacher morale, job satisfaction and motivation, to which I refer in Chapter 1. Essentially, the process is one of self-perpetuation, fuelled by a propensity for unquestioning acceptance of prevailing views. If, for example, teachers are constantly being reminded by the media and by those around them that they have low morale, and that this is because they are not paid enough then, when presented with questionnaire items asking them whether they consider teachers to be underpaid and whether, in turn, pay is a source of dissatisfaction, they are more likely to respond 'yes' than 'no' to both questions.

I am certainly not suggesting that teachers' morale and job satisfaction are not affected by their views on the pay they receive, nor that teachers hold such views only because they are prevalent in the public domain. However, I do feel that oversimplistic reasoning has given rise to many misconceptions which have distorted the picture of teachers' working lives, and that this distorted image has, in turn, obscured the complexity and intricacy of morale, motivation and job satisfaction within the teaching profession.

The impetus for my research was my concern to present a more accurate portrayal of how teachers feel about their work, and of what accounts for how they feel. I wanted to supplement the body of knowledge in this field, to which several studies have already made valuable contributions. Most, though not all, of these have tended to focus more widely on areas of study that encompass or feature peripherally, or even incidentally, morale, job satisfaction and motivation. I felt that there was room for closer scrutiny of a narrow area, and the research reported throughout this book was the means of effecting this. This chapter presents an outline of my research design.

The research design

My research comprises four separate but related qualitative studies. I therefore refer to it as a composite study of teacher morale, job satisfaction and motivation. The main aim of this composite study was to acquire greater understanding of primary schoolteachers' attitudes to their work and to identify the factors that influence these attitudes. Outline information on these four studies is provided in Table 4.1. The four studies that comprise the composite study are described in more detail below.

Table 4.1 Outline details of the research design of the composite study

| Study | Focus of inquiry | Dates | Sample | | Method(s) of data collection |
			No. of schools	No. of teachers	
1) Rockville	Investigation of the morale level at Rockville County Primary School and of the factors influencing it	1988–9	1	12	1) Observation 2) Semi-structured interview 3) Questionnaire
2) School climate	Investigation of the effects on teachers' attitudes to their jobs of the combination of school climate and teachers' professionality	1989–90	2	6	1) Observation 2) Semi-structured interview
3) 'Extended' professionality case studies	Investigation of factors affecting the job-related attitudes of 'extended' professionals	1990–2	4	6	Semi-structured interview
4) Post-ERA follow-up	Investigation of the comparative effects on teachers' attitudes to their jobs of school-specific and centrally imposed factors	1992–3	1	8	Semi-structured interview

The Rockville study

This was a pilot study of factors influencing primary schoolteachers' morale and job satisfaction in a single school, Rockville County Primary School. The school was selected on the basis of its being referred to, anecdotally, as a 'low morale' school in which there was, reputedly, much staff dissatisfaction. Access was facilitated by my being slightly acquainted with a few of the Rockville staff. When I approached the headteacher for permission to undertake the research I made no reference to the school's reputation, of which he seemed unaware, since I felt that this would serve no useful purpose. I simply mentioned that I wished to study teacher morale, and I guaranteed anonymity. He was perfectly amenable to my using the school, and thereafter showed little interest in my research.

Within the Rockville study were three stages of data collection.

Stage 1

This involved informal, unstructured and unsystematic observation of (in the role of part-time classteacher and classroom support colleague) day-to-day life at the school over one academic year beginning in September 1988. In this study observation was a peripheral means of gathering evidence used to support the other two main methods of data collection, of which I provide details below. It was primarily a means of gathering background information and provided me with insight into staffroom group dynamics, for example, and networks of interpersonal relationships – an inroad into appreciating the complexities and intricacies of the school's collegial climate. I was, in a sense, acting as teacher-cum-observer, since I typically undertook classroom support teaching duties for, on average, three half days per week. It was during these periods, as I came and went around the school, that most of the observation occurred. The staff were all aware that I was in a researcher-cum-teacher role, and that I intended to publish my findings, preserving the anonymity of the school and its teachers with the use of pseudonyms. However, since I did not take notes until after I had left the school for the day, my research role was generally overlooked and, in many cases, after the initial few weeks, forgotten for much of the time, after which I seemed to become entirely accepted within the staff peer group. I am aware of the methodological problems associated with roles of this nature, arising out of the potential for bias. Recognising these limitations, I am nevertheless convinced that such roles enable data to be gathered which reflect, with as much faithfulness as it is perhaps possible to achieve, individuals' attitudes to their work and responses to situations and events which occur. I share the sentiments expressed by Pollard (1980, p. 37) when he describes the type of data collection involved in one of his studies:

I have collected the majority of the data from the role of teacher-cum-researcher, with the research aspect having a low salience to many teachers with whom I have worked and talked primarily as a colleague. Because of this involved and non-threat role, most discussions have occurred in totally natural and unforced contexts. The data are thus mainly drawn from backstage, relaxed and unguarded atmospheres and include a large element of 'inside knowledge' to which many teachers may be reluctant to admit when called to account as a 'professional' by some outside agency.

By allowing me to witness day-to-day events, crises, conflicts, personal triumphs and catastrophes, and to be privy both to open discussion and to many private, closeted conversations, the observation phase gave me a sense of and feeling for teachers' diverse perceptions of, and overall levels of general satisfaction with their jobs, their roles in school, their colleagues and the way in which the school was run.

Stage 2

Interviews constituted the second phase of the study, and were carried out in 1989, approximately one year after I had left the school as teacher/observer. They were semi-structured, the schedule consisting of general topics towards which I wished to steer the interview conversations, within which were specific questions which were components of my research questions but which were not necessarily always presented to interviewees in the same way. Twelve Rockville teachers were interviewed. This sample included all the teachers (except the head) who were willing to be interviewed, but most refusals were made on the basis of absence from school due to ill health or personal problems. I excluded the head since I wanted to confine my study to the job-related attitudes of teachers who constitute 'the managed', and who have class teaching or similar responsibilities. In addition, in order to incorporate the perspectives of individuals who were acquainted with the Rockville context, but were a little more detached from the issues directly affecting teacher morale and job satisfaction, and to help balance the subjectivity of my overall assessment of the Rockville situation, following the example of Smith (1978, p. 349), I also interviewed the school secretary and one of the teachers who was employed at the Rockville-based English Language Teaching Centre.

I typically began by asking Rockville teacher interviewees to describe and then to account for their own morale levels. Irrespective of the level of personal morale reported, I asked all interviewees to comment upon specific incidents and circumstances which had occurred in the school, of which I had become aware through my informal observer role and which, I was also aware, had given rise to some contention, disapproval and dissatisfaction. I also asked interviewees to estimate the morale levels of their colleagues – both as individuals and, as far as it was felt possible to generalise, collectively. I asked, too, about conditions of service and non-school-specific issues. The interviews involved much tactful probing as I tried to elucidate the complexity underlying the reasons why individual reactions and responses to situations, circumstances and events differed, though my familiarity with the interviewees encouraged them to be open, honest and direct. It is impossible to provide a comprehensive list of questions employed in interviews of this kind because, although there was a core of broadly similarly worded questions which were included in all interviews, there were also many additional interviewee-specific questions, since this method of qualitative data collection incorporates an element of opportunism and spontaneity. The core questions included the following:

> Can you try to describe your own morale at school at the moment? . . . For example, is it really high, or really low, or rock bottom . . . or whatever? What I'm looking for is factors which affect morale – either make it high or low – can you, sort of, elaborate?

> Are you happy to stay at Rockville? Can you see yourself still being there in five years' time, or even ten years? Are you looking for another job? How desperate are you to leave? *Why* are you so desperate to leave? What do you particularly like about working there?

> How does Rockville rate, compared with the other schools you've taught at? Are you happier there, or do you wish you were still at _____? What are your views on that? Is that a source of low morale, or of dissatisfaction to you? What, precisely, was it that bothered you about it?

> What changes do you think need to be made at Rockville? If you were the headteacher how would you change things? What would be your priorities? Why? Would you retain the policy of _____?

> Some people have said that _____/complained of _____. Have you found this to be the case, or does it not bother you?

> Are you happy with teaching, as a career, in general? Are you glad you chose it? Do you ever feel like getting out of teaching? Why did you choose it, originally?

> What do you like about the job? What gives you the most satisfaction? What makes a good day for you – describe a good day? . . . and a bad day?

> Can you recall any incidents at any time during your career, which have had the effect of raising your morale, giving you a real lift? What about incidents which have demoralised you? Can you recall any?

> Do you find the job satisfying enough? I mean, is it stimulating? Does it challenge you? What aspects of the job do you find challenging? Are there any aspects of it that you could happily do without?

> Are your satisfied with the salary that you receive?

> What are your views on the introduction into teachers' conditions of service of the five Baker days? What are your views on the introduction of the National Curriculum?

Presentation of a list such as this, however, only provides a very general indication of the approximate content, style and nature of the interviews. Many more questions were asked than those in the above list, which identifies some of the main points of departure only and is in danger of misrepresenting the interview content as oversimplified and lacking depth. Interviews were geared to the individual interviewees and aimed at elucidating the background behind their perspectives and attitudes. Moreover, the sample of questions listed above has a tendency to suggest a sequence of interviewee responses and comments which reflect negative job-related attitudes, but sequences of more positively worded questions were used, when appropriate.

Interviews took place either at my home or at the interviewees' homes and, with the exception of one, were tape-recorded. Duration of interviews ranged from 30 minutes to three hours, with an average duration of 75 minutes. All interviews were transcribed by me, and the quotes incorporated into the chapters in Part II of this book are all extracted from transcriptions.

Stage 3

Self-completion postinterview questionnaires were distributed to all the Rockville teacher interviewees. The purpose of the questionnaires was threefold. First, they provided a means of ascertaining the extent to which concerns and issues raised by interviewees as sources of dissatisfaction were shared amongst the whole sample. Secondly, they provided a means of verifying interview-generated information and of revealing discrepancies between comments made by individuals in interviews and their later questionnaire responses. Thirdly, they provided a means of quantifying levels of satisfaction, dissatisfaction and morale.

The questionnaires consisted of statements which were compiled as a result of extrapolation of interview-generated data. Respondents were asked to rank each statement on a six-point scale presented below:

1) I disagree with this statement/I have never noticed this/I don't find this to be the case.
2) I agree that this occurs/I accept this, etc., but it doesn't bother *me*, personally.
3) It is a slight source of dissatisfaction/It bothers me occasionally, but not very much, on the whole.
4) It is not a *continual* source of dissatisfaction, but it has been a source of dissatisfaction on isolated occasions, in the past.
5) This is a definite source of dissatisfaction to me, but I don't let it get me down/I try to ignore it.
6) This is a major source of dissatisfaction to me – it affects my morale at the school. I feel it should be rectified.

The questionnaire statements were all negative in the sense that they reflected what at least one interviewee had reported as a source of dissatisfaction. Thus, the lower the ranking attributed, the lower the dissatisfaction which it reflected. The statements were usually very specific, and included statements such as 'The deputy head is failing to carry out her duties effectively,' and 'The head apparently lacks concern for the children's education'.

The reason why the questionnaire statements were what would generally be interpreted as negative was that, amongst the sample as a whole, relatively few positive statements had been made during interviews. This probably reflects individuals' tendency to focus on sources of dissatisfaction rather than sources of satisfaction, because the former tend to predominate amongst their concerns. The minority of positive statements that were conveyed during interviews were often personal, and the impression I gained from having interviewed 12 Rockville teachers was that few positive perspectives were widely shared. However, my six-point ranking code provided questionnaire respondents with the facility to convey their disagreement with any statement, thus transforming a negative into a positive viewpoint.

The questionnaires also included an item aimed at revealing respondents' desire to remain at Rockville. Respondents were asked to select any number of eight statements or, alternatively, to compose one of their own, which described levels of willingness to stay at the school, ranging from

1) I love working at Rockville and do not, at the moment, have any wish to leave

   to

8) I am desperately unhappy at Rockville and, if a suitable job elsewhere does not come up soon, I will probably just resign anyway.

The school climate study

The second study was more narrowly focused than the pilot and tested the generalisability of, and investigated further, what I had considered to be the most significant findings of the Rockville study: the importance of teachers' professionality orientation on the 'extended–resticted' continuum, as identified by Hoyle (1975), and the importance of school professional climate. I wanted to investigate the combined effects of these on teachers' attitudes to their jobs. I therefore selected two different schools in which to undertake one year's observation and, within each of these schools, I selected three teachers for interview. Access into the schools was facilitated by my acquaintance with, in the case of each school, one of the teachers. Like the Rockville study, the school climate study involved two stages of data collection. Six teachers were observed and interviewed, as in stages 1 and 2 of the Rockville study: three of them employed at Leyburn County Primary School and three at Sefton Road County Primary School. As with the Rockville study, the period of observation provided me with insight into everyday life in the schools.

Since teachers' professionality had emerged in the Rockville Study as a significant issue, the interviewees were selected on the basis of the professionality which they manifested in the varied contexts in which I was able to observe them. From each of the two schools teachers were chosen with the purpose of representing a cross-section of professionality.

'Extended' professionality case studies

In the third study, case studies were built up of six teachers whom I categorised as 'extended' professionals. Categorisation was based upon my observations and day-to-day interaction with them, again as described in stage 1 of the Rockville study and, in the case of those four of them who had acted as research interviewees in my earlier studies, of interview evidence. The teachers displayed disparate degrees of 'extended' professionality but were all, nevertheless, noticeably distinct from their colleagues with respect to professionality. The purpose of this study was, through semi-structured interviews, to provide individual case studies illustrating the significance of teachers' 'extended' professionality on their work and on their job-related attitudes. For four of these teachers, the interviews in this third study constituted follow-ups to earlier interviews though, in the case of one of these teachers, Helen, the initial research interview and the observation had been conducted as part of a study which does not constitute part of the composite study described here.

In the cases of five of the six teachers, data for these case studies were gathered during dual-purpose interviews, which were designed to serve two of the studies. For example, Kay was interviewed as part of the school climate study but, since I had identified her as an 'extended' professional during the observation phase of this study, I was able to gather two sets of related data during her one interview.

The post-ERA Rockville follow-up study

At the time of the Rockville study, which was carried out in 1988–9, the full force of the implications for schools and teachers of the Education Reform Act 1988 (ERA) and, in particular, of National Curriculum implementation and its testing, had not been felt. I therefore conducted a post-ERA follow-up study involving follow-up interviews with the purpose of ascertaining whether or not the importance on teachers' morale and satisfaction levels of school-specific issues was diminished by competing concerns about centrally initiated policy implementation. This study was restricted to Rockville teachers because they were the only ones of my interviewees who at the time of their interviews had not yet been affected by the demands of the National Curriculum. Eight of the 12 Rockville teacher interviewees were reinterviewed in this fourth study. Sample details relating to all four studies are provided in Table 4.2.

Table 4.2 Details of the teacher sample involved in the composite study

Pseudonym	Age at time of first interview	No. of times interviewed	Job status	School	Study(ies) in which involved (as numbered in Table 4.1)
Elaine	35	1	Main scale	Rockville	(1)
Rosemary	52	2	1) A allowance-holder 2) Deputy head	Rockville	(1), (3), (4)
Brenda	39	2	Main scale	Rockville	(1), (4)
Stephen	33	1	Main scale	Rockville	(1)
Barbara	25	2	Main scale	Rockville	(1), (4)
Jane	40	2	Main scale	Rockville	(1), (4)
Pat	41	2	Main scale	Rockville	(1), (4)
Joanne	49	1	Main scale	Rockville	(1)
Susan	30	2	Main scale	Rockville	(1), (3), (4)
Jean	55	2	Main scale	Rockville	(1), (4)
Amanda	45	2	Main scale	Rockville	(1), (3), (4)
Lesley	31	1	Main scale	Rockville	(1)
Hilary	36	1	ESL main scale	Rockville	(1)
Deborah	43	1	School secretary	Rockville	(1)
Helen	42	2	1) B allowance-holder 2) C allowance-holder	1) Woodleigh Lane 2) Ethersall Grange	(3)
Kay	42	1	B allowance-holder	Sefton Road	(2), (3)
Sarah	28	1	Main scale	Sefton Road	(2)
Louise	40	1	Main scale	Sefton Road	(2)
Mark	32	1	Main scale	Leyburn	(2), (3)
Fiona	41	1	Main scale	Leyburn	(2)
Ann	42	1	Main scale	Leyburn	(2)

Achieving construct validity

Clearly, if it is to reflect as accurately as is possible teachers' attitudes to their work, research into teachers' job satisfaction, morale and motivation needs to be based upon shared understanding of how these concepts are interpreted by researchers. This shared understanding constitutes construct validity.

The researcher must develop a clear idea of what key concepts involve and how s/he defines or, at least, interprets them. This construct development need not necessarily precede data collection; it may arise out of the data analysis. My own constructs of job satisfaction and of morale (see Chapters 1 and 2) each developed out of a cyclical elucidatory process of data analysis, questioning inconsistencies, formulating concept-related hypotheses and reanalysis.

Ideally, researcher(s) and subjects should share a common understanding of the key concepts involved and share acceptance of definitions, if these have been developed. This stage is not always easy to achieve. Researchers may have devoted much exploratory thinking to the process of their conceptualisation, which will undoubtedly have been based upon extensive knowledge of work in the relevant field. Research subjects, on the other hand, will be reliant upon more everyday, less specialised interpretations and usages of terminology. They will be less likely to share the researcher's commitment to rigorous conceptual analysis and, in the time available to have concepts and definitions explained to them, may be unable to grasp the intricacies and subtle distinctions which researchers have uncovered over a much greater time span. To help combat this problem it is important that data collection is designed in such a way that it incorporates inclusion of the distinct dimensions of key concepts.

In researching job satisfaction, for example, interview questions should be designed to distinguish between job comfort and job fulfilment (see Chapter 1) factors. Interviewees need not necessarily be introduced to the specialised terminology which the researcher intends to use in her/his written reports of the work, but the researcher's interpretation of this terminology should be reflected in the questions posed, as in the examples from my own research (presented in Chapter 1), when I asked interviewees not to identify factors which affected their job comfort but to identify aspects of their jobs which they were satisfied *with*, but not satisfied *by*. In this way it is likely that understanding is shared, even if terminology is not. I am confident of having achieved this shared understanding in my research, throughout studies 2, 3 and 4. Details of the process involving my achieving construct validity in my research are presented in Chapter 1.

Data analysis

Data analysis involved a prolonged, cyclical process of data reduction, data display, speculative conclusion-drawing, verification-seeking, further data reduction, data display, respeculation and so on. This was applied in particular to interview-generated data, with observation-generated data (since observation had been intended as a peripheral method of data collection) being integrated into the process as evidence used to support, reject or question emerging conclusions.

Data reduction was an incrementally reductive process, involving several levels of coding, focusing increasingly narrowly on categories of increasing specificity before the much broader overview analysis was applied which sought the fundamental source of decontextualised commonality; what I refer to in Chapter 1 as the 'lowest common factor'. First-level coding, for example, involved examining transcripts of interviews for evidence of levels of teachers' morale, motivation and job satisfaction and of factors which influenced these levels. Data display following on from this revealed a small number of general categories. Second-level coding, and several subsequent levels, then reduced data more narrowly into, for example, categories relating to more specific sources of job satis-

faction, motivation and morale, such as: working with children, interaction with colleagues, centrally initiated policy, school policy, school
management, etc. By this reductive process, alongside emerging conceptualisation and reconceptualisation of job satisfaction and morale
(described in Chapters 1 and 2), analysis eventually culminated in uncovering precisely what it was about the factors which were able to influence individuals' morale, job satisfaction levels and motivation, which
did, in fact, allow them to influence them. Clearly, this also involved
examining the individuals themselves.

Since I was working independently it was necessary to test the reliability
of the categorisation which was incorporated into my data analysis. This
was done following the method proposed by Atkins (1984, pp. 257–8) by
using an independent judge, who categorised data from a sample of three
interview transcripts. This revealed reliability of categorisation.

Verification of emerging conclusions was sought from the teacher interviewees both through separate conversations and, sometimes, in interviews. This was opportunistic rather than systematic, but all levels of
conclusion-drawing were subject to this. It was an invaluable aid to elucidation of the issues presented throughout this book. Moreover, towards
the later stages of analysis when I was seeking elucidation on the 'lowest
common factor', my conclusions were verified by a wide range of
teachers who had not acted as interviewees.

Part II

Teachers' working lives

5

A 'low morale' school? Rockville County Primary

Introduction

As I point out in Chapter 2, morale essentially relates to the individual. Nevertheless, it is typically conceived of as a group phenomenon whose consideration may be applied to various levels and compositions of collectivity. It is not unusual, for example, to hear references to the morale of the profession as a whole, of a particular school or school department, or of teachers who may be identified as a specific group, such as primary headteachers. Of all the three work-related attitudinal concepts examined in Part I of this book, morale is the least frequently applied to individuals.

Yet it is important for the purpose of practical application to examine the extent to which group interpretations and applications of morale are accurate and, therefore, appropriate. If morale may, indeed, be school, department or even profession-wide in its applicability, then comparisons between parallel groups which manifest different morale levels would provide a useful starting point for identifying morale-influencing factors. Lessons may be learned from scrutinising low-morale professions, schools and departments, and prescriptive blueprints developed out of examination of their high-morale parallels.

From a management perspective, which this book incorporates, it is perhaps the notion of whole-school morale that is of greatest interest. Headteachers clearly would prefer to lead a high-morale rather than a low-morale staff, and good managers will be anxious to learn how they may best raise, and maintain, morale within their schools.

It is with the notion of whole-school morale that this chapter is concerned. It focuses upon Rockville County Primary which, as I point out in Chapter 4, was singled out as the subject of research on the basis of its anecdotal reputation as a 'low-morale' school; a school in which there appeared, according to hearsay, to be many dispirited teachers. What I present below is an illustrative outline examination of morale, job satisfaction and motivation within the context of a single school. Not only does this case study set the context for later chapters' analyses of specific morale-, job satisfaction- and motivation-influencing factors but it also assesses the validity, and defines the parameters, of the notion of whole-school morale.

Rockville County Primary School: background information

Rockville County Primary School is located in an English industrial town in the Midlands, in what has developed into one of the 'poorer' districts characterised, at the time of my Rockville study in 1988, by badly main-tained terraced housing, condemned property and a generally untidy and dirty, litter-strewn environment. The Rockville area is one in which there has been a steadily growing influx of ethnic minority families, which began in the late 1970s. These families are Indian, Pakistani and Bangladeshi in origin and, at the time of the study, were mainly first-generation immigrants, particularly in the case of Bangladeshi families. In 1988, 99% of the pupils in the school represented these ethnic minorities. Socioeconomic status of the families was very low.

With the exception of the Year 3 class, Key Stage 1 classes and Key Stage 2 classes were housed separately in what had, until September, 1979, been two separate schools, Rockville County Junior School and Rockville County Infants School. Whilst there was inevitably much close liaison, the two schools were run independently of each other. They were situated some 300 metres apart and had adjoining playgrounds through which there was access between the two buildings.

The retirement of the infants school headteacher coincided with the transfer to another headship of the junior school headteacher, facilitating the application of the education authority's policy of amalgamating, at such appropriate opportunities, infants and junior schools into primary schools. The newly amalgamated Rockville County Primary School was led during its first year by acting headteacher, Margaret Kitchen, who had been the former junior school deputy head, and a newly appointed headteacher, Geoff Collins, came from a deputy headship in the north east to take up his post at the beginning of the school year in September 1978.

In 1988 there were 490 pupils on roll and each year group was, un-usually for a state primary school at this time, streamed on the basis of overall ability and/or English language proficiency into two classes.

Excluding the headteacher there were 18 full-time teachers (one of whom was a home–school liaison teacher with a 50% teaching timetable) and four part-time (0.5) teachers. In addition, the school was the site of the town's County Language Service, which was a support teaching unit for children who lacked proficiency at written and/or spoken English as a result of English being their second language (ESL). One classroom at Rockville housed this language centre. Three full-time ESL teachers employed within the County's ESL Service were based permanently at this centre and, although being answerable to the head of the ESL Service rather than to the Rockville head, they were fully accepted socially within, and to outsiders, appeared indistinguishable from the Rockville staff peer group. They used the Rockville staffroom, participated in play-ground supervision and often attended staff meetings. Children who were designated ESL were removed from mainstream schooling daily for programmes of half-day sessions to attend the language centre until they were considered capable of full integration.

When the second phase of the Rockville study began, the deputy head had been hospitalised and it was not known when, or if, her prolonged absence from work would end. Her duties and responsibilities had been taken over by Rosemary, who had been appointed from within the Rock-ville staff as acting deputy head. Alison, who held the post of what was at that time a scale 3 head of the infants department but which became Principal Teacher Status, with an incentive allowance C under the Baker education reforms, took early retirement after prolonged absence from work.

Examining teacher morale and job satisfaction at Rockville

Significant contextual features

It is impossible within the confines of a single chapter to present a realistic picture of the day-to-day ambience, atmosphere and climate of a school, and to illustrate with any degree of accuracy the complex ways in which specific incidents, events and circumstances influence this. What I present below, therefore, is a snapshot; a crude representation of the Rockville context or setting in the form of descriptions of two of its constituent features: the headteacher and his leadership, and the deployment of staff. These are perhaps most clearly described as circumstances or situations which prevailed at Rockville at the time of my study. They reflect the school's micropolitics and institutional bias and were selected on the basis of their having emerged from the data as particularly significant in influencing levels of staff morale and job satisfaction.

The headteacher and his leadership

The role of headteacher is the pivotal role in a school, central to any understanding of the micropolitics of schools (Ball, 1987, p. 80) and of school culture (Nias *et al.*, 1989, p. 95). Coulson's (1988, p. 254) assessment that 'school headship is not at root about skills, rules or procedures but hinges upon the personality of heads and their relationships with others, especially their capacity to lead by example and the capacity to embody key values' was borne out by the Rockville context. The headteacher's personality, his intellectual capacity, professionality and the ways in which he did things – both at a general level and in relation to specific incidents – were the foci of the majority of work-related conversations between teachers in the staffroom, in classrooms, during playtime supervision and in the pub at lunchtimes. In my teaching-cum-observation role I noted that not a single day passed without my having witnessed some teachers' manifestations of concern about the quality of leadership and the repercussions which this was perceived to have upon the way in which the school functioned.

It is important to emphasise that, throughout this book, I present teachers' perceptions of work-related circumstances which were important to them. I do not examine the accuracy of those perceptions nor the degree of objectivity within them. Not only would this be impossible to determine but it is also irrelevant since, even if their perceptions were 'mispercep-tions', this would not preclude their being the bases of their job-related attitudes. Consequently, the Rockville head is represented as he was perceived, but he was perceived with a strikingly high degree of consensus.

The impression I gained of Geoff Collins, the Rockville head, throughout my prolonged attachment at the school matched the consensual perception of the Rockville teachers. Geoff was seen as a very affable, essentially well-meaning but weak head who avoided difficulties and confrontation and allowed himself to be governed and dominated by one or two strong personalities amongst the staff. His management style was the subject of considerable derision; indeed it was generally agreed that he was an exceptionally poor manager.

During research interviews the Rockville staff spoke candidly and were, in most cases, highly critical of Geoff's management of the school:

> I think he finds the management role incredibly difficult . . . to say he's been on two management courses . . . you'd think he'd realise that he wasn't a manager.
> (Susan, Rockville teacher)

> I think he thinks he's doing his best . . . which, I think, he is . . . in his way . . . but, whether it's the right way for the school is arguable, really, you see . . . And, certainly, his management skills leave a lot to be desired.
> (Deborah, Rockville school secretary)

> He's not directing the school – it's the tail wagging the dog! . . . he's in the wrong job – his personality's wrong for this kind of job.
> (Hilary, ESL teacher based at the language centre)

> I think he'd probably say himself that . . . he's not a manager.
> (Brenda, Rockville teacher)

More specifically, Geoff's hierarchical approach to management underpinned much of his overall policy and determined decision-making and responses which proved very unpopular. He had established a senior management team consisting of himself, Margaret, the deputy head and Alison, the next most senior teacher, who had been placed in charge of what was then known as the school's infants (now Key Stage 1) department. Geoff's attitude to management seemed very clearly to be one of blind faith, non-intervention and unquestioning support in relation to those of his colleagues who held promoted posts, even at the lowest level of the promotion hierarchy, but particularly within the senior management team. This attitude was applied without exception to incumbents of promoted posts, not in a personal capacity but in their capacity as post-holders. It seemed to reflect a wider respect for authority, and was applied irrespective of whether post-holders had been promoted by Geoff or whether he had inherited them. It was removed in the event of promoted posts being relinquished, as in the case of a Rockville teacher who had been appointed to the school on what was then a scale 2 promoted post for co-ordinating the school's mathematics education, and who later relinquished the co-ordinator's role when she returned after maternity leave to teach on a permanent part-time basis. Similarly, it was noticeably applied to teachers to whom it had not been previously applied, once they were promoted. Since its hierarchically oriented, rather than personally oriented basis was recognised it was not interpreted as favouritism, but its unquestioning and often evidently irrational basis created much frustration and resentment. Geoff manifested this attitude to management by his apparently blinkered, 'head-in-the-sand'-type manner of refusing to accept criticism of the behaviour, policies and decisions of teachers who held posts of responsibility, particularly those who constituted his senior management team. I recall, for example, overhearing a conversation with a Rockville teacher during my teaching-cum-observing. The teacher had complained to Geoff at having been left alone to teach a large class of reception children (4–5-year-olds) when her co-teacher was sick and when she had seen Alison, the head of the infants department, who did not have responsibility for a class of her own, coming and going throughout the morning on seemingly routine, non-teaching tasks: filling flower vases, stocking bookshelves and transferring the contents of one cupboard to another. She had asked Geoff why Alison had not assigned herself to assist in what she knew to be the understaffed reception class, and she had questioned the deployment of the senior teacher during the rest of that day. Geoff's response was characteristically courteous but unwavering; Alison was, he said, a senior teacher who had been given responsibility and who was to carry out those responsibilities as she saw fit. He would not make Alison accountable for her movements, nor would he assign her to help in the reception class. The issue was not debatable, and the message conveyed by Geoff on this and on many similar occasions was clear: there was no right of appeal against decisions made by senior members of staff. This managerial approach was interpreted by the Rockville staff placed at the lower level of the hierarchy as a combination of stubbornness and weakness. The stubbornness was evident in Geoff's dogmatic refusal to be drawn into any criticism or questioning of the work of senior staff. The weakness manifested itself in his apparent capacity to be influenced, even dominated, by members of his management team: Margaret and Alison during the teaching-cum-observing stage of my study, and Rosemary and Joanne during the interviewing stage.

Geoff's hierarchical approach to management was recognised by all the Rockville interviewees, and the wider repercussions of it, such as the inequality which it created, particularly in relation to decisional participation and influence on policy, were criticised by most:

Interviewer: . . . could you, sort of, go through the sources of frustration that you experience at Rockville – however small or large . . . Could you try to identify them?
Management . . . the sort of hierarchical structure that there is, in that, although all teachers are now main scale, in actual fact, any teacher who has seniority due to the fact that they've had a scale 2 post, is automatically put into situations that he or she might not be suitable for . . . er . . . the way that some people's opinions are taken into account more than others' . . . well, they're treated as . . . just as if they're better than other people and that their opinions are always the ones that matter . . .

Interviewer: . . . are you prepared to say who?
Alison . . . Margaret . . . Joanne and Rosemary . . . He has a management team, doesn't he? . . . without who he can't make any decisions at all – but that doesn't involve everybody . . . I've been *asked* about things . . . but they never take note.

(Susan, Rockville teacher)

He's very proud of his management team! . . . it certainly doesn't involve everybody . . . no . . . 'cos we're not allowed to say anything . . . I just tell him, I say, 'Don't ask me anything, Geoff, 'cos nobody takes any notice of what I say!'
(Jean, Rockville teacher)

He does not treat everyone the same! . . . There's Alison and Margaret, and, I'd say, Joanne Shepherd, as regards her opinion being more important than anybody else's . . . Rosemary's opinion being more important than anybody else's . . . I mean, if a set of things involves them, and they don't like it, then the whole plan is thrown out of the window. But, if a set of changes – somebody else doesn't like – it would go ahead anyway, because he's the boss.
(Patricia, Rockville teacher)

Consistent with the depersonalisation which underpinned Geoff's respect for, and loyalty to, senior post-holders was another feature of his approach to management: an apparent belief that nobody is indispensable. He tended to convey a generally complacent, unruffled fatalistic acceptance of events, summed up by one teacher's description of him:

he doesn't worry about – nothing worries him. To me, he seems like the type who'll go home at night and go to sleep without a worry or a care . . . there's no . . . he's naive, or oblivious, or insensitive, or *something* . . . I don't know what the word is . . . it's just like it's passive – an abdication of responsibility.
(Hilary, ESL teacher at language centre)

Geoff was a religious man, and a practising Christian – an evangelical Anglican – and some teachers attributed his 'que sera sera' approach to life to his deep faith and a conviction that events are ordained by God. Several interviewees commented upon Geoff's belief that his work at Rockville is a mission and, indeed, in general conversation with me on one occasion he confirmed that this was the case. Others had evidently had similar conversations with him:

> God sent him to Rockville – to sort out the community. I'm convinced he thinks that!
>
> (Deborah, Rockville school secretary)

> Er . . . d'you know, for a long time now, I've sat and thought, 'I wonder what makes Geoff tick' . . . and I've *thought* – I don't *know* but I *think* . . . I think he thinks he's got a mission. And, I think, if you think *that* . . . I think he thinks that this is his role in life . . . that God's given him this role . . . and I think, if you think *that*, then . . . *nothing* – no matter what it is that goes wrong – can get you down. So, in that way, I suppose . . . why he keeps on going and keeps coming up smiling, day after day, has always intrigued me [*laughs*] . . . because I don't know why he's not suicidal!
>
> (Brenda, Rockville teacher)

When it was translated into a management approach, Geoff's fatalism or religious faith, if that was indeed the driving force behind it, created an image of a headteacher who afforded limited value to the individual achievements of, and contributions made by, the Rockville staff. This aspect of Geoff's character and the precise way in which it manifested itself in his role as headteacher are very difficult to convey accurately. To present Geoff as being uninterested in individuals would be misrepresentative of his leadership style, which I would categorise as, fundamentally, a version of what Ball (1987, p. 88) identifies as an interpersonal style. Geoff seemed to thrive on interpersonal relationships. In a pastoral-type role he appeared to be concerned about the well-being of all his colleagues equally, as individuals. He endeavoured to maintain good relations with everyone, tried to please as many people as possible, was never bad-tempered, never criticised and was, essentially, mild-mannered at all times. He manifested a degree of equanimity and goodwill which precluded his ever – to my knowledge – falling out with anyone; indeed, it seemed impossible to fall out with him since he brushed off snubs, insults and criticism and refused to be drawn into arguments. He avoided conflict and always tried to allow his sunny disposition and geniality to fight off ill-feeling, dismissing complaints whenever he was able to with a joking response. He was very sociable, and enjoyed one-to-one discussions and chats with any of his colleagues. He was, himself, one of six children and a father of five, and was concerned to promote his ideal of Rockville as, to use his terminology, 'a big happy family'. His fundamentally caring approach to individuals was demonstrated by his often going out of his way to help colleagues who had personal crises or difficulties.

Nevertheless, predicated, it would appear, upon a conviction that everything which happens is ultimately for the best, was Geoff's evident diminution of the significance of specific individuals' roles and contributions. This was reflected in an apparent lack of concern about losing individual members of staff and a sanguine response to manifestations of discontent. He shrugged off reports of widespread dissatisfaction amongst the staff, evidently in the belief that events would take their course and the situation would rectify itself eventually; that if people were unhappy it would be better for all concerned if they left. I have no knowledge of his ever attempting to intervene in or change a situation in order to placate, pacify or retain members of staff. The consequence of this was that many teachers felt undervalued and unappreciated and the only recourse left to those who were dissatisfied with the way in which Rockville was run seemed to be either to grit their teeth and stay, or to leave. Reasoned argument seemed to fall on stony ground and so there was no possibility of exerting influence to change the situation. Deborah's comments convey Geoff's non-interventionist, head-in-the-sand response to problems in his school:

> *Interviewer: Now, is Geoff aware of the morale problem in his school?*
> Oh, yes, I think he is – he just turns a blind eye! . . . like he does to everything that he doesn't want really to get involved in . . . you see, like he always says, 'Well, if you don't like it here . . . ' and that's what he'll say to *anybody* . . . *anybody at all!* – even me, and, I mean, I know he thinks a lot of me, but, nevertheless . . . if I said I was leaving he'd just say, 'Oh, well, OK, if that's what you want to do . . . I'm very sorry . . . it's a shame you're going', . . . but, he wouldn't *bother* – he wouldn't – no! He wouldn't feel like saying, 'Oh, well, perhaps I'd better have a rethink' . . . That's where he loses a lot of his good staff.
>
> (Deborah, Rockville school secretary)

Other teachers corroborated Deborah's views:

> *Interviewer: Do you feel that, if you were to leave, he'd be most upset?*
> I don't think he'd be in the least bit bothered . . . not bothered in the *slightest*! – about *anybody* – not even his management team! Now, *I* don't think anybody's indispensable, either . . . but, on the other hand, if you feel valued.
>
> (Susan, Rockville teacher)

> Oh, he wouldn't be in the least upset . . . if you mention that you're going to apply for another job, he'll say, 'Yes, do', as if, well, you know, 'the sooner you go, the better'.
>
> (Jean, Rockville teacher)

Deployment of staff
During the period of my teaching-cum-observing at Rockville, there arose a situation concerning the deployment of senior teachers which gave rise to widespread condemnation of Geoff's hierarchical managerial approach and which undermined his credibility as headteacher more than any

other situation or event of which I was aware. Having established a management team, Geoff then developed a policy of freeing up the time of his two most senior colleagues in order to increase their availability for management tasks. This involved the senior teachers' not having class responsibilities but being deployed as support teachers. At first, each of them kept to a timetable which deployed them fairly equitably amongst the different classes and left one afternoon free for management duties, but the situation gradually evolved over several months whereby Margaret, the deputy head, abandoned her timetable in favour of operating a system of supporting teachers on a more *ad hoc* basis. This change was announced by Margaret herself, with Geoff's approval, at a staff meeting which I attended. Margaret explained how in future, if no one objected, she would make day-to-day assessments of teachers' needs and deploy herself as she considered appropriate. This would give her greater flexibility, she argued, and was much more workable than rigid timetabling, which had often had to be abandoned when conflicting demands on her time arose.

Whilst, ostensibly, Margaret's initiative was accepted in the meeting, it was heavily criticised in many closeted discussions over the following days. Margaret was generally perceived as a forthright, assertive, even on occasions, aggressive personality who greatly influenced policy by dominating Geoff. Her plans for a discretionary system of self-deployment were greeted with suspicion and generally interpreted as *carte blanche* for her to do what she liked, when she liked.

This initial cynicism proved to have been justified as, gradually, Margaret's decisions about which teachers to support, the activities which she undertook in classes and her movements in general began to be questioned and criticised. Amongst themselves at first, teachers complained, for example, that Margaret was becoming increasingly elusive, that she only went into the classes of teachers whom she liked and to whom she related well, that she typically did not teach in any capacity but often only sat and observed or wandered around chatting to children and looking at their work. There were also increasingly frequent reports of her having failed to appear in any classrooms at all. On these occasions she was often seen chatting at length in the corridors, or sitting in the staffroom drinking coffee.

Whilst Margaret's behaviour attracted condemnation from the growing number of teachers who noticed it and who aired their disapproval in small groups behind closed doors, it was Geoff who provoked the greater outrage with his characteristic, *laissez-faire* response. Whilst a facade of good relations was maintained between Margaret and the rest of the staff, a core group of teachers was becoming increasingly discontented with Geoff's tacit acceptance of what they considered to be Margaret's inappropriate deployment, and with what several reported as his refusal to address the issue when it was brought to his attention.

Attitudinal responses

It is not an unreasonable expectation that these prevailing circumstances and situations, identified and described with much consensus, should give rise to widespread dissatisfaction and low morale amongst the Rockville staff. It is easily conceivable that many teachers would have become demotivated by what was generally accepted as poor management and ineffective leadership, that most felt frustrated at their opinions being disregarded and would be actively seeking posts elsewhere.

Yet this was not the case. The most striking, overall finding to emerge from the Rockville study was the diversity of job-related attitudinal responses. In relation to the deployment of staff, for example, and in particular that of the deputy head, despite unanimous recognition of the situation amongst my interviewees, the effect which it had on job satisfaction, morale and motivation varied considerably. Although there was general increasingly widespread dissatisfaction over the issue – levels of dissatisfaction, and the underlying reasons for it, varied. It was a majority of teachers who were clearly very dissatisfied with what they considered to be an unacceptable situation. The following comments are representative of this majority viewpoint:

> *Interviewer: . . . if you were given the chance of going to another school . . . would you jump at it, or would you be more selective, or what? How desperate are you to get out, in other words?*
> Oh, yes! I'd go to an infants school – just infants.
>
> *Interviewer: And what is it, basically . . . is it just **one** thing that's driving you out . . . is it the management – the hierarchy that you've spoken of . . . or is it a lot of other things?*
> Well . . . waste of . . . er . . . waste of manpower, I think a lot of it is.
>
> (Jean, Rockville teacher)

> I think, if there was a stronger head, people wouldn't get away with what they get away with . . . that's the thing, isn't it? He just allows himself to be influenced so easily . . . Margaret was only doing half a job.
>
> *Interviewer: . . . if **you** were the head what would you have done? Would you have given her full-time teaching responsibility?*
> I'd certainly have given her at least part time – half-time.
>
> *Interviewer: . . . and you'd have expected the rest – the administration – to be done in her own time?*
> Well, that's what they get paid extra for . . . that's what I firmly believe . . . If I have to work two hours a night, somebody who has a deputy headship should be working three . . . otherwise, all it's saying is that you're being paid extra for being in teaching so long . . . A deputy head should have all the responsibilities of a class teacher, *plus* others . . . but the deputy head in our school has no curricular responsibilities, no class . . . you know . . . He's [Geoff] allowed the management team to make up their own job descriptions . . . and these new conditions of service haven't been applied to them – he's just applied them to everybody else.

Interviewer: Why do you, or any of you, not try and tackle Geoff directly about this?
I think we have

Interviewer: And what's been the result?
Nothing . . . there hasn't been any.

(Susan, Rockville teacher)

Well, I would say that my morale at the moment is lower than average . . . because of all the stresses and strains of various things that've been going on.

Interviewer: Yes. Can you elaborate?
Yes . . . mainly with the deputy . . . not doing the job she was supposed to be doing . . . the pressure on other staff . . . everybody's feeling it and, of course, everybody's discussing it, which tends to bring morale down . . . negative views on things . . . I don't think she went round visiting classrooms as it was claimed she did . . . We don't seem to know where she went – this was a question in everybody's minds – 'Where was she?' Now, I went, with Joanne, straight to Geoff . . . because I thought, 'What *is* Margaret supposed to be doing? Where is she?' He said, 'Well, she hasn't got a timetable, as such', and we said, 'Well, she *should* have' . . . Sometimes she'd be in the staffroom – if you had to go in for first aid equipment you'd find her.

But, I don't think Geoff has been strong enough. He should've put his foot down and said, 'Look, you're doing this. I want you to do *this* timetable', but, instead, he lets it come from Margaret herself, and I think it's the same with Alison . . . you know, you get things like, 'liaising with so-and-so' or 'liaising with the nursery school' – I mean, that's too vague. But he lets that pass. Now, you couldn't get away with that as a class teacher . . . Some people are doing less than others, and getting more money for it.

(Elaine, Rockville teacher)

Margaret shouldn't have a job as deputy head . . . Alison shouldn't – well, they shouldn't , really, for what they do and the amount of money they're paid. For the amount of money that they get paid, and the responsibilities – well, they should have class responsibilities *as well as* all those extra responsibilities . . . as far as the conditions of service are concerned – but they *don't!* Whereas, we *do* . . . and, I mean, that's not right!

(Jane, Rockville teacher)

I mean, it's disgusting! I mean, she [Margaret] does have a timetable now, but it's *so* ambiguous and so flexible, it's just beyond . . . beyond reason! . . . Well, to say we've got all these managers, how can the school *be* so mismanaged – it's a farce!

(Patricia, Rockville teacher)

There was, however, a reasonably large minority of more tolerant or complacent views. Several interviewees, like Rosemary and Stephen whose comments are presented below, clearly had managed to detach themselves sufficiently from the situation to allow them to cope with it by not allowing it to impact too negatively on their attitudes to their work:

I think changes are planned for a more efficient carrying out of the deputy headship role . . . and it's not before time, because this has been the root of a lot of staff's dissatisfaction . . . this drifting around . . . That's when dissatisfaction began to creep in . . . I think that was the beginning of it . . . the thing just went from bad to worse . . . and I think a lot of people . . . er . . . felt very low at that point, and, you know, feelings were running high

Interviewer: And how did you feel at this point? Did it bother you?
Not *personally*, because . . . I'd, sort of, organised myself and was getting on with the job that I felt I was employed to do . . . er . . . and I didn't really let it . . . er . . . bother me. I mean, Margaret was timetabled to come into the reception class, but we never ever saw her . . . only on very, very rare occasions when she just breezed in . . . So, personally, you know, I didn't let it get to me, because, if you recall, when you were there, people were getting to the point where something had to be done . . . either *they* had to get out, or they'd to bring in some outside help to remedy things there . . . and, you know, people were talking about going down to the Education Office, and, you know, they had no confidence in management, and so on . . . But, I didn't really want to get involved in that because . . . er . . . I don't know – maybe I'm a bit of a coward . . . er . . . I didn't want any more ill-feeling within the place than there already was . . . and, also, I felt sorry for Geoff in a lot of ways because, as I say, he was a victim of circumstances – the way that he came in, and the strength that Margaret had at that time, with her colleagues around her . . . er . . . I really think he was up against a very confident and a very tough . . . and aggressive . . . person . . . and I think he had to tread very carefully, otherwise, you know, perhaps he could have been destroyed by it.

(Rosemary, Rockville teacher)

Interviewer: . . . people have criticised the way in which there are two members of staff who don't have classes . . . now, how does this affect you?
Er, it doesn't, really – I wouldn't say it affected me all *that* much . . . No, it doesn't get on my nerves as much as it gets on other people's nerves . . . things like that don't really get to me as much, I don't think . . . er . . . if they haven't got a class.

(Stephen, Rockville teacher)

As these illustrative comments show, responses to the issue of the deployment of senior staff were wide-ranging. A majority of interviewees were clearly dissatisfied with the situation: some with the injustice of it, others with the inconvenience and/or increased workload which it imposed on themselves, and some with the irrationality of it. Most were dissatisfied with the headteacher's management of it and laid the blame at his feet. A minority of interviewees took a more tolerant or a more complacent stance, either because they had not allowed the situation to have a significant impact on their work or because they were able to view it vicariously.

Morale and job satisfaction at Rockville

Initially, my intention in undertaking the Rockville study was to reveal the level of morale and job satisfaction amongst the Rockville teachers, and to identify the factors which had influenced these levels. Having picked up anecdotal evidence that Rockville was a school experiencing management-related problems and that many of its teachers were disgruntled with what was vaguely referred to as 'the situation' there, I had expected to find a 'low morale' school, full of dissatisfied teachers who were looking for new posts. The situation was not as simple and straightforward as that, but it served to reveal to me the complexities involved in understanding job satisfaction and morale. By a cyclical process of data analysis, questioning inconsistencies between my findings and what I had found in some of the literature on morale and job satisfaction, reanalysis, seeking verification from research subjects and, again, reanalysis, I developed over time my own interpretations of the two concepts which are presented in Chapters 1 and 2.

It was the diversity of attitudinal responses which made any assessment of morale and job satisfaction at Rockville considerably more complex than I had anticipated. Whilst, clearly, there was widespread low morale and dissatisfaction, it would have been inaccurate to describe Rockville as a low-morale school.

Levels of morale and job satisfaction were high amongst some teachers which, despite these teachers representing a minority, precluded the application of a general 'low morale' label to the school. Moreover, the range of lower levels of morale and satisfaction which emerged was surprisingly wide. A minority of teachers described their own morale and satisfaction levels as being 'extremely low', 'very low' or 'at rock bottom', but other teachers fell within the two extremes. Observation- and interview-generated data, together with the more quantitative questionnaire data which afforded a basic means of quantifying levels of job satisfaction and dissatisfaction, revealed the most dissatisfied Rockville teacher to be Amanda, whose story is presented in the next chapter. Two of the most satisfied teachers were Rosemary and Brenda, who are profiled in Chapters 7 and 8, respectively.

It was particularly interesting that, as I have pointed out, this diversity of attitudinal response did not seem to be a straightforward case of multiple perceptions. As is shown by the samples of illustrative quotations presented throughout this chapter, there was general agreement in relation to what was going on in the school, even between teachers representing the extreme levels of morale and job satisfaction. It was, therefore, not perceptions but responses which were diverse and, whilst situations and circumstances which were clearly acknowledged by all who were aware of them as undesirable did not foster high morale or high levels of job satisfaction, they did not necessarily in all cases lower morale nor give rise to significant dissatisfaction. This clearly precludes morale from being interpreted, as it so often is, as a group phenomenon. It calls into question the validity of the notion of whole-school morale and reveals both job satisfaction and morale to be essentially individual phenomena, as I explain in Chapters 1 and 2.

The individuality of morale and job satisfaction

Why do some teachers accept conditions and situations of which others complain bitterly and are unable to tolerate? Why is it that circumstances, which are described with striking similarity by all affected by them, may develop into a resignation issue for some and yet are accepted with sanguinity by others? The individuality of human behaviour, arising out of differences in life experiences and biographical factors and which underpins the heterogeneity of teachers, is clearly the underlying reason for diversity of responses. However, my findings revealed more specific distinguishing factors emanating from this underlying heterogeneity. Three factors in particular were influential upon the Rockville teachers' attitudinal responses, not only to the school-specific circumstances and situations which I describe above but also to other prevailing contextual conditions which I observed or which were reported to me. These factors, which are inter-related, are *professionality*, *relative perspective* and *realistic expectations*. In the following three chapters, using examples of cases of individual teachers drawn from four primary schools, I illustrate how these factors influence teacher morale, motivation and job satisfaction.

A management perspective: issues for consideration

Table 5.1 is a summary of how their schools' management was viewed by a majority of Rockville teachers. This represents the perceptions of the 'managed'.

Table 5.1   School management as viewed by the majority

Key features of management	Illustrated by	Corresponding effects on teachers' working lives	Corresponding attitudinal responses of teachers
Hierarchical	Decision-making undertaken only by senior teachers	Exclusion from decision-making process	Frustration
Intransigent	Headteacher's reluctance to modify decisions/policy	Incapacity to influence change	Frustration
Laissez-faire	Ineffectiveness and incompetence remain unchecked	Inequitable treatment	Anger
Unreflective	Decisions and policy lack a rational basis	School professional climate impoverished	Dissatisfaction

Key points
- Features of management perceived as positive by managers may be perceived negatively by the 'managed'.
- Management is a potent influence on teacher morale, motivation and job satisfaction.
- Senior staff need to be accountable to colleagues.

- Management approaches need to be constantly evaluated and modified.

Consider

- How would the Rockville *headteacher* be likely to perceive and evaluate his management? What would *he* consider to be its key features? What would he consider to be the corresponding effects of these key features on teachers' working lives?
- Was the Rockville headteacher right to support senior teachers unquestioningly? Should headteachers be receptive to criticism of their senior colleagues? Should loyalty to, and support for, the deputy head take precedence over accountability?
- How important and useful a role did the Rockville deputy head perform? Can the role of primary school deputy head be dispensed with? What alternatives could replace it?
- Had the Rockville head allowed the situation of the deployment of senior staff to get out of hand? Had he exceeded the parameters of acceptable management? Should the Rockville staff have taken more direct steps to challenge the headteacher's handling of the situation? What options were available to them, and which would have been appropriate?
- Was Geoff Collins a satisfactory headteacher? Should he remain in a headship role? If you were a governor of Rockville County Primary School how satisfied would you be with the school's management? How might you have reacted if (1) a Rockville teacher, (2) a deputation of Rockville teachers reported to you the circumstances of the issue of the deployment of senior staff?

6

Voices crying in the wilderness? Dissatisfaction and unfulfilment amongst 'extended' professionals

Introduction

The preceding chapter's description of Rockville County Primary School provided a contextual background against which the Rockville teachers' work-related attitudes could be presented. It highlighted the individuality of morale and job satisfaction, revealing a diverse range of attitudinal responses.

This chapter leads on from the observation that individual teachers respond in quite different and distinct ways to situations and circumstances which are perceived similarly. It is the first of three chapters which each examines the stories of teachers whose cases share commonalties but which, together, consider the heterogeneity of teachers which underlies the diversity of individuals' attitudinal responses. The focus in this chapter is upon teachers' dissatisfaction and low morale, illustrated by the cases of three teachers to whom the category 'extended' professional may be applied.

Amanda, Helen and Mark: three 'extended' professionals

'Extended' professional is a term which is neither familiar to, nor widely used by, most teachers. It was introduced over 20 years by Hoyle (1975), who presented a continuum of teachers' professionality ranging from 'extended' to 'restricted'. Professionality, as described by Hoyle, is not the same as professionalism. Professionality refers to the knowledge, skills and procedures which teachers use in their work, whereas professionalism refers to status-related elements of an occupation (*ibid.*). Professionality essentially combines professional ideology, job-related values and vision. It reflects what the individual believes education and teaching should involve, and incorporates individuals' predispositions towards, and levels of, reflectivity, rationality and, to some extent, intellectualism or, perhaps more precisely, intellectual curiosity. It influences perspectives.

Whilst professionalism principally relates to ways, or even codes, of *behaviour*, professionality fundamentally relates more to ways and levels of *thinking*. Professionality seems to be what Little and McLaughlin (1993, p. 6) identify as 'orientation' – a dimension of teacher-to-teacher interactions and which, they write: 'combines aspects of teachers' value dispositions and depth of expertise . . . Embedded in this dimension are the criteria by which teachers judge one another and the concepts of colleagueship by which teachers may judge more or less congruently the accepted notions of a good colleague.' Hoyle's 'extended–restricted' continuum of professionality identifies, at one end, a model of 'restricted' professionality which is essentially reliant upon experience and intuition and is guided by a narrow, classroom-based perspective which values that which is related to the day-to-day practicalities of teaching. 'Extended' professionality, at the other end of the continuum, carries a much wider vision of what education involves, values the theory underpinning pedagogy and generally adopts a much more reasoned and analytical approach to the job. Similarly, Evans's (1986) characteristics of the 'extended' professional, encompassing most of Hoyle's, present an image of a reflective, intellectual practitioner who also manifests a high level of professionalism through loyalty to the school and colleagues and a commitment to serve pupils' needs.

To anyone who has either been a teacher or has spent prolonged periods of time in schools interacting with teachers, the descriptions and characterisations of 'extended' and 'restricted' professionality ring true and are recognisable, even though the terminology may be unfamiliar. The 19 teachers upon which my research focused represented a wide range of professionality orientations, situated along the 'restricted–extended' continuum. Amanda, Helen and Mark were all what I would categorise as 'extended' professionals.

Their 'extended' professionality became apparent in the course of general, work-related conversation with them. In the cases of Amanda and Mark, who taught at schools where I carried out teaching-cum-observation phases of my research, it was evident in classroom discussions and staff meetings, in the ways in which they worked and, in the case of Amanda, in the complimentary, even slightly reverential, comments made about her by some of her Rockville colleagues. Brenda, for example, spoke of Amanda: 'I respect what she does as a professional *immensely* . . . I mean, I think she's probably the most brilliant teacher that ever – she's probably the most dynamic . . . the most energetic . . . the most gifted – I think she *is*. I think she's fantastic!' Hilary, who taught at the language centre which was housed at Rockville and who had worked extensively with Amanda, corroborated Brenda's evaluation: 'I've got a great deal of respect for Amanda . . . in fact, I would love – I've learned a lot, working with her . . . She's everything that a teacher *should* be . . . Amanda questions development and the intellectual side of things

. . . would consider content, children's needs, suitable assessment.' Their 'extended' professionality was also evident in comments made by the three teachers themselves during research interviews. Mark's description of himself is illustrative:

> I believe passionately in . . . good education, and having sound aims and objec- tives . . . and, you know, having purpose to what you're doing. . . . I don't mean to sound big-headed, but I do look for the rationale behind things and I do look at the theory and the philosophy. I like to read reports and documents.

In particular, each of them manifested an interest in undertaking further study and was either registered on, or seriously considering following, a higher degree or similar long, award-bearing course:

> Every so often I get bored . . . mentally, and I need to take on the next challenge – the next intellectual challenge. And it's important to me . . . er . . . my intel- ligence is important . . . I do need some kind of intellectual stimulus, and so, having done my Open University degree . . . the next thing was my MA.
>
> (Helen)

Indeed, participation in such courses is one of the characteristics identified by Hoyle (1975) as distinguishing 'extended' professionals from 'restricted' professionals, who typically prefer shorter courses of a practical nature.

As the term itself implies, 'extended' professionality involves charac- teristics and qualities which exceed the norm. There is therefore a dis- tinctiveness about 'extended' professionals which allows them to be singled out either from their colleagues in school or, since it is conceivable that there may be schools in which 'extended' professionality permeates the dominant prevailing teacher culture, from the rest of the profession. Either way, 'extended' professionals stand out from the crowd. This dis- tinctiveness was my main criterion for categorisation, which was applied loosely in order to reflect the notion of 'extended–restricted' profession- ality being a continuum rather than polarities. Whilst all those teachers whom I labelled 'extended' professionals manifested characteristics which were clearly oriented towards the 'extended' end of the con- tinuum, they represented different degrees of 'extended' professionality. In the cases of Amanda, Helen and Mark, such a difference was apparent, but this did not preclude there being a striking similarity between the factors which they considered to have been significant in affecting their job-related attitudes, and the kinds of events and circumstances that shaped their separate stories, which are presented below.

Mark's story

At the time of his research interview Mark was 32 years old and had been teaching for six years. He had been at Leyburn County Primary School for the last four of those six years, where he was originally appointed as the science co-ordinator. He was a late entrant to the profession, having left school at the age of 16 with GCE O-Levels and, finding office work unchallenging, embarked upon a four-year B.Ed honours degree course at a local college of higher education so that he could become a teacher.

Mark was, overall, dissatisfied with his job at Leyburn. He was not dissatisfied with teaching as a career. Indeed, he spoke of how he derived job fulfilment from working with children:

> I feel that I've got my fulfilment back in teaching, a bit . . . er . . . through reappraising how I teach certain things, and getting satisfaction out of teaching things better the second time around . . . and . . . just a simple thing . . . I get a lot of satisfaction when children understand a topic I've covered. This year I've had a rethink on how to teach decimals . . . and something as simple as that gives me a lot of satisfaction, when I've tested them and found that they could do it . . . and there've been quite a few experiences like that in the last couple of years, and I've got satisfaction out of it.

His dissatisfaction emanated from school-specific issues – in particular from what he perceived to be poor leadership. He made no attempt to disguise his dislike of Mrs Hillman, the Leyburn headteacher, of whom he spoke very critically. He complained that her highly efficient management presented a false image of a 'good' school and obscured what he perceived to be the lack of sound underlying educational principles and ideologies:

> I was reading a document about four weeks ago . . . and it said that the type of school that looks efficient is one where the head dictates and talks . . . and there's no coming back to the head – no feedback. I mean, our school, it's just . . . Mrs Hillman *says* and there might be one or two things fed back, but there's no interaction – no communication. There's no, sort of, coming to a decision by consensus . . . To me, that's a bad school, but, from the outside, it's run so smoothly in terms of administration and clerical duties and things swept cleanly . . . nice carpets and nice curtains . . . it looks like a good school.

He proceeded to give an example of this superficiality:

> Mrs Hillman *knows* what the right things are in education. She knows that you have a class assembly . . . and combined topics . . . that you involve classes of different age ranges in activities . . . but, it's only superficial – it's not in the sense of . . . we get round the table and discuss, and say, 'Well, we need to do this – let's do something that's meaningful to you and the children' . . . A few years ago she dropped on us a work experience . . . 'Schools' Involvement in Industry' . . . and she dropped on us the topic, 'The World at Work'. And we all had to set up a market place and do different topics related to industry . . . But she just said, 'You're doing this', and everyone was totally bewildered, really . . . most people hadn't had a good training and they didn't know what she was talking about . . . so they just said, 'What shall *I* do?' and so, in the end, she was just *telling* them, 'You do this, this and this . . . ' But it wasn't meaningful, and it wasn't purposeful, and . . . no real benefit was gained by the children . . . but, from an outsider's point of view, who doesn't know anything about it, it looked

like Leyburn was doing really exciting things . . . Leyburn's involved in 'The World of Work', and *she's* involved in the bandwagon of industrial liaison . . . On paper it looks good . . . but, in reality . . . The acid test is whether I'd send *my* children there – and I wouldn't . . . I wouldn't recommend anyone to send their children there.

In particular, Mark condemned Mrs Hillman for perpetuating Leyburn's underlying speciousness through her leadership style, which involved an exceptionally high level of efficiency but which glossed over the surface and swept problems under the carpet, in order to present a false image of a 'good' school.

For Mark, job fulfilment was tied up with translating sound pedagogy and educational principles into practice through school management: 'I want to ultimately be in charge of a school where . . . sound aims and goals and philosophy are thrashed out, through discussion, and put into practice.' He explained how, over several months, he had eventually come to recognise this career path as the one which would be the most satisfying for him:

I think I've changed. I've gone through phases, at times, of wanting to leave teaching to be an academic . . . to go and do research . . . or to write children's books . . . and the most fulfilled I've ever felt in my life was when I was studying at college and writing essays . . . Er . . . I had a word with the adviser, and he said he thought it was fine doing an MA degree . . . and I still fancy the idea, for personal reasons, but I'm back in the groove of wanting to get on . . . as a deputy head, and become a headmaster, which I didn't want to do before . . . The trouble was, I didn't fancy the social problems and the nastiness in-volved . . . and parental conflict. But now I feel that I've got the personality . . . that won't be a problem – I can easily get over that . . . the thing that I feel now . . . I feel that it's always been there, but I have the confidence to know better, now.

Mark's dissatisfaction at Leyburn resulted in his actively seeking a new post though, since he was only prepared to apply for posts which con-stituted promotion, his career ambitions clearly also played a part in his decision to leave. Nevertheless, the frustration which he experienced at Leyburn was evident: 'I'm not happy at the school . . . I didn't think it was desperate . . . but, . . . the other week . . . she [Mrs Hillman] . . . conducted a staff meeting in the usual style, just dropping her decision on us, and I thought, "It's time to go".' His frustration and dissatisfaction emanated from a sense of unfulfilment both at teaching in a school which, despite outward appearances, operated on a functional rather than a rational basis, and at being denied the opportunity to exert any influence on changing this situation: 'I want a position which gives me more clout and more power . . . an involvement in the management of the school . . . to be an integral part of the decision-making machinery – which I'm not.' Mark's case was clearly one of mismatch between his own and his head-teacher's ideologies and values and between the different professionality orientations which they each represented. The headteacher's leadership style was such that her somewhat 'restricted' professionality permeated the whole ethos and culture of the school, making it inconducive to the kind of organisation and practice which reflected Mark's more 'extended' professionality. It was 'professionality clashes' of this kind which were similarly the underlying causes of both Helen's and Amanda's dissatisfaction.

Helen's story

Helen was 42 at the time of her first research interview and had worked as a teacher of early years children since leaving college at the age of 21. When I first interviewed her she held a main-scale teaching post with an Incentive Allowance B at Woodleigh Lane Primary School, but was waiting to take up an appointment in another school, Eckersall Grange Primary, giving her an Incentive Allowance C. She had left college with a teacher's certificate, gained an Open University degree through part-time study and was working for an MA degree. For over a year she had held a part-time (0.25) post at her local university, for which she was seconded from her teaching post. Her university work involved teaching on the primary PGCE course on one and a half days a week.

What distinguished Helen as an 'extended' professional was her dependence upon extra sources of job fulfilment, beyond those which were class teaching-based. She spoke of the job satisfaction which her PGCE course teaching afforded her, and of how her university-based work had prompted her to consider a career in higher education:

> although I don't have to do any, sort of, er . . . 'high level' planning for the students – because I'm not teaching academic courses – I mean, I find *that* taxing enough, presenting it in that new way. So that did keep my mind *well* occupied . . . And then, I think it was just, kind of, being around people at the university, and talking, and partly thinking, you know, 'Could this be the next chapter in my career – actually moving into this?' . . . The way headship is now, that would be preferable to being a head. I think . . . what I've got out of working at the university is a little bit of the things we've just been talking about – about working with staff. Because, I find that, certainly working with postgraduate students, has been like running INSET . . . but at a more basic level . . . and I've found it exactly the same, because you can't just *tell* them things, and you can't just be didactic . . . you actually have to set up situations where they can learn and come to conclusions for themselves . . . But, I am finding that very satisfying . . . working in that way.

Like Mark, Helen experienced much dissatisfaction and frustration in her job, which she attributed to poor management and leadership in her school. She spoke scathingly of her headteacher, complained that he lacked vision, was ineffective and that both the quality of education provided in the school and the prevailing professional climate had been greatly impoverished as a result of his inadequate leadership:

I've just found it incredibly frustrating because decisions are *not* made. I'd even prefer it if decisions were made that turned out to be wrong. I can't stand indecisiveness . . . In my opinion, not only has the school not moved on, but we've actually gone backwards! . . . If it's properly managed it's a very inspiring school to be in, but at the moment . . . it's not the school – it's the head. He's spoiling it . . . Other members of staff like myself, who actually see things in a wider sense for the school, are getting out . . . and I'm the last one to go. All the . . . you know, the 'extended' professionals, are just going . . . There's nobody in that school with any vision – nobody with any educational philosophy – and that's what *really* frightens me to death . . . Because, they think that you just go in and you teach, therefore children will learn. They don't seem to realise what a curriculum really is . . . They're two male members of staff – the head and the deputy – and they cannot see that that has implications for equal opportunities in the school! They seem to think that, because we've got one girl who plays football, that's it . . . and because the names on the registers are mixed they think everything's working okay.

She summed up her assessment of her headteacher: 'He's thick! He is one of the most unintelligent men I have ever met.'

However, despite her extreme dissatisfaction with her present situation, Helen's morale was high at the time of this first interview since she anticipated much more opportunity for fulfilment in the new post to which she had been appointed, and to which she looked forward eagerly: 'I actually feel that I can be part, again, of moving a school on . . . of actually developing and growing in all sorts of ways – all of us, together.' She spoke enthusiastically of the headteacher with whom she would be working at Eckersall Grange, and who had clearly made a favourable impression on Helen:

My new school – my *next* school, . . . when I was in visiting last week they'd got the children's reports back from the head, and, where the teachers had written . . . er . . . say, four or five lines on the children's personal and social development, the head had written a good, sort of, five-inch column . . . And I flicked through a few, and it was different for every child. She knew each child, and she knew what she was writing . . . And that immediately inspired me. I thought, 'This is somebody I want to be allied with' . . . I just *knew* – I like the whole way she is with people . . . she's got a real vision . . . a real educational philosophy.

Helen was one of those teachers whom (see Chapter 4) I interviewed twice, with over a year's interval between interviews. By the time of her follow-up interview Helen was, however, again dissatisfied with her job because her new appointment and, in particular, the school's headteacher, Julie, had failed to meet her high expectations:

Last July . . . I put down a lot of my problems then to being in that particular school . . . especially with that head . . . and . . . it didn't take me long to realise in September that I was having similar problems in the new job . . . er . . . and having to face up to the fact that it wasn't the school, it was *me* – something in me . . . that was causing the problems . . . I get very frustrated seeing heads making a hash of things. And I know that sounds arrogant, because I know the job's . . . awful, in lots of ways . . . But, I *am* disappointed – I'm *very* disappointed . . . I am *very* disappointed . . . The sad thing is that . . . that I guess she still has all that I thought she had . . . vision . . . a sound philosophy . . . but . . . she cannot put it into practice . . . She's been ill. She was appointed head about four or five years ago, and then, after she'd been in the post for just over a year, she had this ME, this . . . viral fatigue . . . And I assumed that she was fully recovered, but I don't think she is. I mean, she uses her energies very badly . . . I mean, she *wastes* time and energy on trivia . . . And she *isn't* actually good with people. She goes through the *motions* of being good with people, but, in actual fact, she's quite autocratic . . . And, although she comes across as being quite democratic, she actually isn't. People can't make decisions, because she will over-ride them . . . And she can't delegate – she has to overlook every little thing you do . . . And she has her favourites . . . she spends a *lot* of time with certain members of staff, and, you know, no time at all with others . . . It puzzled me right from the start . . . she seemed very . . . 'odd' with me when I first went, . . . hardly spoke to me . . . I was certainly expecting some kind of talk about . . . you know, my role in the school, and the set-up of the school, and I got nothing – I had to pick it up as I went along . . . I've had about . . . two . . . bits of positive feedback since I've been there. So, it's just as bad as at the other place, really . . . So, yes, I *am* disappointed – I'm disappointed with the whole set-up.

More significantly, Helen's latest disappointment had the effect, not only of creating dissatisfaction but also of demotivating and demoralising her and influencing her perspective on teaching as a career. She was now disillusioned to the extent that she had begun to doubt whether she would ever find job fulfilment of the kind that she had once experienced when working with a headteacher whom she had respected and admired. This demoralisation had prompted her to reconsider her career path and to redefine her 'ideal' job. At the time of her first research interview Helen had described her 'ideal' job as a headship, in which she would enjoy working with staff in order to provide children with the kinds of experiences which she would want them to have. She had referred to the possibility of embarking upon a career in higher education, but had identified this only as an option. A year later, she was much more committed to a career in higher education:

My ideal, *now* is to be actually working at university or polytechnic level, . . . certainly, that's where I see the future . . . I'm afraid I've just reached the . . . er . . . you know, that stage . . . I'm struggling to keep going . . . what I want to do – what I think's important . . .
Interviewer: And how much of this is to do with the National Curriculum, and how much is a result of school management?
Er . . . it's hard to measure . . . but my feeling is that *most* of it is to do with school management.

Helen had actually applied for a lecturing post at what was then a polytechnic and, at the time of her second interview, was waiting to hear whether or not she had been short-listed. Her decision to escape from what she perceived as the relentless frustrations of working in schools which lacked purpose, by seeking a change of career, makes her case very similar to that of Amanda, the third of my dissatisfied 'extended' professionals.

Amanda's story

Amanda was a late entrant to the teaching profession. After leaving school at 18 with A-Levels she had worked in the Civil Service and then brought up a family before undertaking her training as a teacher, which she completed at the age of 31. Like Helen, Amanda was interviewed twice. At the time of her first research interview in 1989 she was employed at Rockville County Primary School, having been promoted since her appointment to what was then a scale 2 post with responsibility for developing the school's religious and multicultural education. She was, however, seconded on a full-time basis from her post in order to work at the local college of higher education. This seconded post involved both participation in an RE curriculum evaluation project and teaching on the B.Ed course. The secondment to St Catherine's College was for one year initially, with a probable extension to two years. Amanda had held her post at Rockville for four years and, at the time of her first interview, was in her thirteenth year as a teacher. Rockville was her second permanent post, to which she had transferred from South Street County Primary School under the county's voluntary redeployment scheme.

Amanda was an extreme example of 'extended' professionality, who consistently applied such a high level of reflection and analysis to all aspects of her work, and whose apparent perspective on and concept of education was so incisive that she was distinct even from other teachers whose professionality orientation lay clearly towards the 'extended' extreme. Her description of the thoughtfulness and thoroughness which she applied to planning her teaching conveys something of the meticulousness which permeated her practice:

> whatever I did in the classroom, I did it as if it – when I planned for something I planned for it . . . some would say, 'Well, the last time I planned like that I did it for assessment' . . . Now that's how I planned for *everything* . . . that's how I got my job satisfaction . . .
>
> I want my maths systems to be absolutely right . . . and, you know, the first months when you're sorting your children out . . . after those first months I can tell you where anybody in my class is, on any book . . . But I feel you *have* to be able to do that because, otherwise, you can't have children working individually . . . And so, when people say, 'Well, you can't deal with them individually', I think you *can* deal with them individually, but it's hard work and it requires a lot of organisation . . . and so, that's what irritates me, when I hear people saying – not bothering about meeting a child's individual needs – and, thinking of the sort of children *I've* taught at Rockville and at South Street in

particular, if you can't meet the child's individual needs . . . then that child might as well not be at school . . . So, really, you've no *choice*, I don't think. You know, to be effective, you've *got* to meet individual needs – to meet individual needs you've got to be absolutely on the ball yourself and you've got to have a system which is so good . . . er . . . you know . . . the sequence of how you're going to do things . . . which schemes you're going to use for which particular needs, and so on . . . And, also, not only is it a lot of work, but it means that you, yourself, have to keep very 'au fait' with what's available, and when something new is introduced into the school you've got to be able to appraise *that* and your supplementary material in the light of what's going to be mainstream . . . So, I suppose, in a way, a lot of my satisfaction is not coming directly from teacher–child contact . . . it's coming from, I suppose, in *my* way, being as organised as I can . . . being as aware of what's available as I can . . . reading as much as I can . . . and finding out as much as I can about how to meet individual needs *for* children, and putting a lot of time and effort into organising my teaching activity to accommodate what I know is appropriate for those children.

Yet, as with my other 'extended' professionals, her perception of teaching went far beyond a narrow, classroom-bound focus. She saw teaching as a career which incorporated continued personal and professional development, underpinned by constant self-appraisal and self-improvement.

As a class teacher at Rockville, though, Amanda felt constrained by the school's management and by the prevailing collegial climate which, she felt, emanated from the attitudes of those in management roles and of her teaching colleagues. She spoke of her interest in teacher development, and of how her work in higher education had allowed her to pursue this interest, whilst constraints at Rockville had restricted the job fulfilment which she derived from her work there:

The work I like at St Catherine's [HE college] is where I'm supporting somebody in . . . er . . . preparing for school practice . . . where I'm supporting those units of the course which are leading to curriculum responsibility. So, the bits of the higher education work that I like are connected with teaching practice. I also like the management work I'm doing as well . . . you know . . . I like that aspect of the in-service work which is directed at management . . . er . . . management styles . . . er . . . and I like the – I like the bit of sociology that's involved in . . . er . . . the research of the project. But my interest is in . . . er . . . developing the professional competence of teachers . . . Now, you could argue, therefore, that I'm still seeing myself very much aligned to classroom practice . . . so, am I getting *my* satisfaction indirectly through the classroom? . . . Well, yes . . . I *did* get a lot of satisfaction from teaching the children . . . I still would now, but it . . . it's not enough for me . . . And, having gone to Rockville thinking that there was going to be a high level of interaction, amongst my teaching colleagues, which was about professional expertise, increased competence, extending and developing your own . . . er . . . teaching performance . . . er . . . by examining the children's learning and seeing what it needed – your in-service being how you could enhance your teaching and, hopefully, the children's learning as well . . . what I *found* was . . . the image I'd been given wasn't real . . . and so I still found myself in a situation there where, generally speaking, . . . I felt that . . . er . . . I lacked colleagues who saw it as a career or as a profession . . . And, so, what does one do about it? . . . Well, I was fortunate, wasn't I, that the project at St Catherine's came up – I could get my teeth into that . . . the scale 2 post came up – it was contentious . . . er . . . it was an area which I knew quite a bit about, but I had to make it context-related to a different situation – er . . . all those things together gave me the opportunity to work at . . . shall we say, what I felt was stretching myself intellectually . . . it allowed me to . . . er . . . I suppose, develop professionally outside of whatever restraint was being put on it either by the school – the attitude of those in management positions . . . the expectations of those who were determining what was the 'norm' for those children there . . . but . . . I'll be honest with you . . . I am absolutely *dreading* – well, I shan't go back to Rockville . . . I shan't go back after this secondment . . . I shall have to look for a different sort of work if I can't – I can't go back there, and I can't, any more, tolerate . . . er . . . I can't tolerate a shoddy performance!

Amanda's dread of returning to Rockville was generated by her extreme dissatisfaction with the general way in which the school was run. Her own professionality, her ideologies and values were clearly at odds with those reflected in the professional climate which prevailed in the school. Decisions at Rockville were based upon practical rather than educational or pedagogical considerations and were often strategically rather than ideologically-motivated. This imposed constraints on Amanda, in so far as she was often thwarted in her attempts to apply a rational basis to her own teaching, and she was able to exert only limited influence on school policy and practice. More significantly, her realistic expectations of how the school would be run were not met. She was both disillusioned and unfulfilled:

And the other thing that disillusioned me was that it became apparent to me that a lot of the staff there were not competent to deal with the children that they were teaching . . . they had no understanding of, first of all, the background of the children . . . they had no understanding of language development . . . they'd no *real* understanding of helping children with learning needs . . . I mean, when NFER assessment is being used on children who've been in the country for six *months* . . . and are ESL . . . and it's being used *despite* – I mean, I actually asked for my protest to be recorded for those children using that – I felt so strongly about it! . . . and I was told it had always been done; Mrs Kitchen thought it was appropriate . . . I could discuss it with her if I wanted . . . but it would be done. Now, alright, I'm not saying I shouldn't have been over-ruled . . . but that was an indication to me that all the school was saying, in regard of its pupils, was, in actual fact, not so.

Amanda's second research interview took place in 1992, three years after her first one. She had not returned to Rockville. The post to which she had been seconded allowed her to develop contacts through which she was recruited to a team of providers of in-service courses and consultancy. She also successfully completed a part-time MA degree course.

Job satisfaction and morale amongst 'extended' professionals

Underpinning the dissatisfaction, unfulfilment and low morale of these three teachers was the 'professionality clash', to which I have already referred, between them and their headteachers. In each case, the more 'restricted' professionality of the headteachers influenced school climate in such a way that the 'extended' professionals were stifled and constrained by their work contexts.

The significance of the influence of school professional climate on teachers' attitudes and work has been recognised and examined by researchers. Pollard (1982) points out that school climates are both constraining and enabling to teachers and, indeed, work which focuses on teachers' coping strategies is predicated on acceptance that school professional climate is one potential constraint. As Rosenholtz (1989, p. 42) comments: 'the organizational conditions of schools create some of the major problems associated with teacher quality and commitment and, just as powerfully, these conditions mold the strategies that teachers find most acceptable and appropriate to use.' Similarly, both Fullan and Hargreaves (1992, p. 6) and Leithwood (1992, p. 96) emphasise the significance of individual schools for either promoting or stifling teacher development.

Whilst not referring specifically to 'extended' or 'restricted' professionals, some researchers have examined the importance of the degree of congruence between teachers' specific, professionality-related characteristics and the professional climates which prevail in their schools.

Nias (1989, pp. 49, 51) refers to the marginalisation experienced by those of her graduate teacher interviewees who manifested professionality which lies at the 'extended' end of the continuum:

> One of my interviewees put it this way, 'I'm intellectually lonely at school, I'm the only one who reads *The Guardian*, the only one interested in politics or literature, and there is only one other who's ready to talk about art and music'. Similar comments were: 'My educational reference group is certainly not in school – it's a few intimate friends from university and scientists generally' . . . 'I feel intellectually starved.'
>
> . . . none of my interviewees enjoyed working in a school in which they felt they had no referential support. As they said, they needed people on the spot who 'felt the same way as I did', 'has the same philosophy', 'saw things the way I did'.

Similarly, Hayes and Ross (1989) and Veal *et al.* (1989) highlight the impact which schools' professional climates may have on teacher reflectivity. Hayes and Ross's (1989, p. 348) case study of Jennifer, whom they identify as a reflective teacher, illustrates the detrimental effects of mismatch between teachers' professionality and school climate: 'At Northside . . . Jennifer's experiences . . . created defensiveness, lowered self-esteem, extreme dissatisfaction with teaching and, at times, acquiescence to practices which violated her basic beliefs about teaching.' In contrast, they describe her response to working in a climate which was more conducive to 'extended' professionality (*ibid.*): 'In this environment, Jennifer drew on educational literature to develop innovative practices, engaged in continuous self-assessment, and her professional self-confidence soared. In fact, she described her first year at Canter as exhilarating. Her principal shared her perspective, saying that she was one of the best kindergarten teachers he had ever seen.' Clearly, then, the experiences of Mark, Helen and Amanda are by no means atypical.

Impediments to achieving job fulfilment

By analysing these three teachers' cases in relation to my interpretation of the job fulfilment process (which I present in Chapter 1) it is easy to see precisely why they were dissatisfied. Of the eight stages that I identify as constituents of the process, all three teachers were severely constrained at level 3 to the extent that they were frequently unable to proceed as far as this stage. Level 1 of the job fulfilment process – awareness of an imperfect situation – was represented by the perception, common to all three of them, that, in their respective schools, children's learning needs which *could* be met were not being met. This was the fundamental source of their dissatisfaction, and the illustrative selection of interview-generated comments presented in this chapter discloses concerns, complaints and frustrations that may, on analysis, all be traced back to this. That these teachers all recognised this prevailing situation in their respective schools as imperfect on the grounds that it was avoidable indicates their awareness of what, in their view, could rectify it. The extension of this into the formulation of ideas about what *could* be done to remedy the neglect of children's learning needs places them at stage 2 of the job fulfilment process, the formulation of a remedial action strategy (adopting the broad interpretation of 'strategy' I outline in Chapter 1). All three teachers had very clear views about what ought to be being done in their schools in order, ultimately, to serve pupil needs better. Amanda in particular spoke not only of general, school-wide policy but also of specific plans she had wanted to implement in her classroom in order to improve teaching effectiveness:

> When I went to Rockville I was told that the remedial work was done by Margaret . . . and that she did group work . . . and . . . er . . . when I took account of the fact that there were 60 children in each year I could see that, whichever 30 you had, there was going to be a sufficient span . . . so I asked them what happened about remedial help . . . and I was told it was small group work . . . Well, the second term that I was there . . . er . . . I had one child in particular who . . . er . . . needed a remedial reading programme. Now, I didn't know how to go about broaching this, and so I did it . . . sort of . . . generally, in conversation, with Geoff Collins and he said I'd only to mention it . . . to Margaret . . . and it would be attended to.

However, when constraints of one form or another impeded the realisation of the remedial action strategies they had formulated, Mark, Helen and Amanda were thwarted in their attempts to reduce or remove the imperfections they identified in their work. The result of this was often to prevent their progressing beyond stage 2 of the job fulfilment process, as in the example of the outcome of Amanda's plans for the provision of a remedial reading programme for one of her pupils, described in her own words:

> Well, of course, that *never* realised . . . Nothing was done about it, and so, as time went on, I became more and more open in what I was saying to him, and less subtle, I suppose . . . And so . . . er . . . he then said that *he* would mention it to Margaret, that I had this child . . . and she came and she had one hour with the child and left me a box of stuff and she said she'd be back the next day. And she never came back again, and that stuff was on my window sill for two terms. So, when I *said* what had happened I assumed that Geoff would do something about it, and I told him that there was no small group work going on – so he knew about it and did nothing about it . . . The thing, I suppose that disturbed me most was that here were children with real learning needs and they were not being met . . . and what became obvious was that, for the most part, the less able children were allowed to *be* less able . . . and it was put down to either laziness, stupidity, or the fact that they weren't English mother tongue . . . and yet I knew, because of all the language work I'd done, that, generally speaking, nearly *all* their needs could be met . . . and I couldn't do it with 30 in the class.

In some cases it was possible for Mark, Helen and Amanda to progress beyond stage 2 of the job fulfilment process in relation to certain aspects of their work. This was most likely to occur in cases involving their own, independent, classroom-based activities, which were less susceptible to threats to their successful completion than were activities that required or were dependent upon some degree of interaction or co-operation with others. Yet, often, for these three teachers, even if they were able to reach stage 3, the remedial action effected fell short of their ideal, which had the knock-on effect of impairing their progress beyond stage 4. Figure 6.1 illustrates the effects upon their progress in the process of achieving job fulfilment of specific school-imposed constraints which Mark, Helen and Amanda identified.

For the most part, though, these teachers faced many barriers on the path to job fulfilment. Unlike many of their more 'restricted' professional colleagues, these three 'extended' professionals were not content with being able to teach in their own classrooms in accordance with their own ideologies. They were dissatisfied, frustrated and often demoralised if wider school issues, policy and practice failed to conform to standards which they considered appropriate. Their job-related ideals reflected much wider visions than those of many of their colleagues, but this meant that their ideals were less likely to be met. Moreover, the frustration which resulted from this was exacerbated by their feelings of not being

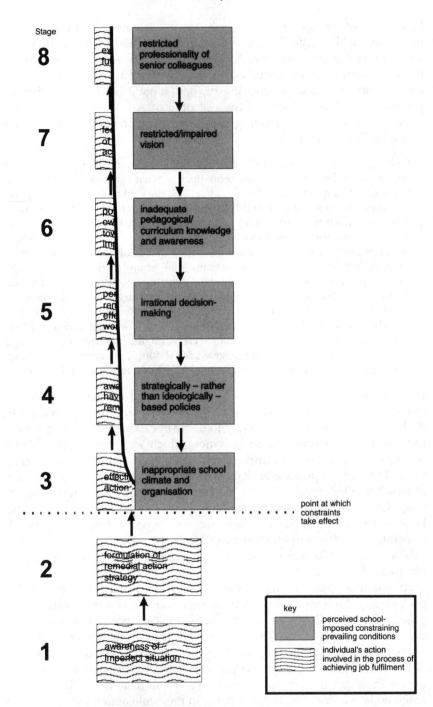

Figure 6.1   Illustration of Mark, Helen and Amanda's impeded progress in the process of achieving job fulfilment

heard, and of making little headway towards influencing their schools' prevailing professional climates. The level and intensity of this frustration are conveyed through Helen's comment, 'I feel like a voice crying in the wilderness'.

This was not the case with all my teacher interviewees, however. Those who found their work contexts to be much more compatible with their ideologies and values enjoyed considerably higher levels of morale and job satisfaction. The next chapter examines the cases of three such teachers.

A management perspective: issues for consideration

Key points

- 'Extended' professionals have distinct job-related needs that place demands upon school management.
- 'Extended' professionals have far- and wide-reaching visions and ideals.
- 'Extended' professionals potentially have much to contribute towards enhancing school effectiveness.

Consider

- From the perspective of 'extended' professionals, what are likely to be the key features of effective school management? In what ways might headteachers incorporate into their school management consideration of the needs of 'extended' professionals?
- How important is it that headteachers are, themselves, 'extended' professionals? Does current school management and headteacher training provision typically encourage the development of 'extended' professionality?
- When making appointments, should headteachers and school governing bodies place greater emphasis on evidence of 'extended' professionality amongst job applicants? What form might such evidence take, and how could the selection process incorporate consideration of it?
- What career development/opportunities are available, within the teaching profession, for 'extended' professionals who may not wish to take on school management roles? Are there enough appropriate career paths available to retain 'extended' professionals? Is the role of advanced skills teacher likely to be one such path? Are the teachers selected for advanced skills teacher status likely to be 'extended' professionals? What new roles could be developed that would be likely to serve the needs of the education system and the teaching profession, whilst also accommodating the needs of 'extended' professionals?
- Are 'extended' professionals too intellectual for teaching? Are they out of place in the profession, or do they represent the ideal towards which the profession should be moving?

7

Keeping on your toes: job fulfilment and high morale through challenge

Introduction

Chapter 6 highlights the similarities between the work-related experiences of three teachers whose dissatisfaction and demoralisation with their jobs were sufficiently great to prompt each of them to seek new posts. This chapter presents quite a different perspective: that of three teachers employed in two schools who represent the most satisfied of my interviewees and whose morale was high. Representing an 'other side of the coin' view from that of their dissatisfied colleagues, these 'high morale' teachers, Rosemary, Kay and Sarah, shared a common, overall satisfaction with their current teaching posts which, in all three cases, fostered a reluctance to consider changing jobs. Just as Mark, Helen and Amanda (identified in Chapter 6), were, for the most part, desperate to leave their respective schools, Rosemary, Kay and Sarah were, for the most part, desperate to stay at theirs.

What makes this contrast of perspectives particularly interesting, though, is that in one case it is the same school from which, on the one hand, Amanda, one of the most dissatisfied of all my interviewees, was desperate to escape and in which, on the other hand, one of my most satisfied interviewees, Rosemary, was very happy to stay. This chapter builds on the contents of the preceding two by contributing to the developing examination of the individuality and diversity of teacher morale and job satisfaction and by presenting evidence which, in later analyses, sheds light on the reasons why some teachers may be perfectly content with a situation which, for others, may be a significant source of dissatisfaction.

Rosemary's story

Rosemary was 52 years old at the time of the first of her two research interviews. Her follow-up interview took place three years later. She was a late entrant into the profession, had trained as an infants' teacher after several years in office work and had been at Rockville since 1973. At the time of my research she was a Key Stage 1 teacher who, in 1989, held an

Incentive A Allowance and, by 1992 when she was reinterviewed, had been appointed to the post of deputy head at Rockville. In the interim she had been promoted to the post of Incentive B allowance-holder, with responsibility for INSET and curriculum organisation and, whilst holding this post, also served as acting deputy head.

Rosemary manifested many characteristics of 'extended' professionality. She was by no means comparable to Amanda who was an extreme example of 'extended' professionality. She lacked Amanda's incisive perception, intellectualism, analytical skills and capacity for reasoned argument, but she was reflective, had a wide vision, sound ideologies and a good understanding of current educational issues and pedagogy. She was investigative, experimental, receptive to new ideas and different viewpoints, and her practice reflected considered decision-making and was rationally based, as the following two separate extracts from her first interview illustrate:

> at the beginning of each year I refer to the background documents and, you know, the files that we have, and check to make sure that I'm covering the things that I *should* be covering.

> and, when I stood back and looked and listened in that classroom, I thought to myself, 'a), somebody's going to get hurt, and b), how can we justify what's going on here if an adviser, or an inspector, or even the head, walked in?' I couldn't justify it, because it certainly wasn't organised. It was chaos! . . . er . . . now, *that's* the sort of thing that I can't cope with.

Rosemary's high levels of morale, job satisfaction and motivation were apparent throughout both of her interviews, and the obvious enthusiasm which she had for her work and the enjoyment and fulfilment that she derived from it were undiminished by the three-year interval between them. In her first interview she spoke of the various challenges that the job presented and of how these energised and satisfied her:

> *Interviewer: Do you find the job satisfying enough? Does it stimulate you?*
> Well, yes, because, I think the way things are done at Rockville, I mean, having different year groups every two years, it certainly keeps you on your toes. And the changes that there've been whilst I've been there . . . I mean, when I went there at first we'd a few Pakistani children, but there were no Bangladeshis, so there have been changes there . . . and, I mean, there are changes that have come about in education itself . . . er . . . and changes in year groups and the children's different needs, and so on, I think keep you on your toes . . . whereas, in a lot of other schools, in, perhaps, more affluent areas, with a good catchment area . . . er . . . the children's needs are not the same . . . and I don't think there are the same changes within the school, and perhaps they don't even change classes. I mean, I know *some* teachers who've been taking the same year group and the same type of ability for most of their careers. Now, to me, you get in a rut, and I think that's where a lot of the dissatisfaction creeps in. I think they tend to look outward for the root of the problems, rather than looking inward.

And now this new county policy of admitting four-year-olds has been thrown at us . . . and, again, you think, 'Oh, my goodness, *why* are they doing this?' But, here again, it's something else to keep you on your toes . . . to get your teeth into . . . and then, at the end of this year, you know . . . we, sort of, had a rethink . . . we'd made mistakes and we're changing those and we're looking at different things. Then this incentive A post came up at school, and, at first, I thought, 'Oh, no, I couldn't do the job' . . . but then I thought, 'Well, why not?' . . . and, again, I felt that it was a new challenge – something else to get my teeth into . . . to have a go at . . . and . . . you know . . . I was prepared and, as I say, after having that first initial *brief* meeting with those members of staff, I felt, 'Oh, yes, there's plenty here to get to grips with and to look at . . . you know . . . er . . . to *help* the staff and the children. And, then again, I suppose this job of standing in for Alison while she's off sick . . . again, it's a new challenge . . . it's something else to have a go at and to get your teeth into . . . and these are all things that keep you on your toes . . . and keep the momentum going . . . and . . . well, it's a challenge.

She summed up her attitude to working at Rockville: 'I'm as happy as I can be . . . with the career. I feel . . . you know . . . quite . . . quite *good* about it because I'm happy at the school. I'm looking forward to the new year.' By 1992, Rosemary had enjoyed many new challenges which her greater responsibilities had brought. When, at the beginning of her follow-up interview I reminded her of some of the things she had said in 1989, and asked her if she felt that, considering the centrally imposed changes which the Education Reform Act had imposed upon teachers' working lives as well as school-specific changes, her attitude to her job had altered, she replied:

Er . . . I think, from *my* point of view, I'm still getting great satisfaction because . . . er . . . everything that comes along, I look at it . . . like . . . well, there's no good sinking down into the depths. These things come along, and they're here to stay . . . for how long, we don't know . . . but . . . you've just got to make the best of it. It's no good thinking, 'Oh, I can't cope with this', because I think that starts you on this spiral downwards. I think you've got to think, 'Well, it's here. What can we do . . . you know . . . to make the best of it?'

. . . I think . . . er . . . it's an attitude of mind. You either get stuck in and make the best of it, or you . . . you know . . . have a change of career and finish altogether.

Rosemary gave several examples of situations which she had found challenging and which, as challenges, gave her a sense of fulfilment when she felt she had responded to them with some measure of success. Some were examples of her own individual teaching successes:

I took on Special Needs, and we decided to make Special Needs a priority for last year. So, I, sort of, got to grips with a lot of that . . . did a *lot* of teaching with small groups . . . But, I found it *very* satisfying, working with these children. Er . . . I had *small* objectives, and, seeing the success there, and the delight from the children *in* that success . . . now, to me, this is what teaching's all about.

Some were examples of school-wide policy which she had either initiated or to which she felt she had contributed. She described at length the process involved in designing, launching, modifying and evaluating a home reading scheme in the school's Key Stage 1 classes – an initiative in which she had played a large part. She summed up: 'And all this seems to have worked, because the 6+ screening results this time were superb! It is *so* pleasing. Er . . . I think we'd only 6% of children in the top infants who scored less than 95 . . . as against the 55% last year! So, it's *working!*' Particularly striking was Rosemary's evident capacity, illustrated clearly in several of the quotations presented above, to turn into welcome challenges situations and circumstances that many teachers might consider to be overwhelming set-backs. In the face of potentially demoralising constraints and difficulties, she seemed consistently to adopt a positive attitude and optimistic outlook which allowed her high morale to be sustained. She referred, for example, to a situation at Rockville whereby the first year of implementation of the end of Key Stage 1 Standard Assessment Tasks (SATs) had, in her opinion, been severely impaired by one of the Year 2 classes having been in the charge of an incompetent supply teacher for a large proportion of the academic year. According to Rosemary, this teacher disapproved of the National Curriculum, disagreed with the testing procedures which accompanied it and, as a result, had failed to keep records and to make sufficient preparation for the administration of the SATs. The legacy of disorganisation and neglect which the newly appointed Year 2 class teacher inherited undermined the testing, and the school's SATs results were so poor and so far below the national average that local education authority advisers and inspectors called the school to account and issued directives for remedial action. Rosemary spoke of this situation:

> So that, again, was another challenge . . . Initially, yes, you feel that it's unfair and people ought to know what we're up against in this school. But, then, you think, 'Well, we've been told to do something about it. We've got to try'. And so, then, it does become a challenge.

It would be misrepresentative of Rosemary to portray her as enjoying a consistently satisfactory, and satisfying, working life. In both her interviews she related incidents which had upset and, sometimes, frustrated her. In her 1992 follow-up interview, by which time she had been appointed deputy head, in response to my asking what aspects of her work, if any, frustrated her, she referred to what she considered to be the unhelpful and unco-operative attitudes of some of her colleagues:

> There are so many with negative attitudes . . . Whatever we bring to staff meetings from the senior management team, and we ask for ideas, thoughts, discussions . . . and then, when something's decided, there are always the few people who . . . don't agree with it, pick holes in it . . . but don't necessarily come forth with any suggestions. Er . . . and that, to me, is annoying.

> What I find *most* frustrating is when an agreement is made and people, for whatever reason, don't adhere to it.

She also spoke of the upsetting effect of interpersonal clashes which sometimes occurred in her management role:

> I think . . . I've always prided myself on being an organiser . . . an organised person. And I think this has stood me in good stead, really, in the management role. And, yeah, it does give me satisfaction when it works . . . Er . . . the other side of that is . . . I get very upset – and it *does* upset me, to the extent that I have sleepless nights, and can't get it out of my head – if I feel that somebody's been upset by what I've done, and feels that they've been hard done to. I do try *not* to tread on people's toes. But there are times when . . . er . . . for all sorts of reasons, decisions have to be made quite quickly. And it *has* been levelled at me, over this past year, that I *have* done things without consulting people . . . er . . . maybe some people feel that they haven't been consulted as fully as they ought to have been, but, as I say, for various reasons, sometimes, it isn't always possible to do that. But I do *try* to speak to people before taking action or making a decision.

Since many of the Rockville interviewees had, in both their interviews, been critical of those who held management roles and, in particular, of the head, for allowing what were generally considered to be unsatisfactory situations and circumstances to prevail, I asked Rosemary if she had found the head's management a source of frustration or dissatisfaction. She identified only one specific complaint: the head's non-interventionist, *laissez-faire* approach to staff management. Referring to staff who failed to adhere to agreed school policy, she criticised the head's reluctance to insist on their conformity: 'In some instances, I don't feel that the head has dealt with them properly. Er . . . some of these instances, I think, wouldn't have got to the point that they had, if he'd nipped them in the bud.' She was otherwise generally satisfied with the management of the school:

> Er . . . there are times when *I* find it frustrating . . . er . . . and I know that a lot of staff feel that he . . . he is a bit . . . too soft. Er . . . but I can understand the way that he operates. In looking back, there are a lot of instances where it's worked out well for the school.
>
> . . . I'm quite happy, basically, with the way things are run. And I feel comfortable in that, if I *don't* agree with something, I know I can go to him and say, 'I'm sorry, I *don't* agree with you on that', and . . . er . . . we can discuss it . . . and I feel quite comfortable with it.

It was clear that Rockville suited Rosemary. She felt at ease with the school's professional climate, had no real complaints about the headteacher and was reasonably satisfied with staff relations and, for the most part, with her colleagues. She had no wish to leave Rockville and planned to stay there until she reached retirement age. Her morale was high, she was motivated and she was fulfilled.

Rosemary was one of the most satisfied of my teachers, and her case exemplifies a good match between teacher and school. Similarly well matched with their school, Sefton Road Primary, were Sarah and Kay.

Sarah's story

At the time of her interview in 1990 Sarah was 28 years old and had been teaching for six years. She had been at Sefton Road Primary School since 1987, when she was appointed music co-ordinator on what was then a scale 2 post of responsibility. This was her second teaching post. She taught a Year 4 class.

Based upon my observation of her in my teacher-cum-observer role at Sefton Road I consider Sarah to fall into a category of 'broadly extended' professionality. She demonstrated reflectivity, generally considered carefully the content and design of her lessons, evaluated what she did, was receptive to alternative viewpoints and was very willing to exchange ideas with colleagues. She worked well and co-operatively with others, particularly with support teachers who shared her classroom. She was, however, manifestly less analytical than were the other 'extended' professionals in my sample, seemed less inclined to value research and theory as bases for practice, showed no real interest in attending in-service courses which were not predominantly practical and, on a day-to-day basis, seemed to operate at a lower level of intellectual application and awareness than did her more 'extended' colleagues. Despite these distinctions, which influenced my categorisation of her as an 'extended' professional being qualified by the adjective 'broadly', Sarah showed promise, in a largely indefinable manner, in relation to her professionality. Compared with my other 'extended' professionals she was young and relatively inexperienced as a teacher. In many respects she characterised the early-career-stage teacher's prioritisation of day-to-day practicalities. Yet she seemed likely to develop into an 'extended' professional eventually, if her capacity to cope with what she considered a demanding job, were to increase. She was conscientious, caring, committed and enthusiastic.

Sarah was very happy at Sefton Road. The school was in a working-class area of a small Midlands industrial town with a large Pakistani community. In 1989, there were nearly 600 pupils on roll. Of Sefton Road's pupils, 70% were from the Pakistani community. The teaching staff comprised 21 full-time teachers, excluding the head, and two part-time (0.5) teachers. The school had two deputy heads: John, who taught a Year 6 class and who was responsible for overseeing the Key Stage 2 classes, and Emily, who taught one of the reception classes and was in charge of the infants department. Each also had curriculum co-ordination responsibilities.

Phil, the Sefton Road head, had a very different style of leadership from that of Rockville's Geoff Collins. Phil was very personable in an extrovert way and managed staff through a predominantly interpersonal process that incorporated a great deal of exclusivity and one-to-one interaction. He left teachers in no doubt about what he thought of their work. Making explicit his own educational ideologies and preferences, which veered very much towards child-centredness manifested through a caring but firm teaching approach and innovative, stimulating, but well-planned activities, Phil was generous in his praise of those whose practice conformed to a style of which he approved. To varying degrees, as he told me in conversation, he was happy with most of the staff, and most of them had been appointed by him. He chose teachers with care and with a view to transforming the school from what he had, at the time of his appointment to the headship eight years ago, considered to be an out-moded, lack-lustre institution, staffed in the main by 'old guard', 'restricted' professionals, into a vibrant, exciting 'on-the-ball' type of school. Those who had witnessed his progress generally agreed that Phil had 'turned the school around', though rather more through a process of erosion than of explosion but with sufficient forcefulness to ease out one way or another most of the teachers who did not share his clear vision.

Phil lavished favour, in the form of personal attention and explicit approval, on those whom he identified as competent teachers. With these teachers he exchanged personal confidences, shared jokes and spent time in conversation after school. He would visit their classrooms to observe what was going on and to provide positive feedback yet, unlike his Rockville counterpart who showed no interest when breezing in and out of classrooms in what the pupils were doing and who would engage solely with the teacher, Phil's visits to classrooms always focused on children's activities. Those teachers with whom Phil was unimpressed were usually treated cordially, but received no such personal attention. Phil's leadership style incorporated blatant favouritism, based on his perception and recognition of professional competence. What resulted from this was a school professional climate characterised by a competitive collegiality which, in the cases of many teachers, seems to have been directed towards securing, or to have been sustained by, Phil's approval.

Attributing it to Phil's influence, Sarah spoke of how this good-natured, friendly rivalry spurred on many of the Sefton Road teachers to greater effort and hard work:

> It's like an undercurrent . . . He [Phil] doesn't *say* it . . . but he doesn't *realise*, I don't think, just exactly how much is expected of you . . . But he doesn't think it comes from him, though . . . because he was discussing with me once – I was saying that it's a hard school to work in – because he was saying he was finding it hard to find staff – quality . . . and he said that people outside perceive it to be a hard school, and I said, 'Well, it *is*', and he said, 'But, why? What is it that makes it hard?' and I said, 'Well, it's the standard to work to' . . . But *he* said that he didn't think it came from him, and I said, 'Well, it comes from . . . everybody's gee-ing each other up all the time'. But we also work to his

expectations. But he didn't realise that – he thought it was *us* that were making ourselves work hard.

The Sefton Road climate suited Sarah. She fitted in well at the school and, though she found the pressure to meet the high standards of expected performance a source of stress at times, she was content to stay there:

> I really like it here . . . er . . . but I know that you have to work a lot harder here than in a lot of places, and I don't know whether I'll always be prepared to put that work in . . . I mean, at the moment, I'm happy here because . . . I just like the feel of working here . . . but I go home and I feel as if I'm under stress and I feel drained . . . and, sometimes, I think, 'How long can I keep this up?'

At various points throughout her interview she identified specific sources of job satisfaction. As was the case with most of my interviewees, Sarah derived fulfilment from successful teaching experiences: 'Er . . . one thing is . . . definitely, getting the children going. If you know that you've motivated them and done something really well . . . that's the most important.' It was clear, however, that school-specific factors were also very influential on her job-related attitudes. She referred to the good staff relations at Sefton Road: 'Now, the thing about here, as well, is that when you go into the staffroom you don't usually hear anybody griping about anybody else . . . and everybody goes in and sits down and gets on . . . we are fairly easy going.' But it was her relationship with the head that essentially underpinned her day-to-day job satisfaction and motivation levels. The extent to which Sarah received personal attention from Phil seemed crucial in distinguishing a good day from a bad day, as one of her anecdotes illustrates particularly well:

> I was ignored today. Er . . . and I was *really* hurt, actually. It was pathetic, but I get really easily offended and Phil came up to me and – he was walking past me and I said, 'Hello', and he just looked straight through me and went towards another member of staff . . . and, admittedly, that person had been ill yesterday . . . but he went up to that person and made a great big fuss of them . . . and, well, I don't begrudge *that* but I begrudge the fact that he didn't even have a minute to say, 'Hello' – a second – all it needed was, 'Hello'. But I felt rebuffed . . . I felt really hurt.

On the other hand, it was attention from Phil, in the form of recognition and praise, that seemed to be a very important driving force behind Sarah's positive attitude towards working at Sefton Road:

> I think I really do seek the approval of other people . . . I try to overcome it, but I think I . . . I *need* praise and I need criticism . . . and I'm not very good at taking criticism . . . but I still need it. That's one reason why I left my last school because . . . I could've got on with what I was doing all day long and, no matter what I put in, I didn't get, 'Oh, that's good', or anything . . . I didn't get any criticism, either. I got nothing . . . and I was doing a heck of a lot there. I mean, I hate to think of it being like that, but I feel like I'm one of the children . . . I really do try to praise the children, and I always think of myself – how *I* feel –

and I need encouragement . . . Phil gives us a hundred times more encouragement than my last head did . . . and it . . . because the staff is so big it's hard . . .
but I still need it all the time . . . I *need* it . . .

Interviewer: Which is more important, praise from colleagues or praise from Phil?
Oh, it's got to be Phil. But I also feel good if John says something . . . because
John is so good, and you think, 'Gosh, if *John* says that . . .' I would say that I
wouldn't be as motivated anywhere else . . . I don't think there'd be anywhere
where I'd feel like this.

Interviewer: Is it Phil who's motivating you? Do you do it, sort of, to please him?
Er . . . I would say that's probably true . . . but I would also say that you see so
much going on elsewhere in school and you're lifted by that.

Kay's story

In 1990 Kay was 42 and had been at Sefton Road for six years, where she
was appointed science co-ordinator on an Incentive B Allowance. She was
a Key Stage 2 teacher, had entered the profession with a teacher's certificate and had studied in-service for a Diploma in Advanced Studies in
Education (DASE).

Like Sarah, Kay enjoyed working at Sefton Road and felt comfortable
with the prevailing culture of hard work and the expectations that it
generated of high standards, competence and conscientiousness. Her description of this culture was consistent with that of Sarah: 'a lot of what is
expected of us isn't actually . . . stated . . . it's what you *feel* is expected
. . . nothing's actually *said* . . . but you feel that a high standard is expected of you.' Like Sarah, Kay believed that the culture emanated principally from the headteacher and was shaped by a generally consensual
acquiescence, on the part of the staff, in his vision of how he wanted the
school to develop. The pressure to sustain high standards of professionalism and performance and to reach high levels of competence originated,
she felt, from Phil's expectations: 'I suppose it just comes down to his
expectations of us . . . Sometimes I think he wants blood out of us.'

Kay's professionality was manifestly more 'extended' in orientation than
that of Sarah and this, coupled with her greater experience and seniority,
afforded her the respect and credibility which allowed her to play a proac-
tive role, alongside senior colleagues, in shaping the school's professional
climate and ensured that she was often consulted in the decision-making
process. The extent of her satisfaction with her job is indicated by Kay's
reluctance to leave Sefton Road, despite her ambitions to secure a deputy
headship, which had prompted her to make several applications:

Interviewer: Now, do you enjoy it here?
Yes.

Interviewer: How much?
Well, it has its bad days . . . I suppose everywhere does. Well, I mean, I'm
applying for other jobs, but it isn't because I'm unhappy here . . . and I feel that,

because I'm happy, it gives me a position of strength when I'm looking for other jobs – I can be selective . . . I'm not grabbing at straws, you know.
Interviewer: So, you obviously enjoy it here, Kay—but it's not, in itself, a retainer?
It is in *some* respects because, even if I was offered another job, I would still consider it very carefully . . . er . . . because your peace of mind *is* important . . . If I was going to move to somewhere where I *was* unsettled, or where I did feel unhappy, then I just wouldn't go. I'd rather stay put.

In response to my asking her to consider what aspects of her job contributed towards a 'good' day, Kay identified both job comfort and job fulfilment factors:

Interviewer: What pleases you most? What could happen to you in a day that would really give you a lift?
Well . . . some of it is feedback from kids . . . when you feel that you've done something . . . that's really rewarding . . . er . . . and I like my big, fat pay cheque . . . you know . . . the more, the better, and if I can improve on that, then I will . . . and I do enjoy the peer group, as well, and that's one of the reasons why I shied away from the idea of moving to a very small school, at one stage . . . because I felt that I would miss a big staff . . . I always think that, in a big staff, there may be people that you *don't* get on with . . . but there's bound to be people that you *do* get on with.
Interviewer: And do you feel that you're getting everything you need from this school?
Yes.

It was clear, too, that, like Sarah, Kay considered Phil's leadership style to play an important part in determining her happiness at work. His influence on her job satisfaction and morale levels extended beyond his simply spurring her on to greater effort by a few well chosen words, to his capacity for enhancing her role as a senior teacher by involvement in managerial decision-making. In this respect, as Kay herself acknowledged, Phil's propensity for favouritism added a somewhat whimsical dimension to his management in so far as he appeared to consult more frequently and to a greater extent with those teachers whom, at any one time, he favoured, than he did with others:

He definitely has his blue-eyed favourites . . . he has a flavour of the month every now and then, and if it's not your turn . . . I do feel, occasionally . . . I feel a little bit . . . left out. At the moment they're having these little meetings in the infants and I . . . er . . . I just feel, occasionally . . . not that I should be *involved* with that, but that I'm being ignored, to a certain degree . . . I mean, if it comes to status . . . I'm not particularly one for status . . . but, if it does come down to it, I have equivalent status, as a B allowance-holder, to Mary Burton . . . and, at the moment, I feel that she's included in decisions and discussions, and all the rest of it . . . and I'm *not* . . . I used to have more say. I think that was when the previous deputy was here . . . before Emily was appointed. Phil used to confide in me much more than he does now. I was involved a lot more in . . . what you might call the management. But, recently, my involvement's just been in the science.

Despite what she perceived as a diminution of her own favoured position in relation to Phil, Kay acknowledged his readiness to listen to all teachers' views and ideas and recognised that his predominantly open, fair and democratic management secured the likelihood of his supporting her initiatives and enabling her to continue to derive satisfaction from her work:

> If you come up with an idea and say, 'I'd like to try this', and you can justify it and it sounds pretty good, then he'll back you . . . I think he does like to see you trying out new ideas . . . not just jumping on the bandwagon, but . . . like . . . saying, 'Well, I think this would be a good thing to do' . . . He'd very rarely stop you from trying out something that you wanted to have a bash at . . . as long as it fitted in with the school.

Essentially, Kay considered Phil to be an enabling rather than a constraining factor. She shared his ideologies and his vision, felt comfortable within the professional culture he shaped and was satisfied with him as a leader and a manager.

The common thread

Quite apart from the high levels of morale, motivation and job satisfaction they sustained, the three teachers profiled in this chapter shared another common characteristic – that of professionality orientation. Based upon evidence obtained from the observation phases of my study, my professionality-related categorisation (see Chapter 4) located them all towards the 'extended' end of the 'restricted–extended' professionality continuum, as interpreted by Hoyle (1975).

This commonality in relation to professionality orientation is important to the incremental analysis of teacher morale, motivation and job satisfaction that is built up throughout Part II of this book. It is important because it dispels any notion that 'extended' professionality is an automatic precondition for dissatisfaction, frustration and low morale: a blind alley along the job fulfilment path. It reveals that 'extended' professionals are capable of sustaining positive job-related attitudes, in the right contexts and under the right conditions.

For Rosemary, Sarah and Kay, the contexts and conditions that were right were, quite simply, those which, in relation to each of them, facilitated the job fulfilment process. Each of these three teachers worked within a professional climate that suited her – one in which she felt comfortable, which was compatible with her own educational ideologies and which was enabling rather than constraining. More specifically, each was, through her work context, presented with challenges she was able to meet. It was through meeting these challenges that job fulfilment was experienced and, through their continued recurrence, that job fulfilment was sustained. The nature of the challenges varied from individual to individual and from context to context. Sarah and Kay both described the Sefton Road professional culture as demanding and as one which clearly was perpetually challenging. Here, the challenge was to sustain a sufficiently high standard of practice to win collegial respect, retain professional credibility and, the most demanding of all, to secure the approbation of the headteacher. Rosemary's challenges took a different form. They were not a pervasive cultural constituent. They were individual, clearly definable and varied problems whose solutions were neither simple nor straightforward. It was through seeking solutions to the problems that Rosemary was challenged, and through effecting these solutions that she experienced job fulfilment. Moreover, unlike Amanda, who had been constrained by the same context in her efforts to meet challenges, Rosemary was advantaged by her managerial role and her senior status within the school. These resulted in her being enabled, since they were valued by the headteacher. The Rockville head allowed Rosemary to meet challenges unimpeded, because she constituted part of his management team. To be fair, he would have afforded Amanda the same privileges had she been a member of his management team; but she was not. Not only was she not a member of the Rockville senior management team but she was also opposed in what she wanted to do by a member of that team, the deputy head, and, since the headteacher's respect for seniority meant that he would always support senior teachers, Amanda was doubly disadvantaged by contextual circumstances.

More than any other teachers whose cases are presented in this book, the cases of Rosemary, Kay and Sarah provide positive illustrations of Steers *et al.*'s (1996, p. 19) comment: 'The need for achievement is perhaps the most prominent learned need from the standpoint of studying organizational behavior. The challenging nature of a difficult task cues that motive which, in turn, activates achievement-oriented behavior.' Rosemary was able to proceed unimpeded through the job fulfilment stages, partly on account of her seniority and partly on account of her compatibility with the school climate in which she operated, which was rendered more compatible with her ideologies by her influence upon it, which, in turn, stemmed from her seniority. Kay and Sarah not only generally proceeded unimpeded but were also often facilitated by the context in which they worked in their progress towards achieving job fulfilment. The challenges posed by the competitive climate and by the expectations of the headteacher assisted their reaching stages 1, 2 and 3, and the remaining stages were made more attainable by the recognition of their efforts they frequently received. Unlike those teachers profiled in Chapter 6, these three teachers were advantaged by not only being presented with challenges in their jobs but by also being given the resources for meeting those challenges.

Not all teachers, however, welcomed challenges. The next chapter focuses upon three teachers whose perspectives on their jobs were quite different from those of teachers who have featured hitherto.

A management perspective: issues for consideration

Key points
- Positive job-related attitudes are sustained when teachers are supported in their efforts to meet challenges.
- School management may provide the means whereby teachers are presented with challenges.
- Through their leadership styles, headteachers may facilitate teachers' progress through the job fulfilment process.
- School leadership is a potent influence on teachers' motivation.

Consider
- What are the key features of motivational leadership? Would these be equally capable of motivating all teachers? Are 'restricted' professionals likely to be motivated by the same kinds of factors that motivate 'extended' professionals?
- Is it the professional responsibility of headteachers to motivate staff? Should teachers be expected to be self-motivated? Are self-motivated teachers likely to be easier to manage? Are they likely to sustain higher levels of job satisfaction, morale and motivation? Is the motivation of teachers likely to be a source of job fulfilment to headteachers?
- In what specific ways might headteachers provide teachers with challenges in their work?

8

Keeping the job in perspective

Introduction

Teachers do not all share the same levels of commitment to their job. For some, it is a major part of their lives; they may devote many hours of what might otherwise be leisure time to work-related tasks, the job is extremely important to them and they afford it extensive consideration and high priority. Others may perceive it differently. To them, teaching is just a job rather than one of the most significant features of their lives. They may carry out their duties conscientiously and they may enjoy the work, but it is not their 'centre of gravity' (Goodson, 1991).

Vroom (1964, p. 144) describes this commitment-level factor as 'ego involvement' in one's job. Goodson (1991, p. 42) refers to 'definitions of . . . professional locations and of . . . career direction'. Lortie (1975, p. 89) labels it engagement: 'People differ in their readiness to involve themselves in work; to some it is a major engagement; to others, something less.' His study, involving interviews with nearly a hundred American teachers, included examination of the relationship between engagement and work satisfaction. His sample represented a wide range of engagement with teaching, from those for whom the job was evidently a major preoccupation: 'one heard statements like "teaching is my life". Such teachers connected travel and other activities to their classroom work; teaching was definitely the master role which organized other aspects of their life', to those described as 'relatively passive, with low commitment . . . their interest in work was low' (*ibid.*, pp. 93–4).

My own sample of teachers included a similarly wide range of commitment levels, and some of those who manifested high engagement with the job are the foci of Chapters 6 and 7. In contrast this chapter examines the cases of three teachers for whom work was not such a key aspect of their lives. It considers the extent to which morale, job satisfaction and motivation are influenced by teachers' prioritisation of, and perspectives on, the job in relation to the rest of their lives.

Three cases of limited prioritisation: Brenda, Ann and Louise

The teachers profiled so far in this book have all had in common a similarly high level of commitment to their jobs, which complemented the 'extended' professionality that they all shared to a greater or lesser extent. It would be inaccurate to represent them all as workaholics whose lives centred around their work and who allowed teaching to consume all their energies; indeed, some of them made a point of clarifying that there were self-imposed limits to what Lortie (1975, p. 92) refers to as 'the proportion of life space' taken up by teaching. Nevertheless, it was clear that each of them afforded the job high priority, devoted considerable time to it and ranked it as a key component in her/his life – an activity they anticipated they would greatly miss if it were not there.

Brenda, Ann and Louise, upon whom this chapter focuses, represented a lower level of engagement. They were distinct from those teachers identified in Chapters 6 and 7 in relation to the importance which they attached to the job within the rest of their lives. They were by no means uncommitted, unenthusiastic or lazy. Each cared about her work, took pride in it, was conscientious and reliable and wanted to do a good job. In all three cases, though, these teachers' lives did not revolve around their work; rather, they made it quite clear that their work was fitted into their lives in such a way that they did not allow it to encroach upon other things that mattered to them. For them, there was considerably more to life than teaching. These teachers kept the job in perspective.

Brenda's story

In 1989 Brenda was 39 and had been teaching at Rockville County Primary School for four years, the first three of which she spent as a full-time class teacher, and the last year as a 0.5 permanent floating support teacher. The reduction to part-time status had been instigated by her as a strategy for coping with the competing demands of her working, and her personal, life. In her first interview she explained precisely what had prompted her to reduce her teaching commitment:

> I think . . . well, I felt – I still *do*, to a certain extent – to be a full-time teacher, you need about 36 hours in every day! [laughs]. I felt that there was no room for any thing else in my life . . . there was no room – if I wasn't *doing* it, I was *thinking* about it. So . . . you . . . sort of . . . would come home from a day's work . . . and do whatever marking there was, and then preparation . . . and you'd be thinking about it all the time . . . even at weekends you were always thinking about it . . . and I felt that, basically, everything else in my life was going . . . There was no room for anything else . . . no time for the children . . . and . . . you know . . . just . . . I couldn't be bothered doing anything else . . . that sort of thing . . . And I decided that life's not about that . . . So that's why I decided to go part time.

As a coping strategy, her change of status had evidently been most successful. Brenda was enjoying high levels of job satisfaction, morale and motivation. In her 1989 interview she spoke of the positive impact which the reduction of hours had had on her attitude to her work:

> My feelings about the job that I'm doing? . . . Er . . . I'm very happy doing it at the moment – whether or not it's so much the *job* . . . or whether or not it's the fact that the job fits in totally with my lifestyle . . . that's probably what it *is* because when I was doing the job full time, I didn't feel as good about it.

> *Interviewer: Are you happy with teaching as a career?*
> It's what I – it's a thing . . . I mean . . . I don't do many things very well . . . I'm not a high flier at *anything* – I never have been – and teaching's one of the things that I do moderately well. So I'm quite happy with it.

> *Interviewer: And you're a lot better off with part-time – you're much happier with part time?*
> Oh, *much* happier! . . . Yes, it's ideal . . . Yes, I've done it for 12 months now, and . . . er . . . as far as I'm concerned, it is really ideal. Perfect.

Brenda was one of the most satisfied of the Rockville teachers and was quite distinct from her colleagues in her non-judgemental response to the circumstances and situation at the school, outlined in Chapter 5, that many acknowledged to be sources of dissatisfaction. Her sanguine attitude seemed to combine tolerance and understanding with a degree of complacency:

> Er . . . Margaret *wasn't* doing her job properly, and hadn't done, probably, for half the time, or more, that *I've* been there . . . She wasn't on the ball in a lot of ways . . . I mean, she was supposed to oversee in the classrooms . . . that was her job . . . and quite often, though, I can't remember seeing her – having said that, if you had a *problem* . . . if you had to go to the doctor's, or something . . . you know . . . she was always there, and the first to offer to come in and help . . . *always*. Er . . . people said that they didn't know where she *was* at certain times. You couldn't pinpoint her down . . . and things like this . . . so, I suppose, in all fairness, now, if you asked *her*, she'd say that she wasn't doing her job properly . . . I mean . . . she knew all about what people were saying about her . . . It was just . . . the whole atmosphere was *awful*! . . . I mean, people were, sort of, in *this* camp, or *that* camp . . . it was just the whole situation, really . . . it was *awful*! Er . . . it was, you know, sort of . . . nasty, and not very nice . . . The thing that gets me down is that people don't seem to be able to see other people's strengths – just their weaknesses . . . People may be going through things which you don't know anything about, at all . . . and that may cause them to act in the way that they act, and, therefore . . . you know . . . you can't say, can you, really? So, in a lot of ways, I think you've probably got to say as little as possible . . . and try and just get on with the job and, if anyone's in trouble, just try and . . . do your best for them. That's all you can do . . . in the hope that, when, and if, you're ever in the same situation, that people will be . . . reasonably friendly with you . . . But, there doesn't seem to be much tolerance.

Clearly, Brenda's predisposition towards tolerance of others' weaknesses was an important influence on her morale, motivation and job satisfaction. However there were in addition two inter-related factors whose combined effect allowed her, within the context in which she worked, to sustain a positive attitude to her job. These were her professionality orientation and her job-engagement level.

On the 'restricted–extended' professionality continuum (Hoyle, 1975), I would locate Brenda somewhere around the mid-point, but gravitating rather more towards 'restricted' than towards 'extended' professionality. She did manifest some characteristics of 'extended' professionality, but certainly not enough to warrant her being categorised as an 'extended' professional. Her teaching was, for the most part, intuitively- rather than rationally-based, some of her ideologies appeared to reflect prejudice and restricted vision and she had little interest in professional development through in-service courses, particularly long, award-bearing courses that incorporate educational theory. Her response to my asking if she had ever considered undertaking such courses illustrates her professionality-related perspective on work:

> I think it's a question of your personality . . . and I know what I *want*, but it's much more widely spread. I love doing things like . . . building walls . . . cement-mixing . . . and decorating . . . I also love going long walks with the dog . . . and, to me, that's very important – if I couldn't do that, then . . . you know . . . that's what was wrong before . . . I don't want to concentrate on one thing – I'm not that kind of person . . . I need to . . . fritter, in a lot of ways . . . I feel that's the way I am, and . . . you know . . . I realise this. I mean, it may not be everybody's ideal.

This comment also illustrates something of Brenda's prioritisation of the different components of her life, and it is this prioritisation which, together with her professionality, was a key factor in sustaining her high levels of morale, motivation and job satisfaction amidst the managerial and collegial crises that were unfolding at Rockville. These two influential factors are inter-related in so far as her low level of engagement impacted upon and shaped Brenda's professionality. 'Extended' professionality demands a high level of engagement and high prioritisation of the job; it is impossible to attain without these, and Brenda was without them. Yet because she was able to keep the job in perspective, affording it limited priority in relation to her life as a whole, she was, as she herself acknowledged, much more impervious than were most of her colleagues to the dissatisfying and demoralising effects of prevailing circumstances and situations:

> *Interviewer: . . . did this situation ever bother you at all . . . or are you the sort of person who thinks, 'Well, I'll get on with my job and they can do what they like'?*
> I think, again, it very much depends on how you feel – I mean, if I was a career teacher . . . if I was going – I mean, say, like Susan Ashcroft, or somebody like

that, who obviously wants to get on – er . . . I think then, probably, I would feel much more strongly about it. I think teaching is . . . I mean, I *enjoy* the job – I like doing it . . . I really do . . . but . . . to be perfectly honest . . . it's not my *life* . . . and, therefore, the things that happen aren't *crucial* . . . whereas, they would be to other people, perhaps . . . I just think that, now . . . in the last four or five years – I suppose it's a maturity – the things that mattered before don't matter now . . . I'm just interested, basically, in living each day for the day, and being happy with it . . . and happy with what I'm doing. I'm probably very complacent now, but . . . alright, I'm complacent.

Moreover, her somewhat more 'restricted' professionality than that of some of her colleagues reflected her narrower vision and interests which, in turn, shaped her ideals and defined her concerns. Her focus was essentially classroom bound and did not, for the most part, encompass school-wide issues and policies. It was for this reason that Brenda's working life remained largely unaffected by the headteacher: 'But, why should it make any difference what the head's like? . . . It doesn't make any difference to *me* . . . I don't see why the head *should* bother you . . . because, really, Geoff has very little influence on *me*.' Since he allowed teachers the freedom to practise as they liked, Geoff Collins, the Rockville head, had very little impact upon Brenda's work and, even though she recognised it as such, his poor management was of no real concern to her. Brenda placed great emphasis on good staff relations, and collegiality was an important source of job comfort to her. Moreover, provided that she was able to carry out her own work without interference and in the way which suited her, she was perfectly happy. Unlike some of her colleagues, whose ideals would only be met if the whole school as well as their own classrooms conformed to their vision of good educational practice, Brenda's ideal was realisable and, indeed, realised.

Ann's story

Ann was employed at Leyburn County Primary School as a Key Stage 2 teacher. In 1990, when I interviewed her, she was 42 years old and in her seventh year at Leyburn. Teaching has been her only career. She left college in 1968 with a teacher's certificate. Like Brenda, Ann had, at the time of her interview, recently reduced to part-time (0.5) status, though in Ann's case the reduction of hours was precipitated by her having been diagnosed as suffering from breast cancer. This diagnosis occurred after my teaching-cum-observing phase at Leyburn, when Ann had been a full-time teacher of a Year 6 class.

Ann's professionality was generally marginally more 'extended' than 'restricted', but insufficiently so for me to categorise her absolutely as an 'extended' professional. Although she was reflective and receptive to new ideas and alternative viewpoints, her teaching seemed often to be rather more intuitively- than rationally-based and she gave no appearance of applying analysis to the evaluation of her practice. She acknowledged the value of educational research and theory to practice and was impressed by colleagues whose teaching was evidently informed by theory, but she had never been interested in undertaking a course of study herself.

Ann's case has much in common with Brenda's. Both women functioned at levels of engagement which allowed them to keep the job in perspective. Predictably, her recently diagnosed illness had impacted upon Ann's relative perspective on her work, and her decision to reduce the number of hours she worked had been based upon her now wanting to make her life less crowded, since it was not certain whether she could be cured. Nevertheless, the limited prioritisation she afforded her job predated her illness. Ann's description of her general level of commitment and effort reflected conscientiousness and interest in the job, but not excessive output:

> I always left at four o'clock when I was full time . . . Well, I think I always work fairly hard . . . I think I've worked fairly hard wherever I've been . . . because I've enjoyed it . . . I mean, there are some times in school when you get a bit tired and you're not, perhaps, working as hard as you could be . . . you get a bit jaded.

> *Interviewer: Have you ever been really fed up and lost interest so that your work's been affected?*

> Yes . . . but, it's never lost . . . I don't think anybody's noticed . . . I, personally, have been a bit fed up – you know, when you get the odd class that, really . . . well, you know . . . and you've got them for a whole year . . . and something goes, and you lose . . . perhaps . . . the spark . . . and you're ticking over . . . you're *functioning*, but you're really going through the motions. Yes, I've been like that, from time to time. But, I don't think it's such that anyone else would notice . . . Oh, that happens occasionally . . . but never to the extent of . . . of looking for another job, or retraining. Partially because I don't know what else I would do. If I knew what I could do to get an equivalent salary, then I *may* try.

Like Brenda, Ann derived much pleasure from collegial relations. Indeed, it seemed that the staffroom peer group was the most enjoyable feature of the job for her. She liked all her colleagues, except for the headteacher, Mrs Hillman. Moreover, when she recalled previous teaching jobs she invariably highlighted interpersonal relations amongst the staff:

> I like the staff where I am now . . . and I know them. . . . I think we definitely have a culture of collaboration.

> At my second school . . . there were only three of us – three women and John, the head – and we were just all friends together, and he's a great raconteur – he'll tell a really good story . . . I mean . . . we were just like one big happy family, really.

Ann was, on the whole, satisfied with her job. She was critical of many aspects of Mrs Hillman's leadership, and recognised in the headteacher all those shortcomings that her colleague, Mark, had identified (see Chapter 6). Indeed, when she was speaking of her job at Leyburn her comments were predominantly related to the headteacher and her leadership. She complained of what she perceived as Mrs Hillman's poor interpersonal skills and, in particular, of how these impacted upon the Leyburn working environment:

> She falls down in her personal relationships . . . I mean . . . er . . . the year after I went there she had Stephen Miller there, who was instrumental in setting up the junior department. And he worked his *socks* off for her! Er . . . I think she really appreciated what he'd done . . . he was very dynamic, and full of ideas, and *very* talented . . . very hard-working . . . Er . . . and he got this job as deputy at Peterfield School . . . and she let him know with a *memo* in his register, telling him when he could start his new job! . . . Well, how impersonal! . . . and I was notified that I was music co-ordinator, through a memo! . . . if I wanted to discuss it with her, I could, it said. I mean . . . in a *small* school . . . because, I mean, it was much fewer staff then . . . is *that* the way you do it?

She spoke, too, of her disapproval of the headteacher's managerial style which, though it was ostensibly consultative, in reality, Ann believed, stifled opportunities for staff participation in decision-making and was, in fact, quite autocratic:

> now, you wouldn't think she's a dominating person, but she is, really . . . er . . . she makes it *appear* very democratic . . . and that we all have a say . . . but, when you sit back, after a staff meeting . . . who's won? Well, it's always Mrs Hillman . . . and that's because no one really voices an opinion or voices what they really, really feel . . . because she has a way of being very scornful . . . I've seen her do it with the deputy head a lot, and I just wonder whether it's *that*, at staff meetings . . . whether you *don't* say anything in case you get that . . . that scornful tone she can sometimes put on . . . and belittle you – I mean, she *can* do it – she can make you look – and feel – very small . . . But she chooses people, when she appoints, that are malleable . . . and . . . er . . . pleasant . . . and not the sort to rock the boat . . . I think it's people who don't have any unpleasant-ness about them, or any . . . er . . . who don't go in for 'scenes'. You see, *I* don't like any unpleasantness . . . er . . . and I said my piece about the directed time . . . er . . . and I've said my piece on one or two occasions – but I could never say it . . . I could never do it with a really nasty tone.

Again, like her Leyburn colleague, Mark, Ann criticised what she considered to be Mrs Hillman's overconcern for the fabric of the school at the expense of pedagogic concerns:

> She'll check the record books, and she'll check that everybody's where they should be, and she'll frown on you if she sees you walking around anywhere when you should be in your room and nowhere else . . . but the actual *content* of what you're doing . . . I don't think she bothers one jot! . . . In fact, I would say my main criticism of her . . . is that she's too much wrapped up in the fabric of the school . . . the actual bricks and mortar . . . and the fact that the toilets are operating . . . I know all these things matter . . . and I know it *does* matter that the environment you provide for the children is a good one . . . but I think . . . er . . . *that* seems to matter more than the work. So long as she has curriculum

guidelines there, and your schemes of work . . . I mean, you could be doing a weekly liar . . . if, on paper, everything fulfilled all the criteria . . . if all your records and everything fulfilled – so that if anyone from County Hall came in, it would all be there . . . I think *that's* what matters . . . and I don't *feel* that she's unduly concerned about . . . er . . . what's going on.

Unlike Mark, though, Ann was happy to stay at Leyburn. When I asked her, after she had spoken in fairly glowing terms of one of her previous headteachers, John, whether she would prefer to work at his school than at Leyburn, she replied that she would prefer to stay at Leyburn because she enjoyed good relations with her colleagues. This factor, the staffroom camaraderie, she said, was placed higher in her ranking of preferred job-related features than were John's good leadership qualities, even though she considered him to be professionally competent and pedagogically sound as well as pleasant and personable. It was her higher prioritisation of interpersonal factors than of educational issues as job satisfaction determinants that distinguished Ann from her colleague, Mark. This distinction reflected their different professionality orientations and, related to this, their different levels of engagement with the job. Essentially, and in common with Brenda from Rockville, Ann's job satisfaction was not dependent upon her headteacher. She was adequately content to be permitted to teach in her own classroom in the style that suited her and, though she found much in Mrs Hillman to criticise, the source of her criticism was less important to her than were the aspects of the job with which she was satisfied. In a sense, the criticism was half-hearted. Mrs Hillman, as Ann herself points out, did not interfere in teachers' work as long as it appeared to be running smoothly, and Ann's comment about the likely insignificance to her job satisfaction of the impact of any headteacher's leadership is strikingly similar to Brenda's questioning (presented above) why she should be concerned with what the headteacher is like:

> I don't think a head would make me leave – if I was happy with the staff and happy with myself in the classroom . . . *unless* it was a total shambles. But I don't think I would leave unless the head had changed things so radically and made life unpleasant . . . and then, of course, I would.

> *Interviewer: So, you could cope with ineptitude, could you?*
> I don't think that would . . . I wouldn't be *happy* about it . . . but I don't think it would make me move.

Ann's limited prioritisation of her job, as well as her professionality orientation, meant that she was relatively unconcerned about the sort of issues which typically bother more 'extended' professionals (and teachers who are more engaged in their work). Certainly, there were aspects of Leyburn's functioning as a school that Ann would have liked to see improved, and these features were sources of dissatisfaction to her. But because she was, for various reasons, able to put the job in perspective and because the things that were most important to her were satisfactory, these sources of dissatisfaction took on more of the status of irritants than major dissatisfiers. She was able to derive fulfilment from her unimpeded work with her own class, and collegial relations were a key source of job comfort. Unlike the frustrated 'extended' professionals whose cases are presented in Chapter 6, Ann clearly did not *need*, even though she may have *preferred* it, to have the school in which she worked conform precisely to her conception of an ideal educational establishment whose organisation was underpinned by, and reflected her interpretation of, sound principles and ideologies.

Louise's story

Louise taught at Sefton Road County Primary School. She did not have permanent status. She taught full time, and had responsibility for a Year 5 class but, when I interviewed her, she was employed on a one-year temporary contract, having spent a large proportion of the previous year as a supply teacher at Sefton Road. She was interviewed in the summer of 1990, shortly before her temporary contract was due to expire. She was going to leave Sefton Road at the end of the school year, and had been appointed to a school in the private sector. She was 40 years old and had taught for ten years, though without ever having held a permanent teaching post.

I would categorise Louise as a 'restricted' professional. Her teaching was intuitively based and generally reflected a low level of classroom competence and organisational efficiency. Her lessons were not always well planned nor well thought-out and her teaching in its entirety lacked coherence in its structure. She did not seem to be committed to any specific educational ideologies or principles. She took little interest in school policy and organisation.

Louise seemed to enjoy teaching and, in her own way, was quite conscientious. She was pleasant, good-natured and co-operative. She established a good rapport with her pupils and managed their behaviour reasonably successfully, but her commitment to and engagement in her work were probably lower than that of my other interviewees. The effort that she expended on the job was by no means exceptionally low; indeed, she seemed to consider herself quite hard-working and, had she been employed at another school rather than at Sefton Road, she may not necessarily have been noticeably different from her colleagues in relation to commitment, conscientiousness and competence. At Rockville, for example, she would not have stood out from the crowd. At Sefton Road, though, with its hard-working, competitive climate (described in Chapter 7) Louise was like a fish out of water.

Her case bears similarities to those of Brenda and Ann. Like them, she found collegial relations a great source of pleasure. Louise was well liked on a personal level by many of her colleagues even though, on a professional level, it was generally recognised that, within the school's professional culture, she was in effect a deviant. She was included in whatever staffroom camaraderie there was time for, within the pervasive busyness and work-related focus of activity, and she sometimes socialised with colleagues after school.

Louise was also similar to Brenda and Ann in relation to the limited prioritisation she afforded her job. She valued her personal life higher than she did her working life and established clear parameters of what she was prepared to accept as the demands of the job. However, she differed from Brenda and Ann with respect to levels of job satisfaction, morale and motivation. She was not happy at work. She was most dissatisfied with the management of Sefton Road and with the headteacher's leadership. It failed to motivate her and, throughout the time she spent there until she was appointed to a new post, her morale was low.

Louise blamed her negative job-related attitudes on Phil, the Sefton Road head. She found the school's professional climate, which she attributed to Phil's leadership style, very uncomfortable. It was too demanding and stressful for her and, more particularly, it required of teachers a level of commitment, conscientiousness and industriousness that she considered excessive. Working at Sefton Road, in Louise's view, involved a level of effort that exceeded the parameters of acceptability she had drawn up for herself. She provided an example of a particular incident that highlighted the very different expectations held by Phil and herself of the demands of teaching at Sefton Road:

> they were having this Asian week . . . so, everything had to be done for this, and he [Phil] was very worked up about it . . . he wanted everything to be absolutely wonderful. But, you see, when I came into that classroom it was bare . . . totally bare . . . so I had to start from scratch . . . I got one full board covered, but then he came in and he said, 'Oh, you'll have to come in at the weekend and you'll have to fill all the boards – all the lot – because it's Asian week next week and it's *got* to be done'. So he gave me a key and then he took me round to Mary's classroom, and he said, 'Now, do look around and get ideas from other classes'. And he said, 'I know you're on your own and, as you know, Mary is. Maybe you don't feel as she does, with you only being here for a year, but, you see, she's doing all these cushions for the children . . . you know . . . sort of . . . doing them at night' . . . Well, I was just . . . gobsmacked . . . utterly – I was dumbstruck. I just thought, 'Who the heck do you think you are?' . . . I wish I could've come back at him and said, 'I'm sorry; I've got a personal life . . .' And I *know* Mary's on her own, but she's making school her whole *life* . . . But . . . I mean . . . he'd no right to say that to me. It was assuming . . . really . . . putting me down . . . and I was quite horrified by it.

It was clear that Louise neither shared nor supported Phil's vision. She found the climate of hard work and competitiveness oppressive and incomprehensible. It was entirely alien to her:

if I'd been at Sefton Road when I was actually assessed for my probationary year I just couldn't have coped. I believe Phil has you doing lesson plans *all the time* when you're a probationer – whereas I only did them when the adviser was coming in.

I feel that he uses his staff to the utmost – I don't know why they all work so hard . . . and it's all for the glorification of *him* . . . and I don't like that either. But everybody runs around for him like chickens with their heads cut off – they're not like human beings; they're like automatons . . . and everybody's like that because of . . . the pressure . . . which I've never found in any other school . . . and I've worked in enough!

Interviewer: So, you'd say there was a distinct climate?
Oh, yes!

Interviewer: How would you describe it?
Well . . . I find it stressful . . . a stressful climate . . . I mean . . . there are only so many hours in a day . . . and I feel that, with Phil, he wants 110% off everybody . . . and I think that's asking too much . . . Actually, d'you know what I think it is? . . . I think it's a bit of 'keeping up with the Jones's'. Everybody wants to do better than everybody else . . . it's almost . . . like on a street, or whatever. I've come across these people who have to 'keep up with the Jones's' . . . they're a certain type of person that does it – I'm not one of them, of course – and sometimes I think there's a lot of this rivalry . . . wanting to do better than the others have done.

Moreover, Louise was extremely cynical of Phil's motives. In most respects, her views of Phil and of working at Sefton Road contrasted strikingly with those of most of her colleagues, including Sarah and Kay, whose cases are presented in Chapter 7. In their interviews, Sarah and Kay had remarked on how pedagogically sound they considered Phil to be, and of his great concern for the children's welfare and education. Louise's perspective was quite distinct from theirs. She spoke of Phil:

Personally, I think he's just interested in creating a good show . . . but that's personal and I might be wrong . . . but that's the impression I've been given . . . that the most important thing to Phil is to put on a good show.

Interviewer: Do you think he has the children's interests at heart?
No . . . no. I know he's very *good* with them . . . er . . . no . . . I don't think he's interested in their well-being – he definitely wants to create a good show, to impress people coming in – it's definitely, to me, a show school . . . to impress other people.

She then described an incident that, she felt, illustrated her point:

We were all having to put up some displays with an ecology theme, and I got this idea from Jill which Jill thought was okay . . . but . . . again, I made the mistake of having *all* the children doing art work. They were doing three things. First of all they were starting off with a pencil drawing, doing an abstract design . . . then they had to copy it in paint, and then, again, in chalk. It was such hard work, but, again, if I'd known the school then, as I do now, I would've simply taken my six best artists and let *them* do work for the display. So I eventually managed to pick out the best and pinned them up on the wall outside – and they were there for two days, pinned up. Then I stapled them one night, and the following morning he [Phil] came in . . . and he was genuinely embarrassed . . . and he called me out of the classroom and he said, 'I'm sorry, but it's not good enough, so it's got to come down'. And he said, 'But, don't worry, Jill's going to put some stuff there'. Well, I was just absolutely demoralised – *totally* demoralised!

Interviewer: Why was it not good enough, did he say?
Well, looking at other work . . . he just said, 'For Year 5, it's not good enough. It's not professional enough'. And I realised that when I saw other people's work, but I realised what they'd done . . . they'd just taken the best. It has to be 'top show', and you've to pick out your best children and get *them* to do something. And, to me, I, personally, don't like that . . . because I don't like top show. But, alright, the work produced was *super* . . . but, again, it's *knowing* what to do. I was just lost.

Louise was desperately unhappy at Sefton Road, and was anxious to leave as soon as she possibly could. On one occasion, after Phil's manner with her had upset her, she had complained to the LEA's Director of Education and asked for a transfer to another school. She told me that her request had been very sympathetically received, but the director had flattered her, told her that she was strong enough to cope and, very kindly, persuaded her to remain at Sefton Road.

She spoke of her relief that she had secured another post, obviating the need for her to remain at Sefton Road: 'I couldn't *bear* to go back there. I couldn't bear it.' Yet it was not the work itself that Louise disliked. She apparently enjoyed teaching, and she spoke of schools where she had been very happy. One of the major sources of job satisfaction, for her, as for Brenda and Ann, was collegial camaraderie, and she had been happiest at schools where colleagues had been friendly and supportive:

Interviewer: Can you describe the sort of climate that suits you, then . . . where you've been happy?
Er . . . where there's a lot of hard work going on . . . but where there's humour in the staffroom . . . when you get in the staffroom and you have a laugh . . . you have a joke . . . and if there's anything wrong, you know that you can say it . . . and you'll get back-up. I like working in a school where there's support . . . where you can have adult conversation and adult humour and . . . any problems, you can discuss it with anybody . . . I've *always* got on with people, socially . . .

Interviewer: So, the socialising aspect is very important to you, is it?
Yes, *very*, because . . . with children, you're isolated. You can be very lonely . . . and, so, it's desperately important, to me, that you get on in an adult way with others.

*Interviewer: And, yet, even though, **now**, you have good relations with the rest of the Sefton Road staff . . . you still wouldn't want to go back there after the summer holiday?*
No . . . because there isn't the socialising in the staffroom . . . all of my friends from school I see *out* of school. In school I know that there's going to be no time for any conversation.

When she summed up her attitude to her job at Sefton Road, it was, once again, on Phil that Louise focused, attributing her low level of job engagement to him: 'You see, I cannot give my all to somebody that I don't like and respect. That says it all, really.'

Shared perspectives and different attitudes

Making comparisons between English and French primary school-teachers, Osborn and Broadfoot (1992) highlight an attitudinal distinction that reflects job engagement or, using Vroom's (1964, p. 144) term, ego involvement: 'At their most extreme, then, a French teacher's perceptions of her role centred on "meeting one's contractual responsibility" and an English teacher's on "striving for perfection" (Osborn and Broadfoot, 1992, p. 4). Although it would perhaps be inaccurate to represent the three teachers profiled in this chapter as reflecting the extremity of low engagement in their work associated with French primary schoolteachers, it is nevertheless clear that none of them seemed unduly concerned to 'strive for perfection'. By keeping the job in perspective, Brenda, Ann and Louise were not of the category of teachers whose working lives are the focus of Spencer's study, and whom she describes (1984, p. 293): 'Regardless of whether they took paperwork home or had extra-curricular duties, all teachers were influenced while at home by school-related factors in ways that made their work an ever-present reality.' They do, however, manifest comparable perspectives on their work to that held by one of Goodson's (1991, pp. 35–6) teachers, who describes himself:

'You don't understand my relationship to the school and to teaching. My centre of gravity is not here at all. It's in the community, in the home – that's where I exist, that's where I put my effort now. For me the school is nine to five, I go through the motions.'

The key factor, according to Ball and Goodson (1985, p. 18), seems to be that of identity: 'The ways in which teachers achieve, maintain, and develop their identity, their sense of self, in and through a career, are of vital significance in understanding the actions and commitments of teachers in their work. Identity is also a key to apprehending the divisions between teachers.' High levels of commitment to, and engagement with, the job reflect strong work-related role identities, such as those held by the teachers profiled in Chapters 6 and 7. The three teachers upon whom this chapter focuses, on the other hand, evidently held much weaker identities as teachers, which were superseded by other identities. Lortie's (1975, pp. 90–100) research findings revealed, contrary to his expectation ('All else being equal, we expect higher engagement to be associated with higher satisfaction, as in the adage that one gets out of life what one puts into it' – *ibid.*, p. 89), that teachers who reported higher involvement did not report higher satisfaction with teaching (*ibid.*, pp. 91, 99):

The system of effort-involvement and net satisfaction, then, is not in balance; there is, in fact, a tendency for satisfactions and contributions to be negatively related.

The system of career rewards, in sum, works most satisfactorily for those who give teaching less than full commitment; 'gainers' are teachers who plan on short-term or less than full-time engagement.

In two of the three cases presented in this chapter, Lortie's findings were borne out. Brenda and Ann were both – but to a different extent – satisfied with their jobs. Louise, however, was not. Despite having shared perspectives on their jobs, the job-related attitudes of these three teachers differed. Indeed, Brenda and Louise represent polarities on the job satisfaction, motivation and morale levels continuum.

The reason for the distinction is to be found, once again, in consideration of the importance of contextual factors and, in particular, in examination of the degree of match between teachers and their work contexts. If teachers afford their work relatively low salience, or relatively low priority in their lives, they are more resilient to factors that might easily develop into sources of dissatisfaction for their more committed colleagues. As this chapter has illustrated, situations that for some teachers might escalate into resignation issues have much less impact upon less committed teachers because, essentially, the job is less important to them. Under such conditions, it is much easier to sustain high, rather than experience low, job satisfaction because fewer things in the job matter. The kind of job satisfaction that is sustained however, is, by the same token, more likely to be job comfort than job fulfilment because there are too few aspects of the job which are considered sufficiently important to develop to the extent of their becoming sources of job fulfilment. There are likely to be fewer 'troughs' in the working lives of low-commitment teachers, compared with those of their more committed colleagues, but there are also fewer 'peaks'.

This, at least, is the case where teachers are permitted within their work contexts to be relatively uncommitted, and where there are few or no pressures on them to be otherwise. This scenario constitutes a good teacher–institution match, which is the key to achieving positive job-related attitudes. This was not the case for Louise. Hers was most definitely a case of teacher–institution mismatch. Herein lies the key to the distinction between her and Brenda's and, to a large extent, Ann's, levels of job satisfaction, morale and motivation.

The headteacher is particularly important in determining the extent of teacher–institution match (which is such a crucial job satisfaction-, morale- and motivation-influencing factor). The next chapter examines in detail precisely what features of school leadership contribute towards shaping teachers' work contexts in ways that impact upon their attitudes to their jobs.

A management perspective: issues for consideration

Key points
- Teachers vary in the extent to which they prioritise their work.
- Low job engagement may, under certain conditions, help safeguard against job-related dissatisfaction.
- Their job satisfaction, morale and motivation are influenced by the extent to which teachers' work contexts are conducive to their job engagement.

Consider
- Are Brenda, Ann and Louise the kinds of teachers that would be likely to make valuable contributions to the schools in which they work? What, if anything, do such teachers have to offer?
- How might 'low engagement' teachers be best managed by head-teachers? What staff management strategies would be most appropriate? Should such teachers' preferences for low engagement be accommodated, or should they be encouraged towards higher levels of engagement? How effective, and appropriate, was the Sefton Road headteacher's management of Louise?
- Is there a place, within the teaching profession, for 'restricted' professionality?

9

The leadership factor

Introduction

Out of the four chapters immediately preceding this one, the most strikingly common factor to emerge as influential on teachers' morale, job satisfaction and motivation is school leadership. Whether it was the extent to which it enabled or constrained teachers, created and fostered school professional climates that were compatible with teachers' ideals or engaged their commitment and enthusiasm, the leadership effected by their headteachers was clearly a key determinant of how teachers felt about their jobs.

In some cases the impact headteachers have on the job-related attitudes of teachers is not obvious. Headteachers who adopt *laissez-faire* styles of leadership, for example, may be considered to exert very little influence on the school-specific circumstances and situations that potentially affect teacher morale, job satisfaction and motivation. In the context of my own research, Geoff Collins of Rockville County Primary School was one such case; indeed, many of the Rockville teachers considered him to have less influence than had specific colleagues. Fundamentally, however, this was not the case. Like all headteachers, the Rockville head was, by virtue of his position, the school's most influential member of staff as the relative influence exerted by his colleagues was effectively determined by the extent of his influence. The headteacher is, therefore, the key influence on his/her school, since his/her leadership, whether it be autocratic, democratic *or laissez-faire* sets the tone of the school's micropolitics and establishes the parameters within which other sources of influence may operate.

In Chapter 5, the headteacher's leadership was identified as one of the significant prevailing situations that gave rise to dissatisfaction amongst many of the teachers at Rockville County Primary School. In Chapter 6, frustrated and demoralised 'extended' professionals complained of school-specific circumstances, for which they all blamed their respective headteachers, of whose management and leadership they were highly critical. High levels of morale, job satisfaction and motivation reported by teachers profiled in Chapter 7 were attributed by them, in part, to leadership that was perceived as either satisfactory or good. Chapter 8 presented the cases of teachers who were either demoralised by or unimpeded by and, as a result, satisfied with, their respective headteachers' leadership style. This chapter synthesises these leadership-related data and supplements them with other research evidence of the importance of leadership on teachers' attitudes to their work, highlighting the ways in which it influences job satisfaction, morale and motivation.

Headteachers as leaders: key influential features

In relation to the headteachers of the three schools in which I carried out observation, I built up composite images from my own impressions and those impressions conveyed by the staff in these schools. Interview-generated evidence of other headteachers' leadership styles which was revealed, for example, when teachers spoke of headteachers with whom they had previously worked, supplemented these impressions and from these combined data there emerged commonalities. I was able to categorise the substance of these impressions into five inter-related features of headteachers as leaders which I consider to have been particularly significant in combining to influence teacher attitudes. These are: *personality, interpersonal behaviour, 'mission', professionality* and *management skills*.

Personality

In this section my intention is to convey an idea of how the different headteachers were perceived as men and women rather than as head-teachers, and of how these perceptions influenced teachers' attitudes. It is impossible to separate completely an individual's work-related self from his/her non-work-self since each impacts upon the other. Most teachers, when speaking of headteachers whom they knew, included reference to their personalities. They were able to speak of their heads as people, as distinct from as heads, but the sources of their perceptions of what were considered to be heads' 'non-work' selves were inevitably teachers' professional relationships with them.

There was an evident ambiguity in the extent of some teachers' recognition of the personality–leadership link. On the one hand, in many comments it was implicit that personality was considered to determine, and be reflected in, leadership:

> *Most* women can't do with somebody who's incredibly tolerant and lets everybody be happy . . . As a person, I respect Geoff . . . but, er . . . I think on the whole, a lot of women together can't do with someone like Geoff.
>
> (Brenda, Rockville teacher)

> The head at Rydal . . . well, again, that was her own personality . . . She . . . er . . . she was insecure – very insecure, really – and her way of doing it was to

blame others for anything that was going wrong . . . er . . . very sharp-tongued . . . er . . . but a very well organised person . . . if she was going to do something she did it well – whatever it was was done well. But, she was a very stringent person – not very gracious . . . again, somebody who couldn't say, 'Please' and 'Thank you' . . . and she wasn't at all sure of herself, but, then again, it was her first headship . . . and she could be a real . . . tyrant – *very* unpleasant.

(Ann, Leyburn teacher, speaking of a former head)

On the other hand, teachers often distinguished between certain aspects of personality and of leadership, separating the 'person' from the headteacher:

It isn't a job for him, really . . . he's not a manager – as a *person*, he's very nice – but, as a manager, he's the worst head I've worked for, by a long way – a long way.

(Jean, Rockville teacher)

As a *person*, I really like him, but I don't think, as a head, he's good at his job.

(Elaine, Rockville teacher)

Jack McNulty, the head at St Paul's, where I used to be . . . he's grand . . . I mean, he's a nice bloke . . . er . . . I wouldn't say he's super efficient, though – but he's very amenable.

(Jane, Rockville teacher, speaking of a former head)

The implication of comments such as these, which effectively draw a line of distinction between headteachers' 'work selves' and their 'non-work selves', is that leadership quality is not necessarily reflective of personal qualities; that likeable people do not always make good heads.

The impression I gained of the Rockville headteacher's personality, for example, was that he was both likeable and generally well liked. He was, as one of my interviewees described him, 'a nice bloke'. Yet these qualities were not incorporated into overall assessments of Geoff's leadership which, as earlier chapters demonstrate, were generally very negative. They were, rather in the ambiguous way to which I have already referred, identified on the one hand, as compensatory or even redeeming qualities which served to preclude assessments of Geoff being entirely negative. On the other hand, they were also identified as factors which contributed to what was considered to be Geoff's inadequate leadership. In other words, many of those aspects of Geoff's character which made him likeable were, for the most part, given very poor rating as leadership qualities. More significantly, as the example of Geoff's leadership (described more fully in Chapter 5) illustrates, headteachers who are liked on a personal level are equally capable as those who are not of engendering negative job-related attitudes amongst their colleagues. A 'nice' personality in a headteacher offers no safeguard against staff dissatisfaction, demotivation and low morale emanating from his/her leadership.

Attitudes are continually being formed and re-formed in response to a cycle of social interaction, of the actions which result from this, of interpretations and evaluations of these, and of responsive, attitudinally directed social interaction and action. Interpersonal behaviour is therefore a key component in attitude formation. The next section examines the interpersonal behaviour which headteachers applied to their jobs, and the attitudinal responses which this provoked in the teachers who were affected by it.

Interpersonal behaviour

Interpersonal skills are clearly a key constituent of leadership. Socially, psychology and management studies have long recognised *consideration*, which Argyle (1972, p. 147) interprets as 'employee centredness', as a leadership dimension. Halpin (cited in Nias *et al.*, 1989, p. 96) describes consideration as 'behaviour indicative of friendship, mutual trust, respect and warmth in the relationship between the leader and the members of his/her staff'.

Coulson (1988, p. 259) identifies *interpersonal competence* as one of eight features of successful school leadership. While Ball (1987, p. 100) questions 'whether styles of headship are independently selected or acquired by incumbents or are, in part, extensions of individual personality types or personal psychologies', Coulson (1988, p. 260) contends that management style is a facet of interpersonal behaviour and as such, is 'an integral part of that individual's way of being'. He emphasises the importance in headteachers of temperament and sensitivity to others and suggests (*ibid.*, p. 262) that 'to a large extent it is interpersonal competence which differentiates more successful from less successful heads, at least in the eyes of teachers'.

Nias *et al.* (1989, p. 105) identify some of the specific aspects of interpersonal behaviour manifested by heads of schools 'which offered a positive model of adult relationships' and which fostered collaborative cultures:

> Staff were almost always welcomed, thanked and praised either directly or by reference to the children's work or behaviour. The frequency, consistency and quality of these acts of appreciation demonstrated that mutual consideration among colleagues stemmed in part from, and/or is reinforced by, the heads' behaviour. Moreover, the heads played an important part in establishing an atmosphere in which allowance was made for the health and personal commitments of staff. Heads were quick to comfort those staff who faced family sickness or problems and did what they could to accommodate unexpected events in the personal lives of staff.

They refer to heads' awareness of the importance of 'how they behaved as people' to teachers' comments about their heads' personal qualities (*ibid.*, p. 106), and to heads' membership of staff peer groups (*ibid.*, pp. 106–7):

> None of the heads was aloof or isolated from their respective staff group. They joined in, particularly in the staffroom, where they were frequently to be found

drinking coffee, chatting, listening and laughing . . . All five heads were members of the staff group. Whilst it was accepted by almost all staff that their heads performed a dual role – leader and member – the quality of the heads' behaviour as members appears to have added to their credibility as leaders . . . All in all the heads earned considerable respect from their staff.

Within my own work, the Rockville case demonstrates particularly well, however, that good interpersonal skills alone are inadequate for securing headteachers' credibility amongst, and respect from, their colleagues. Geoff Collins was a social animal. He seemed to thrive on interpersonal relationships and clearly enjoyed one-to-one discussions and chats with any of his colleagues. He was frequently to be found in the staffroom or in classrooms, often long after the school day had ended, engrossed in light-hearted discussions with one or two colleagues usually, though not always, on school-related issues and through which, in a convivial atmosphere, his ideas and plans or his responses to those of teachers would be articulated, explained and rationalised. In a pastoral-type role he appeared to be concerned about the personal well-being and welfare of all his colleagues, equally, as individuals. He was always very willing to assist colleagues with problems and difficulties in their personal lives and was supportive in times of domestic crises. Typically this was not just moral but practical support, and the Rockville staff knew that he could be relied upon in this way. The school secretary's assessment of this aspect of Geoff's personality and interpersonal behaviour reflects general consensus:

> He's a good *person*. He's good-hearted person, is Geoff – you'd go a long way to find anyone . . . I mean, if anyone's ill . . . straight away – no messing! He would go for Margaret's prescriptions when she was off sick, because she'd got no one to go for them, and all this sort of thing . . . He's very good like that.
>
> (Deborah, school secretary)

It was often Geoff whom members of staff would ask for lifts into school in the morning when their own cars were being serviced, and this occurred even when it involved Geoff going out of his way. One teacher who was stranded one Saturday in town with her two preschool children when her car broke down, and who needed to return home quickly, phoned Geoff to ask for a lift when she could not reach her husband. He came willingly. When the teacher thanked Geoff by leaving a tin of biscuits for him at his house, Geoff told her at school the next day that he appreciated the gift but that it really was not necessary at all. 'If you can't do something for somebody to help them out, it's a poor show,' he said. This comment sums up an important aspect of Geoff's interpersonal behaviour but one which, to some extent, backfired on him throughout the course of specific significant events and developments by contributing to the evolution of an unhealthy social and organisational climate at Rockville.

Contrasting with Geoff Collins' caring, solicitous behaviour, however, were some headteachers whose poor interpersonal skills and perceived insensitivity to others' feelings and needs, when incorporated into their leadership, provoked negative job-related attitudes amongst their staff:

Oh, I think she's [Mrs Hillman] ignorant and she's really egocentric . . . you can't talk to her about anything which is to do with hard work without her relating it to herself . . . but, whenever *you* try to relate anything to yourself or to your own personal interests, she changes the subject.

And the other thing that bothers me . . . she hates people being off sick . . . it's a weakness; it's a sin . . . no matter what – if you've got cancer – her only concern is how long you're going to be off, not whether you're going to die! And she gives certificates to children who've been in school every day . . . so, you might work your arse off – you might be a star – but if you get chicken pox, or if you have your tonsils out, you don't get a certificate. I think, if she'd been a mill-owner, people would've got hurt on the machines because conditions wouldn't have been right . . . and I think she would've exploited people . . . and I think that reflects her personality.

(Mark, Leyburn teacher)

Interviewer: So . . . you don't regret that you'll be leaving Leyburn in a few weeks?
No. I did have regrets at first . . . but something happened . . . I think it was Mrs Hillman's manner once when she came back into school one day during her secondment . . . and other things took precedence with her over the staff – we didn't even get a, 'Good morning' . . . there was this fervent activity . . . and I thought, 'No, I've got no regrets' . . . I think, perhaps because Mrs Hillman's been away . . . out of the school . . . and it just hit me once . . . I thought, 'I will resent her coming back' . . . The tension has eased this year, with Mrs Hillman being seconded, and Felicity in charge. If you're ill you know you'll be sent home by Felicity . . . whereas, at the end of last year, Mrs Hillman came into the staffroom and told us how many days off the whole staff had had together! 'Thirty days off!' she said . . . but I don't think that's bad for ten members of staff. But everybody felt guilty. Well, you *shouldn't*. I mean . . . if my children were ill I used to go into school after my husband had come home, to prepare work . . . to make up for the time I'd had off. But I'm fed up of feeling guilty.

(Fiona, Leyburn teacher)

Mr Black . . . was awful to us – *awful*! He was very bitter . . . and we couldn't do anything right . . . You couldn't talk to him about anything . . . I mean, he was very rude to people . . . he was *awful*.

(Joanne, Rockville teacher, speaking of a former head)

Evidence from the Rockville study suggests that teachers' frustration, dissatisfaction, low morale and demotivation, arising out of what is perceived as poor leadership, remain relatively unaffected by approbation of leaders' interpersonal behaviour. This illustrates a low correlation between levels of approbation of leaders' interpersonal behaviour and leadership-influenced job-related attitudes. Yet this low correlation only seems to be applicable in cases where leadership-influenced job-related attitudes are negative. In cases where they are positive, there is a much higher correlation:

> And she worked with staff in the way that she worked with children. She had – I don't know what it is about her . . . but she made you want to do your best – and not just for *her*, but for yourself . . . You weren't working *for* her – you weren't working to please *her* . . . but she suddenly made you realise what was possible . . . and you, kind of, raised your game all the time.
>
> (Helen, Woodleigh Lane Primary School, speaking of a former head)

> he would bring in Mars bars and say, 'I think we all deserve this' . . . and sometimes he'd say, '*I'll* take the kids this morning – you get on with some work', and he'd keep them for a good hour, or so . . . We were just like one big happy family . . . I mean, I think we were *too* friendly, really; he needed slightly more distance . . . but, of course, it was too late by then; we were already friendly, and he couldn't go back . . . But, you worked every bit as hard for somebody like him . . . every bit as hard.
>
> (Ann, Leyburn teacher, speaking of a former head)

This higher correlation probably reflects perceived causality; teachers attribute their leadership-influenced, positive job-related attitudes to, at least in part, the leaders' interpersonal behaviour of which they approve.

Mission

'Mission' is identified by Nias *et al.* (1989, p. 95) as one of their six dimensions of leadership, and is interpreted both as a reflection of headteachers' 'principal beliefs both about personal relationships and about effective educational practice' (*ibid.*, p. 97), and as pointing the direction for the school and reflecting the school's underlying philosophy (*ibid.*, p. 98). In Nias *et al.*'s five collaborative schools, the headteachers 'provided their school with a mission based on their educational beliefs which, in turn, helped to develop or sustain the school's culture' (*ibid.*, p. 122).

Coulson (1988) does not use the term *mission*. He refers to head-teachers' *vision* for their schools (*ibid.*, p. 257), which heads strive to realise through the organisational cultures they nurture. Webb and Vulliamy (1996, p. 308) also refer to headteachers' 'vision and beliefs' as guiding their direction of the school, and Southworth (1994, p. 18) writes of 'leaders with a vision . . . able to project it in such a way that others become committed to it.' Similarly, Wallace and Huckman (1996, p. 314) write of heads' promoting 'beliefs and values' amongst staff.

I interpret mission, in the context of school leadership, as a strategic plan aimed at realising a vision. A mission is a sense of commitment towards a goal. It provides focus, direction and purpose to leadership. It reflects beliefs and values and influences leadership behaviour: in particular, decision-making and policy formulation. I do not believe that leaders will always necessarily have a 'mission'. Many will have a vision of how they would like their school to develop, without having the strength of commitment and the focus associated with a mission. Some may even lack a clearly defined vision.

The extent to which teachers and heads share a vision, or even a mission, will clearly influence job-related attitudes. Dissonance may give rise to dissatisfaction and low morale, while congruence in relation to the images towards whose realisation staff want to work is likely to motivate. Those of my teachers who recognised and shared their heads' visions manifested high levels of job satisfaction, morale and motivation. Their willingness to work with their headteachers in their missions of realising these visions afforded them many opportunities to experience job fulfilment since they were then generally supported, rather than constrained, by school policy and decision-making. It was partly the facilitatory outcomes, in relation to her own work, of her co-operating with her headteacher in trying to realise their shared vision that enticed Kay to remain at Sefton Road rather than move on for promotion (see Chapter 7). Similarly, it was the job fulfilment and professional development opportunities presented by her working in what she perceived to be a well led school, within a climate shaped by a real sense of direction and purpose, that underpinned Helen's praise of a headteacher for whom she had once worked:

> She had a very strong educational vision . . . Now, up until that time – I mean, I'm a much slower learner – I was piecing together my educational philosophy and, a lot of the time, just . . . you know, struggling to get by . . . er . . . and she really just turned me round like nobody else ever has done . . . She was very, very challenging on a direct level.

However, it is through examination of cases of dissonance that the importance of vision and mission in relation to teachers' job-related attitudes becomes most apparent. Nias (1980, p. 268) identifies as a key source of dissatisfaction amongst her sample of primary schoolteachers the frustration experienced from working in schools where there was no sense of purpose. Indeed, this was given by five of her interviewees as a major reason for their resigning. Freeman's (1986) case study of teacher stress amongst secondary schoolteachers provides evidence to corroborate this. Analysis of questionnaire-generated data identified four stress-inducing factors that accounted for 81.4% of the variance. Of these four, 'loss of purpose and poor organisation and management' accounted for 54.4% of the variance:

> Factor 1, which accounted for over 50% of the variance seemed to describe the ethos of the school, as recorded in other areas of the case study. It tended to describe a hopelessness and a helplessness, relating to a lack of purpose, loss of direction, loss of knowing what they were doing for the pupils.
>
> *(Ibid.*, p. 10)

In my study, the 'extended' professionals who worked in schools where the headteacher did not appear to have a clearly defined mission, nor an explicit vision of what s/he wanted to achieve in relation to the children's education, were frustrated and demoralised. Lack of purpose and lack of direction in relation to the pursuit of educational goals do not conform to 'extended' professionals' ideals. Helen's comments about her head-teacher at Woodleigh Lane convey the intensity of the frustration that had prompted her to seek a new post:

> He's never set me any challenges, and he's never once noticed what I've done . . . And I've never once had any feedback. And I said to him, in one of my really bad moments, I said, 'I could be teaching them Swahili, hanging by their heels from the light fitting, and you wouldn't know!' . . . He doesn't collect in any planning books, he doesn't know what people are teaching! He hasn't a clue! . . . I mean, he doesn't know the children . . . he doesn't know the children by name. He's written a comment on their reports that've gone home yesterday . . . and he's put exactly the same comment on every child's report, because he doesn't know them. He doesn't know who they are.

At Leyburn, the headteacher's vision was interpreted by her staff as being focused on the physical environment rather than on the substance of what was provided for the children's educational needs fulfilment. Her mission, they felt, was to create and sustain a well resourced, clean and attractive and well run establishment, but that this mission reflected over-sight of consideration of the purpose for which the establishment should be run was a source of dissatisfaction to them:

> I think she likes to make sure that she provides a lot of equipment . . . and good teachers . . . but, otherwise . . . I don't know . . . I don't know if she has the academic interests of the kids at heart, to be honest. I really don't . . . because I think that, if she *did*, she would ensure that she would be there to help in the classrooms, rather than in the office . . . But, she aims to have a very tidy school . . . her aim is that school does not reflect the outside world . . . so, there's no litter . . . no grafitti . . . that's what riles her . . . untidiness . . . or wall displays that haven't been changed. That's very important to her.
>
> (Fiona, Leyburn teacher)

At Rockville, it appeared that Geoff Collins' leadership was influenced by a mission. The term was employed, in relation to Geoff's leadership, by several of the Rockville staff. Geoff's mission reflected his sociability, his concern for others and his religious faith. It was not pedagogically or educationally oriented, but pastoral in nature. It reflected Geoff's evident ideal of Rockville as a 'family' and it encompassed a solicitude relating to the personal needs of the staff at least as much as and, in the opinions of some teachers, more than those of pupils. It incorporated an interest in enhancing and sustaining good relations between the school and the community which it served. Rockville was not a community school, but Geoff gave every indication that he would have been happy for it to be so. His promotion of good relations within, and outside of, the school seemed to be of greater concern to him than the children's education. Staff welfare did, on occasions, appear to take precedence over pupil achievement. Whilst most of the Rockville staff accepted Geoff's evident commitment to his pastoral mission with good-humoured equanimity on the grounds that it did no harm, a minority of teachers was resentful of what they interpreted as misplaced energy which contributed towards neglect of what they felt the school's main focus and purpose ought to be.

Particularly scathing in her condemnation was Amanda, who is profiled in Chapter 6 as the most extreme example of an 'extended' professional. She was also one of the most dissatisfied of all my teacher interviewees. Her dissatisfaction with Geoff's making allowances due to her ill health for what was universally accepted as the underperformance and increasing incompetence of the deputy head, developed into wider criticism of this feature of Geoff's leadership:

He doesn't understand that a school is an institution which is set up for the learning of the children, and that the satisfying of the staff's personal needs is incidental to that. Now, alright, you've to acknowledge that if somebody's had a bereavement then there's a need for that member of staff which is, in actual fact, affecting the institution . . . but, it's a temporary thing. The school does not have to provide that person with a parent . . . all it has to do is support . . . you know . . . the peer group supports the teacher through the bereavement, don't they? Now, Geoff thinks that the effectiveness of the institution's purpose . . . it's diminished by . . . the lack of fulfilling of the teacher's personal needs. So, for example, we hear, 'Well . . . you know . . . she doesn't really like one of those boys and so that's why she's sharp with people here' or 'She has a lot of problems, you know' or 'She's not well, you know', without any recognition of the fact that he's actually saying, 'It's all right for this institution not to function for the purpose it's here for because somebody else has a need . . . which this institution isn't here to fulfil, anyway . . . but, never mind, we'll impede what's going on here . . . we'll diminish what's going on here . . . we can't actually *meet* the need of that person, as an institution, because it's not something that we're here for' . . . it's actually saying, 'It's okay not to do your job right, because there's something about your life which is lacking'. Now, that's not on, as far as I'm concerned. You wouldn't allow a doctor to kill somebody or – alright, that's a drastic thing – but . . . you know, would it be alright to keep on giving the wrong drug? Or, if you observed that they weren't actually dressing a wound correctly, would you let them keep on doing it? You'd either say to them, 'You need to go home' or you'd change the duty they have, wouldn't you? . . . You wouldn't *excuse* bad performance . . . Now, that's happened a lot at Rockville, hasn't it? – a lot! So, again, it's bad management, isn't it? It's a bad management technique . . . and a total misunderstanding of what school is for! You know . . . it's rewriting the social system . . . So, he was quite happy for the performance in school to be diminished because somebody had a personal need. Then, when it came to the point whereby . . . you know . . . it was a crisis . . . he was quite happy for the whole school – the whole staff – to suffer whilst he, then, tried personally to meet the needs of Margaret!

(Amanda, Rockville teacher)

For the most part, Geoff's educational beliefs were not made explicit. Many teachers remarked that they had no sense of what his views were on teaching and learning methods, curriculum development or, indeed, any educational issues. He simply did not convey any impression of having applied any depth of analysis to any issues of this kind. He appeared to be oblivious to the activities which went on in classrooms and never commented on specific projects. He just allowed teachers to teach precisely as they liked unhindered and, to a large extent, unobserved by him.

It was not unusual to see Geoff bustling around the school, coming and going in the course of routine tasks and popping in and out of classrooms. His purpose in doing so, though, was not to monitor as was the case with Webb and Vulliamy's primary headteachers (1996, p. 311). Indeed, when he breezed in and out of classrooms, Geoff seemed to be oblivious to the pupils' presence. Consistent with his sociable nature and, to some extent, with his pastoral-type mission, his interruptions of classes were in order to engage with teachers. Sometimes on these occasions he would digress from his original intention of passing on a quick message, confirming an arrangement or even seeking opinions, and become engaged in lengthy conversations without any apparent concern for the disruption to the class which might ensue.

Clearly, Geoff's mission was not based upon educational beliefs, as was the case with Nias *et al.*'s headteachers (1989, p. 122). Unlike these heads Geoff did not, therefore, appear to operate at two levels: at a high level of abstraction and at the level of day-to-day actions (*ibid.*). He seemed to operate only at the lower level. In some respects, Mrs Hillman at Leyburn was considered by many of her colleagues also to operate mainly at this lower level. Helen's perception, too, of her headteacher's leadership of Woodleigh Lane Primary School was that it involved engagement in day-to-day actions and no high-level abstraction, and some of my teacher interviewees referred to similarly low-level leadership on the part of heads with whom they had once worked. This lower level of operation was consistent with and reflected what many of my teachers identified, though without employing the term, as their headteachers' 'restricted' professionality.

Professionality

The concept of professionality and its facets and dimensions are examined in more detail in Chapter 6 (see also Evans, 1997). Here I provide an illustration of, and an outline overview of teachers' attitudes to their headteachers' professionality.

Where there was a fairly good match of professionality orientation between teachers and their heads, positive job-related attitudes were likely to emanate from approbation of school leadership. Professionality reflects values and ideologies and it underpins and informs decision-making and practice, so congruence between teachers and heads in relation to these is a sound basis of a climate of mutual respect and consideration. Such a climate is more likely to be enabling rather than constraining and this, in turn, facilitates progress along the job fulfilment process. This was clearly illustrated by my research findings. Essentially, teachers who veered towards 'restricted' professionality were generally satisfied with the leadership effected by headteachers who were, themselves, similarly 'restricted' in their professionality. Conversely, teachers whom I categorised as 'extended' professionals were generally dissatisfied with, and frustrated and demoralised by, such leadership unless they were sufficiently influential to over-ride it. I emphasise, however, that this was the general picture and that there were exceptions to this generalisation.

At Rockville, the leadership reflected 'restricted' professionality. Geoff Collins' 'restricted' professionality manifested itself in different ways, though never more blatantly than through his reactions and responses to the gradual development of, and opposition posed by, a reflective subculture within the Rockville staff dating from the appointment to the school of a significantly influential 'extended' professional, Amanda.

Geoff was very evidently out of his depth intellectually, and specifically in relation to his knowledge and understanding of educational issues, alongside those of his colleagues whose professionality was, to varying degrees, located much nearer to the 'extended' end of Hoyle's (1975) continuum. It was these comparatively more 'extended' professionals who were the most aware of Geoff's shortcomings and who identified them as such during research interviews, though without specific reference to Hoyle's (*ibid.*) terminology, which is not widely recognised amongst practitioners:

> He's inadequate, because he's no sense of direction . . . he lacks depth in educational development – in the development that *should* be going on in the school . . . er . . . his perceptions . . . so that he's inadequate.
>
> (Hilary, Rockville-based ESL teacher)

> they're taking a much broader view of headship now . . . there *is* the opportunity to appoint people who have management skills but also who are sound, not necessarily in *teaching*, but in curriculum development work . . . in implementing change . . . in assessment of need . . . structural need in a school, perhaps . . . I don't mean *learning* need . . . and people who are good at inter-relating in a peer group . . . But, the problem is . . . that when you think of some of the heads we're talking of . . . where would you fit Geoff Collins into that? He's neither pedagogically sound, nor is he – you see, Geoff Collins wouldn't get a headship now!
>
> (Amanda, Rockville teacher)

> If the head gave a bit more . . . direction to the school, I think we'd work together better . . . If I was in charge I'd be . . . thinking more about curriculum . . . and setting goals and things . . . but, I mean . . . there hasn't been any

direction . . . I've only got limited experience of heads . . . er . . . and my first head was fairly poor on curriculum but good on public relations . . . er . . . the second head was poor on both . . . and . . . er . . . Geoff seems *quite* good on the public side . . . er . . . but, then, not very good on the curriculum.

(Stephen, Rockville teacher)

Geoff's rather 'restricted' professionality was reflected in his typically blinkered views on many educational matters, and his apparent incapacity to apply indepth analysis and enlightened perspectives to the reasoning behind his decision-making. His myopic vision, coupled with his characteristic intransigence, deprived him of the intellectual requirements for post-ERA headships. He was not one of the new breed of higher-calibre primary head that has begun to emerge gradually since 1988.

It was not only the Rockville teachers who were frustrated by the leadership that emanated from their headteacher's 'restricted' professionality. Helen, at Woodleigh Lane, whose scathing criticism of her headteacher is included in Chapter 6, was sufficiently dissatisfied with and demoralised by what she perceived as her headteacher's intellectual shortcomings that she had found a new post. Mark, at Leyburn, was another victim of teacher–headteacher professionality clash. His assessment of Mrs Hillman's professionality incorporated reference to what he considered to be her incompetence at classroom practice:

> She doesn't give a shit! She's not concerned. If she goes into someone's class, she doesn't *teach*, she just sits and goes through a box of files . . . And, I thought she was strict, but once, she took my class . . . and while I was in the hall with the advisers and teachers from different schools I could see my kids running around and jumping over chairs, and all sorts of things . . . and I thought she must have gone back to her office, but when I went back to the classroom she was just sat at the desk and she showed no interest in the education of the children and the activities which they were doing . . . I just think the place is how a school should *not* be. And when I've been on courses and they've offered models of leadership and management technique and communication . . . and everybody slags off their head . . . but, it's just marginal things with them. Here, it's just *everything* – the whole thing! . . . the school . . . everything is wrong . . . but it looks right from the outside . . . It's just a model of how *not* to be, as far as I'm concerned.

(Mark, Leyburn teacher)

On the other hand, leadership that reflected more 'extended' professionality, since it was more likely to provide challenges and meaningful direction and less likely to stifle or constrain teachers' professional development, offered many more opportunities to experience job fulfilment. It was this kind of leadership that was offered by Phil, at Sefton Road, and to which his staff for the most part responded well.

Amongst teachers who respected it, and responded well to it, 'extended' professionality in headteachers was an effective motivator. It often impressed teachers, provided that it incorporated competence at classroom practice, and in cases where it exceeded teachers' own 'extended' professionality it established an exemplary model of professional behaviour. It gave headteachers the professional credibility that my research evidence reveals to be essential for motivating teachers. Ann, from Leyburn County Primary School, spoke of a head with whom she had once worked: 'He was Montessori trained . . . he'd done a Montessori course . . . oh, he could blind you with science . . . Oh, yes! I mean, he's doing a M.Phil now . . . He was very much more educationally aware than Mrs Hillman . . . He was very well read . . . and he cared very much about the children.' However, professionality alone was clearly insufficient as a constituent of leadership for fostering positive job-related attitudes. The most potent leadership-related influence on teachers' attitudes to their work was school management.

Management skills

The ways in which teachers were managed, as members of the staff of an institution, greatly influenced their levels of job satisfaction, morale and motivation. So influential was headteachers' management that it could make the difference, as preceding chapters have illustrated, between teachers being fired with enthusiasm and commitment and their dreading going to work on Monday mornings. Identifying successful staff management, though, is by no means simple and straightforward, since teachers differ in relation to how they prefer to be managed. Consideration of the implications of individuality and heterogeneity in relation to what influences job-related attitudes is an important feature of this book, and it features in later chapters. In this section, I present an outline of aspects of management that generally were either notably successful in fostering high levels of job satisfaction, morale or motivation, or that engendered negative attitudes.

The teachers involved in my study, for the most part, manifested concern to be listened to, to feel that their views and opinions were taken seriously and to be able to have a say in the running of their schools. In some cases, particularly those of more 'restricted' professionals or those teachers whose level of engagement in their work was quite low, it was often only in matters that impacted directly upon their own teaching that they wanted to be involved. In other cases, teachers' interests were much more widely spread and many teachers, particularly the more 'extended' professionals, wanted to influence school-wide policy and decision-making. Headteachers whose management tended to be consultative were therefore generally successful at securing high levels of job satisfaction, morale and motivation amongst those who valued opportunities to be heard. Phil, at Sefton Road, was such a headteacher. Although he sometimes operated a rather unsystematic and spasmodic approach to consultation, most of the Sefton Road staff felt that if they had an idea to suggest, an issue to raise, or a concern to express, Phil would give it serious consideration and make a reasoned response. In this sense, Phil was perceived predominantly as an enabling leader. This allowed the Sefton Road teachers greater opportunities for experiencing job fulfilment, and their recognition of this motivated them and helped sustain high morale.

Some of the other headteachers of whom my interviewees spoke, as well as the two other heads in whose schools I observed, seemed to varying degrees to have adopted less consultative approaches to management, but with the result of provoking generally negative attitudes amongst their staff. It was, for example, his exclusion from his school's decision-making process that prompted Mark's decision to leave Leyburn (see Chapter 6). Not all teachers shared Mark's level of concern to influence decision-making; some were quite content for and, indeed, some even expected their headteachers and other senior colleagues to make most decisions. What most teachers did want, though, was the assurance that if they *wanted* to be heard and taken seriously, they would be. In this respect, the Rockville headteacher's management skills were perceived as deficient.

Geoff Collins' management reflected some features of interpersonal leadership, as identified by Ball (1987, p. 88). His avoidance of conflict and his fear of confrontation, for example, were reflected in his evident preference for consulting with individuals on a one-to-one basis rather than addressing larger groups. On the other hand, he manifested certain characteristics which Ball (*ibid.*, p. 109) applies to the 'authoritarian head':

> Such a head takes no chances by recognizing the possibility of competing views and interests. Opposition is avoided, disabled or simply ignored. No opportunities provided for the articulation of alternative views or the assertion of alternative interests . . . Indeed, the authoritarian may rely, as a matter of course, on conscious deception as a method of organizational control.

In many respects, in relation to the managerial strategies which he employed, Geoff Collins was recognisable in Ball's description. Several Rockville teachers mistrusted Geoff, doubted his integrity and provided examples of his having misled them or even blatantly lied to them. In addition, an overwhelmingly consensual criticism of Geoff was that, though he often went through the motions of listening to and sometimes even soliciting teachers' views, he generally disregarded them. To many, this was a major source of dissatisfaction and demotivation:

> *Some* heads think that they're already doing staff appraisal – *our* head thinks that he's already doing staff appraisal! And, actually, what he's doing is causing more trouble than it's worth . . . People feel it's a waste of time, anyway. He's either not heard, or he's heard and he's thought, 'she doesn't know what she's talking about, so we'll do such-and-such, instead'.
>
> (Amanda, Rockville teacher)

If somebody told me I was going to be at Rockville for another five years I'd go into another job . . . I just think . . . er . . . I'm probably more aware of the situation, now . . . and more . . . frustrated, really . . . I feel that I ought to be able to have more influence on it than I obviously can . . . whereas . . . when you go into teaching at first, you know that you can't . . . but now I feel that I ought to be able to . . . but, I can't.

Interviewer: Do those in charge ever ask your opinion about anything . . . and take notice of it?
Oh, yes. They *ask*, but, no, they don't take any notice . . . because it's only a token gesture . . . Well . . . one example that's happened recently and that's fresh in my mind is the moving of children from class to class . . . where the children are streamed and a child makes progress . . . or doesn't . . . and you, perhaps, want a child to move up, or don't want him to move . . . or, whatever . . . well, you're *asked*, and then your opinion isn't taken into account.

(Susan, Rockville teacher)

overall, I think Geoff does what he wants – and I think staff are consulted as a matter of good manners . . . He's very sincere at pretending. He'll listen, and you think he's taken in some of your points, but, in the end, he goes his own way.

(Elaine, Rockville teacher)

I think, now, that he [Geoff] tends to listen and then just do the opposite to what you want . . . I sometimes wonder if he listens to find out what – I don't know . . . I don't know if it's a deliberate action, or not – I mean . . . we come out of staff appraisals – and we *all* feel like this – I mean . . . you tell him what you think in these staff interviews, and . . . we got just the opposite of what we'd asked for!

(Pat, Rockville teacher)

In a sense, the extent to which teachers' opinions are considered reflects the recognition afforded them. Recognition of teachers, in its widest sense, was the key attitudes-influencing aspect of headteachers' management. This includes recognition of teachers' needs, efforts, capabilities and achievements. It involves taking notice of teachers.

Headteachers who were aware of what was going on in their schools and of what teachers were doing, who showed a genuine interest in everything that was happening around them and who carefully monitored the activities that went on were the best motivators. The Rockville and Leyburn heads did not fall into this category, nor did Helen's headteacher at Woodleigh Lane. However, Helen spoke of a former headteacher whose management had incorporated interest, awareness and recognition of what her staff needed in terms of professional guidance and direction:

I mean, she insisted, right from the start, that we do a planning book every week, and she had that in, first thing on a Monday morning – and, woe betide you if you had any lame excuse as to why the book wasn't there! And she would read those on a Monday morning, and have them back to you by playtime! . . . with copious comments, and, 'why don't you . . . ?' and things like that. So she, kind of, developed . . . er . . . you know, what you were doing, and asked questions . . . And . . . what she was focusing on, as it became apparent through all her notes that she was writing, was actually the children's experience – 'cos what most people write in a planning book is what they're going to *teach* . . . which isn't the same thing at all . . . Er, so, in that way she challenged people. She then spent a lot of time *in* the classroom . . . and, she'd remember what you'd put in your planning book, and so she came round to see it in practice, and asked you how it'd gone on.

Recognition of teachers' efforts and achievements through praise was perhaps the most effective motivator. Teachers who were given positive feedback on their work by their headteachers reported higher levels of job satisfaction, morale and motivation than those who were not. Recognition of this kind, when it was merited, was a key feature of the Sefton Road headteacher's management. Phil would make a point of conveying to teachers his satisfaction with their work. He would compliment them on their latest wall displays, on their plans for particularly interesting activities of which they had written in their weekly record books or on the progress they were making with specific children of which he became aware as he went in and out of classes, monitoring the work in his school. In this respect, his management style seems similar to that of John, a headteacher with whom Ann, from Leyburn, once worked:

> Well, at one school, Littlefield, we had a head who was a very good motivator and was very free with his praise . . . and he would come into your room and say, 'Oh, it looks lovely in here; oh, you *are* working hard!' . . . It was the praise business . . . *and* he worked hard himself . . . you knew where you stood with him . . . But . . . er . . . he was a good motivator, and I think it was just that one little word of thanks every now and again that did it.

Many teachers, however, who received no praise or, indeed, feedback of any kind from their headteachers were dissatisfied and had become demotivated and demoralised by their efforts remaining unrecognised. Helen's analysis of precisely why she was dissatisfied with her headteacher's management and leadership focused on this issue:

> I *think* it was the lack of recognition that really bothered me . . . that, whether I do it or don't do it, he doesn't think any different of me . . . I think it's that . . . As I say, in my classroom, he's never once come and said, 'Oh, that looks a good piece of work you've done with the children.'

Similarly, Fiona, Ann and Mark's comments about Mrs Hillman, the Leyburn head, highlight how detrimental had been the effect upon their job-related attitudes of her neglect of recognition of teachers' efforts:

> She once said to someone, 'You never tell staff how well they've done . . . because it makes them stop trying'. Now, to motivate people, you give them feedback . . . and it makes them drive on.
>
> (Mark)

> Fiona's leaving because of *her*, yes . . . it's *totally* because of Mrs Hillman. She lost Mrs Earnshaw – a very conscientious . . . er . . . hardworking person . . . because she wanted something doing *yesterday* . . . and when it was done you

always felt that it wasn't done as well as she would've liked it to have been done . . . er . . . she *never* gives praise! . . . Er . . . this is one of the first rules of teaching kids . . . and we all like a bit of praise . . . and she never, ever, gives praise . . . You never know quite where you are with her – or whether she likes you – or whether she thinks you've done a good job.

(Ann)

She doesn't stand there and look, but she knows everything that's going on, and she can recall and sometimes throw it back to you . . . or make a comment about something . . . but, if it's favourable, it should be done at the time, and if it *isn't*, then, likewise, it should be done at the time . . . but we never knew whether we were doing the right thing . . . I just no longer want to work for her . . . it's just the fact that she'd never *say* . . . she'd never say . . . you got no feedback. I mean, if somebody's not doing the job properly, you should have them in your room and tell them – but there's not even *that*.

Interviewer: Do you need feedback from the boss?
Yes, definitely!

Interviewer: And Mrs Hillman doesn't provide it?
No.

(Fiona)

By focusing on leadership features that have been revealed as particularly influential on teachers' attitudes to their jobs, this chapter has identified some of the ingredients for a recipe for successful school management. But it is important to emphasise that, since teachers' tastes are diverse as the chapters in this part of the book have illustrated, there is no school management recipe which is guaranteed to satisfy every appetite for satisfactory, and satisfying, work experiences. However, there are basic underlying principles relating to how to deal with staff that might usefully be applied to developing new approaches to school management which aim to foster positive job-related attitudes amongst teachers. These are presented in Chapter 11.

The next chapter draws together the evidence that has been presented throughout Part II of the book of what it is about their working lives that influences how teachers feel about their jobs. It examines what it is, essentially, that makes teachers tick and, conversely, what makes them cross.

A management perspective: issues for consideration

Key points
- Being liked, on a personal level, by their colleagues does not preclude headteachers from being considered ineffective, or generally poor, as managers and leaders.
- Positive job-related attitudes are likely to occur when teachers and headteachers share a vision of how they want their school to develop.
- 'Extended' professionals are likely to be frustrated, dissatisfied and demoralised by headteachers who do not have a clearly defined, and acceptable, vision.

- Recognition of teachers' efforts, in the form of feedback from respected headteachers, is a key feature of motivational school leadership.

Consider
- From the evidence presented in this chapter and in preceding chapters, what specific features of school leadership and management emerge as being particularly ineffective at fostering positive job-related attitudes amongst teachers?
- From the same evidence, what, conversely, emerge as key features of positive leadership? Would all teachers be likely to consider these leadership features as positive?
- What, if any, parallels are identifiable between class teachers' responsibilities towards, and management of, their pupils, and headteachers' responsibilities towards, and management of, their teacher colleagues?
- Do headteachers have too much influence upon, and authority within, their schools? Is there a case for considering more democratic school management structures? What form might these take? How effective are they likely to be?

10

What makes teachers tick?
What makes teachers cross?
Completing the picture

Introduction

This chapter draws together the different constituents of an understanding of teacher morale, motivation and job satisfaction and assembles them to make a more complete elucidatory picture of what, at a generalisable level, makes teachers feel the way they do about their work. The different constituents of this understanding of job-related attitudes have been presented as the foci of the other chapters in this part of the book. In Chapter 5 the focus was on the diversity of teachers' attitudes to what they all generally perceived consensually. This revealed individuality as a key constituent. Chapter 6 illustrated the importance of teachers' professionality orientation in explaining why teachers respond as they do to specific situations and circumstances, and Chapter 7 highlighted the need for teachers to be presented with challenges they are able to meet. Level of prioritisation of the job was presented in Chapter 8 as an important influence on attitudes and, in weaving together the key leadership-related strands that were identifiable in preceding chapters, Chapter 9 focused on teacher–headteacher compatibility as a significant factor accounting for diversity of levels of morale, job satisfaction and motivation. This chapter applies a deeper level of analysis to the composite picture that takes shape when these separate constituents that have been identified, and examined, are merged.

In Part I, I examine the three key concepts that constitute the book's subject: job satisfaction, morale and motivation. In order to present these examinations, which incorporate my own conceptualisations and definitions as well as those of major theorists and researchers in the three different fields, I had to include some references to my research findings, whose analyses directed my construct formulation and informed the thinking that underpinned my definitions. To some extent this involved pre-empting the process that was to follow in later chapters – that of gradually, through the presentation and examination of research findings, elucidating what determines teachers' job satisfaction, morale and motivation levels. This was, I feel, inevitable if explanations and inter-pretations of the key concepts were to be presented before the research findings. Moreover, it reflects the cyclical, elucidatory process (to which I refer in Chapter 5), of conceptualisation, data analysis, reconceptualisa-tion and reanalysis and which, in turn, illustrates the difficulties involved in wanting to study a concept which is unclearly defined, but whose definition is dependent upon elucidation of its properties and constitu-ents through study.

This chapter, in a sense, takes up the 'trilogy' of the 'stories' of job satisfaction, morale and motivation where it was left off at the end of Part I. It supplements the 'trilogy' with the colourful illustrations Chapters 5–9 provide, incorporating realistic, contextual authenticity and, by way of providing a denouement, presents a general, widely applicable picture of what teacher morale, job satisfaction and motivation are all about. This picture is more complete than the separate, vignette-type ones that have featured in preceding chapters because, although it is informed and col-oured by their contextual specificity, in order to provide greater elucida-tion it is, in its final form, free from contextual specificity. It is formed by taking the lowest common-factor level of analysis of Chapters 1–3 and adding to it meaning, relevance and practical applicability by injecting into it empirically based consideration of what this analysis looks like when it is applied to the context of primary schoolteachers in the UK.

Understanding teacher morale, motivation and job satisfaction

Deeper analysis of my research findings, particularly those presented in Chapters 5–9, reveals the substance of teacher morale, motivation and job satisfaction to incorporate specific properties and constituent features. These are a predominant influence of context-specific factors; individual-relatedness; professionality orientation-relatedness; relative perspective-relatedness; and realistic expectations-relatedness. I examine each of these in turn below.

The importance of contextual factors

One of the key findings of my research was that job satisfaction, morale and motivation are predominantly contextually determined. Interview evidence corroborated the impression I had gained during the obser-vation phases of the study that the context of teachers' working lives represents the realities of the job and, as such, has a much greater impact upon job-related attitudes than do factors such as centrally imposed pol-icy or teachers' conditions of service, including pay. Only one of my interviewees, Jane, a mainscale Rockville teacher who had reached the top of the salary scale, was dissatisfied with teachers' pay. The same teacher also made reference to the wider issue of the demoralising effect of teachers' low status in society. Only one other teacher, Kay, who held what was then an Incentive Allowance B, identified pay as a source of satisfaction. A few teachers even identified pay specifically as a relatively unimportant factor in relation to motivation: 'I haven't looked at my payslip for the last 12 months . . . and I don't know why – it's not a driving force any more. At one stage I used to long for pay day and look carefully at how much I'd got . . . but it doesn't bother me any more' (Mark, Leyburn teacher). In all cases, it was school-specific factors that teachers identified as the most significant influences on their job satisfaction, morale and motivation. Issues such as the introduction of the National Curriculum, which was intended as the main focus of the post-ERA follow-up study, the imposition of contractual hours and the five Baker days designated for in-service training, were either relegated to subsidiary levels of importance in teachers' assessments of what affected their morale and/or job satisfaction, or were assessed within the context of their own school situations, and in relation to how these contexts shaped them. Pat, for example, in her 1992 follow-up interview, spoke of how the Rockville management was a constraint on her doing her job, including her implementation of the National Curriculum:

> You ask yourself, 'Why am I bothering? Why am I giving up time in the evenings . . . time in the holidays, to do work which is not directly related to the class, to find that . . . it's being ignored?' – or to find that you go to a management meeting with the head and he doesn't even know what a Core Study Unit is for history! He hasn't even bothered to read the document before he speaks to you!
> (Pat, Rockville teacher)

Particularly interesting, though, were some teachers' responses to my asking whether centrally initiated factors affected their attitudes to the job. None of my post-ERA follow-up interviewees had actually identified ERA-imposed factors as being significantly influential on their own job satisfaction, morale and motivation levels when I posed open-ended questions about how they felt about their jobs. It was clear from their comments that any impact which the National Curriculum, for example, had had on their working lives had been superseded by that of school-specific issues, such as management and staff relations. Yet, my asking them to talk specifically about the National Curriculum prompted responses which seemed to be intended to conform with the popular belief that its introduction has demoralised and demotivated teachers. It was almost as if these teachers felt they would be 'letting the side down' if they failed to identify the introduction of the National Curriculum as a negative influence on teachers' job-related attitudes. In doing so, however, they seldom spoke subjectively; rather, they conveyed the impression that they were passing on second-hand knowledge. They did not refer to specific colleagues whom they knew to have been demoralised by the demands of the National Curriculum, nor did their evaluations include reference to their own experiences. Moreover, when I probed deeper by asking if they could provide any subjective illustrations of how the introduction of the National Curriculum had lowered their morale or job satisfaction, most were unable to offer any, and those examples that were related, such as that of Pat, only served to highlight the influence of negative school-specific factors. Rosemary's comments in her 1992 interview are illustrative of the generality with which complaints about the National Curriculum were made. These are particularly interesting when considered alongside some of her other comments about her attitude to her work, presented in Chapter 7, which convey a strong impression of a teacher who sustained high morale by adopting a positive response to change. She responded to my asking her to move on to consideration of the extent to which centrally imposed factors, such as pay, conditions of service and the introduction of the National Curriculum, had influenced her morale and job satisfaction:

> I don't think pay really enters into it. If a pay rise comes along, everybody's happy. People can always use extra money, but . . . er . . . I think . . . people would be happy with pay as it is – I don't think we've done too badly over these last few years, anyway; I think we've had *good* increases – a lot of other things have affected morale . . . I think . . . you know . . . the coming of the National Curriculum. The thinking behind it was good . . . er . . . and you can understand why it was done . . . but, the *way* it was done . . . the speed . . . er . . . was all wrong, and this is what gets teachers' backs up more than anything. There've been so *many* changes in such a short time . . . not only *those* changes, but, they're bringing changes to *those* changes . . . for instance, the maths and the science. The dust has hardly settled . . . people are just coming to terms with the National Curriculum in maths and science, and the attainment targets are changing. So, it means a lot of changing and planning of the curriculum in school . . . and it's these *changes* that people are not happy with . . . It *is* frustrating, and you feel sorry for the co-ordinators who put a lot of work in, and they write the policies, and they link it to the National Curriculum, and then . . . it's all changed. And so, they've got to rewrite and . . . er . . . make changes. The same with the record-keeping, and the assessment. Er . . . and I think there's a lot of criticism at both government and at county level, in that they don't give enough guidance.

> (Rosemary, Rockville teacher)

Similarly, Kay, who also reported high levels of job satisfaction, morale and motivation, highlighted in a rather detached way some of the frequently identified problems that had accompanied the introduction of the National Curriculum:

> *Interviewer: Do you have high morale?*
> At the moment, yes. I think it does come and go . . . but, at the moment, I'm thinking of next year, and what I'll be doing with my class . . . er . . . but, it does vary a lot . . . I think, over the last few years, it's been very low with a lot of people, and outside influences affected that . . . And I think, with the National

Curriculum . . . people, at first, felt very threatened by it, and that made morale very, very low . . . because you just felt that you'd been doing this job all these years and nobody was satisfied with you . . . you know . . . what more did they want? Everybody felt they were doing their best . . . but, somehow, it just wasn't good enough. I think, now that we've looked into it a bit more we can cope with it, and most people feel *fairly* happy about . . . at least doing *some* of it . . . you know.

(Kay, Sefton Road teacher)

Consistent with this are the findings of the 1991 Warwick study into the effects on Key Stage 1 teachers' working lives of the introduction of the English and Welsh National Curriculum. Evans *et al.* (1994) report how school-specific factors, such as leadership and collegiality, greatly influenced the attitudinal effects on teachers of the implementation of the reforms (see, in particular, p. 188).

Positive influences on morale and job satisfaction were predominantly school-specific, as the following examples illustrate:

Well, I enjoy the children; the sort of children that I work with . . . and I like, to an extent, the freedom that you have in your own classroom.

(Susan, Rockville teacher)

but, I mean, when you get a child who comes in who's never been to school before – who can't even hold a pair of scissors, can't speak the language or anything . . . and, within, say, six months you can watch them blossom and cope with things and . . . you know . . . the children . . . the children are lovely! The children still have the magic that our children have lost . . . This, this 'awe' – this wonder of the world and the enthusiasm . . . because our children are . . . well, spoilt . . . But the Asian children have that real joy of everything you show them. I mean, at Eid we went to Smithfield Park, and, I mean, they should be used to it by now, but there was one little girl who'd never ever been in Smithfield Park! . . . and, the flowers – she was just in absolute ecstasy! She just kept saying, 'Oh, the flowers . . . the pretty flowers!' and she just went on and on . . . she really was captivated with them . . . You'd have thought you'd given her the world!

(Pat, Rockville teacher)

the one thing at Leyburn, in many ways, is that there's a good social mix – partly because most of the teachers are from a working-class background – and there's lots of humour and experiences that we can all relate to . . . like, a sense of humour . . . *that's* important.

(Mark, Leyburn teacher)

The reason why it is school-specific issues, situations and circumstances that evidently take precedence as morale-, motivation- and job satisfaction-influencing factors is that they constitute teachers' working lives. It is at the context-specific level that teachers carry out their work. Centrally initiated conditions or, indeed, any conditions that emanate from outside the contexts in which teachers work only become real for and meaningful and relevant to teachers when they become contextualised. Until they are effected within the contexts in which teachers work, such conditions are, in reality, non-operational; they exist only in abstract form as ideas, principles or rhetoric. They do not constitute reality.

The introduction of the National Curriculum does not, therefore, impact in a real sense upon teachers' lives until it is introduced into their contexts – their schools. The low status of teachers in society does not, as an issue, encroach upon a teacher's life until it is introduced into it: in the form of a derogatory remark or a self-conception that reflects consciousness of belonging to a profession which is held in low esteem, or a perception of being unfavourably compared with other professionals. The problem of class sizes does not become a problem for teachers until it occurs in their own schools. It is only within the contexts of their own lives that things matter to people; although, sometimes, this contextualisation may involve only consciousness and may not be dependent upon direct, activity-based experience. Under these circumstances, issues that, for example, are at odds with ideologies, offend sensibilities or conflict with values, constitute introduction into people's lives and, therefore, realisation through contextualisation.

It is also important to recognise that it is within the context in which teachers work that policy and initiatives that emanate from outside this context are, through their realisation, adopted, adapted, institutionalised and effected in ways that may make them more or less acceptable to teachers than they were in their conceptual form. It is at school level that government-imposed reforms or LEA initiatives may be effected in ways that are palatable to, or that alienate, teachers through the institutionalisation process they adopt. Those who take responsibility for implementing externally imposed change into schools have much capacity, for buffering teachers against or, conversely, exposing them to the worst anticipated effects of the changes. Externally imposed change is never introduced into schools with a uniform level of intensity. Policy implementation varies from school to school. This was found to be the case with the introduction of the English and Welsh National Curriculum. Evans *et al.* (1994, pp. 100–6), reporting the findings of the Warwick study into the effects on teachers' lives of the introduction of the National Curriculum, identify four approaches to implementation: the 'head-in-the-sand' approach, the 'paying lip service' approach, the 'common-sense' approach and the 'by the book' approach. Each approach reflected a different level of intensity of implementation and, as such, affected with different levels of intensity the working lives of teachers. It is at school level rather than at Whitehall that teachers' working lives are affected.

Job comfort and job fulfilment: comparisons with Herzberg's theory
My teachers experienced job fulfilment through the process illustrated in my model, presented in Chapter 1. It was through feeling a sense of significant achievement that job fulfilment occurred, as in the example

provided by Mark in Chapter 6 of his reappraising and improving the way in which he taught decimals to his class, or as in Rosemary's example in Chapter 7 of her having made a significant contribution to the implementation of a home reading scheme, which she believed to have been extremely successful in improving standards of reading.

Herzberg (1968) identifies five specific factors that lead to job satisfaction: achievement, recognition (for achievement), responsibility, advancement and the work itself. In Chapter 1 I suggest that these five 'motivation factors' (*ibid.*) may be reduced down to only one key job fulfilment factor – achievement. The other four I argue, are either contributors to, or/and reinforcers of, achievement. This reinterpretation of what Herzberg identifies as motivators is based largely upon my research findings. It was certainly the case, for example, that recognition in the form of feedback on their work from respected colleagues and, in particular, from their headteachers, was widely identified by my teachers as a motivator; its absence from their working lives was, in the cases of many teachers, a source of dissatisfaction and, conversely, teachers who received it reported it as satisfying. But I believe that it is not the recognition in itself that is the source of job fulfilment. Rather, the recognition only serves to reinforce, confirm or even introduce to teachers a sense of their work's being of sufficiently high standard to warrant their feeling a sense of achievement. My point is strengthened by consideration of the example of a hypothetical case of a teacher who knows her/his work to be, in certain respects, inadequate but who nevertheless receives positive feedback on it from colleagues from whom its inadequacies are obscured. The recognition for her/his achievements would not be a source of fulfilment to the teacher since s/he would be aware that it was undeserved. This was borne out in the context of my research by Sarah's comments in Chapter 7 that, although she sought praise from Phil, the headteacher, she also appreciated recognition from John, the deputy head, because this constituted praise that was genuinely merited. Essentially, it is not recognition for achievement but achievement itself that is fulfilling. Similarly, advancement and responsibility, which Herzberg identifies as motivators, are not in themselves sources of job fulfilment. Rather, like 'the work itself', they are paths that may lead to the individual's being provided with opportunities for experiencing job fulfilment, and they may also serve as forms of recognition that reinforce a sense of achievement. In his application of the term 'motivator', however, I believe Herzberg to be quite justified. These factors are, indeed, motivation factors. The difficulty with Herzberg's theory, though, is that, because of its neglect of consideration of conceptual clarity, it is flawed by its failure to distinguish between motivation and job satisfaction.

Herzberg's (1968, pp. 75–6) contention that the removal of 'dissatisfiers' does not lead to satisfaction, because those factors that are capable of satisfying are distinct and separate from those that may create dissatisfaction, was not borne out by my research findings. This is partly because, as I point out in Chapter 1, my reconceptualisation of job satisfaction involves its bifurcation into two separate concepts: job comfort and job fulfilment. What this means is that the kinds of factors that Herzberg identifies as 'hygiene' factors are those which I would categorise as job comfort factors. Herzberg's finding that the removal of 'dissatisfiers' – which, according to him, are all 'hygiene' rather than 'motivation' factors – does not lead to job satisfaction, and that this constitutes the basis of a 'two-factor' theory, arises out of his failure to recognise that job comfort is entirely separate, conceptually, from job fulfilment. Had he recognised this, he may have reasoned that the removal of 'dissatisfiers' may potentially create job satisfaction, but that the particular kind of job satisfaction that is created by the removal of 'dissatisfiers' is job comfort rather than job fulfilment. My findings do not corroborate Herzberg's in this respect, because they reveal positive as well as negative job comfort factors. These positive job comfort factors are those aspects of their work teachers are satisfied *with*, but not *by*; they are satisfactory, but not satisfying. Good staff relations was one such factor, convenient working hours was another. Brenda, for example, (Chapter 8), was dissatisfied with her working life until she reduced from full-time to part-time status, allowing her more time for the non-work-related activities she wanted to pursue. This illustrates how the removal of 'dissatisfiers' may, in fact, potentially create job satisfaction, but the effectiveness of the illustration is predicated upon acceptance of a wide interpretation of job satisfaction.

Herzberg (*ibid.*) also contends that the opposite of job satisfaction would not be job dissatisfaction but rather *no* job satisfaction. This contention arises out of his perceiving 'dissatisfiers' to be, to use his terminology, 'hygiene'-related. Yet my findings revealed many sources of dissatisfaction amongst teachers that, on deeper analysis, could be identified as negative job fulfilment, rather than exclusively negative job comfort, factors. What revealed them as such was their potential to lead to job fulfilment, if they were removed or modified. Mark's exclusion from the decision-making process at Leyburn is one such example. The Sefton Road headteacher's criticism of Louise's work is another. The hierarchical management structure at Rockville is another. It prevented Amanda and Susan from exerting an influence on, and from changing, those ways in which the school was run that conflicted with their images of what a school should, ideally, be like, and within which they might be enabled rather than constrained in their pursuit of job fulfilment.

In her second follow-up interview in 1992, after she had left teaching to take up educational consultancy, Amanda spoke of the fulfilment she derived from her work. She explained how (despite the satisfying elements of teaching), because contextual factors had constrained and frustrated her, her current job was preferable to teaching because there were fewer constraints, and because it had greater potential for personal and professional development. She responded to the question, 'Can you describe your ideal job?': '*This* job . . . Because the job is so developmental, and . . . because it's to respond to . . . context, financing . . . changes in educational thinking . . . constantly'. She then explained how she had developed whilst doing the job:

The work I'm doing is so personally and professionally – not just *satisfying*, but . . . well, I think fulfilling is *more* than being satisfied . . . but, it's so energising. It's made me into such a creative person that . . . I would become a different person if I went into something such as a deputy headship . . . I don't think it'd have the same effect if I went back into *teaching* – I think, I wouldn't *cease* to be creative . . . but I feel *so* sustained and energised by the work I'm doing . . . I got so much satisfaction out of teaching, but . . . you always have constraints, so the actual satisfaction of teaching was *high*, but constraints were there . . . I have satisfaction in the work I'm doing now, partly because of the freedoms that I have. So, you create your own way of responding . . . For some LEAs I design my own courses . . . I offer them to the LEA, simply go, deliver them, and come away . . . Consultancy work . . . well, obviously, you're expected to be ahead of whatever else is going on there, because they're consulting you . . . yes, you're creating your own agenda. There *are* constraints – some of them, financial, a lot of them, time . . . At the moment . . . work overload causes a degree of . . . I suppose . . . well, not *dis*satisfaction . . . but, it's frustrating, because there are some things I could do better, given time . . . I know that some of the work I'm doing . . . it lacks rigour . . . or . . . it could have greater . . . intellectual . . . er . . . but, then, you see the response of people! I mean, people are so easily . . . well . . . pleased . . . Teaching wasn't as developmental for me, personally or professionally, as *this* job is . . . I find that very satisfying. I suppose I have to say that I've *become* a different person . . . Well, no . . . not different . . . but, I've become more of a person . . . because of the work I'm doing now . . . and that may be, partly, because . . . the constraints are of a different kind . . . At Rockville I think I was an influence . . . on colleagues. The way you dealt with the children . . . what you would stand up for . . . the fact that you took a developmental view of the work you were doing . . . that you tried to be reflective in what you were doing. I think that actually influenced other people in the school . . . So there was always a *second* tier of activity. But, I think now, I see *many* tiers of activity . . . so, er . . . some advisers that I work with, substantially . . . I see an influence on what other advisers are doing – how *they* regard their curriculum, in the light of the work that I've done with that LEA . . . I see a tier whereby . . . er . . . some of the work that I've been doing in . . . er . . . agreed syllabus consultancy . . . meeting with academics in education, academics in theology, people within the churches . . . actually impacting it upon *them* – people actually writing and saying, 'That has been a momentous input to my *own* thinking on this particular subject' . . . so, yes . . . there are the teachers that you direct, and sell to . . . there are the people that you're working with as a peer group . . . there are those whom you actually consider to be . . . intellectually . . . academically . . . well, superior . . . advanced . . . beyond you, developmentally . . . and yet you're feeling, yes, you're having some impact on *them* . . . but, through the teachers, you're also having an impact on *children* . . . So, I think there are far more facets to the job

... and, although I've said that satisfaction is in terms of *me*, and how I view myself ... and what I think, professionally, I'm capable of ... and have the potential to do ... *some* measure of that has got to be how people respond to what you do ... I think there's also the boomerang factor, that what *that* experience ... *that* contact ... or the impact that *that* has made on them ... then makes on you. And that, to a large extent, I think, was an incomplete circuit when I was at Rockville.

The essential point is that factors such as those I present above as illustrations of negative job fulfilment factors may normally only be *potentially*, rather than absolutely, identified as such at a general level. This is because, since job satisfaction is very individual, what may lead to fulfilment for one teacher is not guaranteed to do so for others. It is often only on closer analysis that what many teachers identify simply as sources of dissatisfaction may be revealed as negative job fulfilment factors. Teachers themselves may often fail to make the analytically-based connection that links their dissatisfaction to lack of fulfilment. In some cases, too, sources of dissatisfaction that are common to several teachers may only constitute negative job fulfilment factors for some; for others, they may simply be negative job comfort factors. Again, this reflects the individuality of job satisfaction. Analysis of my Rockville study findings, for example, revealed that the issue of the deployment of senior teachers was, in Amanda's case, a negative job fulfilment factor because it constrained her by impacting upon her own class teaching and, in particular, by preventing her from meeting all of her pupils' learning needs (see Chapter 6). This reduced the amount of job fulfilment she could, potentially, have experienced. In the cases of other Rockville teachers, however, the same issue seems only to have been a negative job comfort factor where, for example, it was the principles of equity and fairness that seemed to be uppermost in teachers' minds.

The final point I wish to make in relation to considering how my research findings correlate with Herzberg's two-factor theory concerns Herzberg's identifying specific 'hygiene' factors, such as salary, staff relations and supervision, as factors that are capable only of creating dissatisfaction. These 'hygiene' factors, Herzberg contends, are not capable of satisfying. Again, this contention clearly arises out of Herzberg's failure to recognise the ambiguity of job satisfaction in its widest sense. My research did reveal what Herzberg identifies as 'hygiene' factors to be capable of providing job comfort – though I accept entirely that they are incapable of providing job fulfilment for teachers. The point is, though, that I believe the reason why Herzberg uncovered only evidence of dissatisfaction rather than satisfaction in relation to these factors lies with individuals' natural predisposition towards highlighting the unsatisfactory features of work rather than the satisfactory ones. Wall and Stephenson (1970, p. 65) make this point about Herzberg's findings: 'Our results have shown that employees tend to exaggerate the importance of hygiene factors as determinants of dissatisfaction for social reasons . . . It is not surprising that hygiene factors are picked on; they are both more tangible and are traditionally the overt causes of dissatisfaction.' Typical positive job comfort factors, such as clean and tidy working environment, ample parking space, proximity of place of work to home and use of a staffroom, are often so taken for granted they are overlooked; they are considered part and parcel of the job and, as such, are seldom singled out for recognition as satisfiers. Yet because they are expected to be available, their absence is invariably noticed, and identified as an unsatisfactory aspect of the job.

The individuality dimension

It is the individuality of job satisfaction, morale and motivation that makes them complex to understand. At the descriptive level such as is required, for example, for reporting findings, the individuality dimension poses no problems. It is simple and straightforward to report that, arising out of the heterogeneity of teachers that reflects individuals' different and individual biographical details, what satisfies one teacher does not necessarily satisfy all teachers, or that what motivates some teachers may not motivate others. Simple recognition of the individuality dimension represents the third of the five levels of understanding or elucidation of job satisfaction to which I refer in Chapter 1. It reveals the inaccuracy and inadequacy of explaining job-related attitudes through sweeping generalisations, or even typologies.

Evidence of the individuality of job satisfaction, morale and motivation permeated my research findings, and is incorporated into Chapters 5–9. It is reflected, for example, in Louise's dissatisfaction with the leadership of Sefton Road Primary School, and her failure to be motivated by the headteacher who so successfully motivated Sarah and Kay; in Brenda's acceptance, with equanimity, of the circumstances and situation at Rockville that prompted Susan to declare she was 'pretty desperate' to leave the school and Amanda to vow 'I *shan't* go back to Rockville'; and in Fiona's decision to leave Leyburn because she no longer wanted to work for Mrs Hillman, whilst Ann could not envisage wanting to leave a school on account of the headteacher.

Analysing the individuality dimension to reveal its key constituents is not simple and staightforward. The individuality of job satisfaction, morale and motivation arises out of their fundamentally involving needs fulfilment. These job-related needs are determined by individuals' conceptions of their ideal selves-at-work, within the wider conception of their ideal whole selves. The job-related needs that emerge determine job-related goals, towards the achievement of which individuals are motivated. It is by goal achievement and, hence, needs fulfilment that job satisfaction may occur, and through the anticipation of continued, sustained or repeated job satisfaction that morale is affected. Most or, indeed, all these stages are likely to be unconsciously approached and reached, and all of them are entirely individualistic. It is this that underpins and explains the individuality dimension.

However, understanding that the reason why what satisfies one teacher does not satisfy another is that each teacher has a distinct set of individual needs, whose fulfilment s/he is unconsciously seeking, is of very limited practical use. What need to be uncovered, representing the fifth of the stages of elucidation identified in Chapter 1, are the practically applicable, contextually-influenced clues that help to explain in a more meaningful way what accounts for the disparity amongst what teachers identify as sources of job satisfaction, morale and motivation. In order to reach this stage of elucidation, I examine in turn below professionality, relative perspective and realistic expectations – the three key, inter-related constituents of the individuality dimension within job satisfaction, morale and motivation I identified earlier in this chapter.

Professionality

Amongst the Rockville staff, not only was a wide range of professionality orientations evident but there was also a close correlation between proximity to overall 'extended' professionality and low morale and dissatisfaction. At first glance, this may suggest that 'extended' professionals are generally more susceptible to dissatisfaction and low morale than are 'restricted' professionals. Consideration of the cases of Mark and Helen (Chapter 6), alongside that of Amanda supports this conclusion. Yet within my sample as a whole, a wide range of professionality orientations was evident and, as I have illustrated in earlier chapters, my findings revealed some 'extended' professionals, such as Kay and Rosemary, to manifest high levels of morale, job satisfaction and motivation, whilst some 'restricted' professionals, like Louise, were clearly very dissatisfied. Once again, it is the importance of contextual factors that accounts for this disparity between similarly oriented professionals. It is the degree of congruence between teachers' professionality orientations and those reflected in the contexts in which they work which is the key issue. At Rockville, the correlation between 'extended' professionality and dissatisfaction would certainly have arisen out of the mismatch between individuals' professionality orientation and the professionality orientation reflected in the school's prevailing professional climate or institutional bias which, in turn, was influenced by the headteacher's professionality. The most striking example of such mismatch was that between Amanda, who was very clearly an 'extended' professional, and Geoff, the headteacher, who manifested more 'restricted' professionality. Evidence of the mismatch pervaded Amanda's research interviews in which she expressed the frustration and exasperation which resulted from the constraints imposed by the school's management and the policies that were implemented. However, it was Hilary, the ESL teacher, who summed up most succinctly the mismatch which gave rise to Amanda's low morale and dissatisfaction:

> Geoff can handle the challenges that Margaret [the deputy head] can present, because they're plain . . . uncomplicated decisions. Whereas, he won't approach Amanda because . . . she challenges his position too much, and he's inadequate . . . he's inadequate because he's no sense of direction . . . and he can't handle Amanda . . . because she challenges every aspect of his approach to the job . . . Avoiding Amanda, he avoids the issue – where he *can*, he'll avoid the issue – never facing up to the reality of the facts of it . . . It's because he lacks depth in educational development – in the development that should be going on in the school . . . er . . . his perceptions . . . so that he's . . . he's inadequate . . . All Geoff wants is someone who will take the management responsibility and run the shop . . . and 'run it' means maintaining all the routine organisational things . . . Amanda questions development and the intellectual side of things . . . and that's the side Geoff can't handle. It's a much lower level of decision-making that goes on at management level – not *curriculum* development . . . and he's got people who'll make the organisational decisions *for* him. Amanda would consider content, children's needs, suitable assessment . . . and he doesn't want to know! He's not interested!

Since professionality orientation reflects the width of vision which underlies attitudes, perspectives, practice and other job-related behaviour, it influences the nature of teachers' responses to the situations and circumstances which confront them. Teachers who manifest characteristics of 'restricted' professionality, whose perspectives of their work are very classroom bound and who are relatively unconcerned about wider school issues in so far as these may be seen to have limited impact upon their own classroom practice, will tend to be relatively unperturbed by policy and decisions which primarily affect wider, more remote, issues. Those teachers whose professionality affords such issues greater prioritisation, though, will be more likely to be dissatisfied and demoralised by any incongruence between their conception of what *should* be going on in their school and what *is* actually going on. Amanda's case is the most extreme example of such incongruence amongst the Rockville staff. Her ideologies were increasingly at odds with those reflected in the Rockville prevailing professional climate. Similarly, Louise was mismatched with Sefton Road's predominantly 'extended' professionality-influenced climate. Had these two teachers exchanged teaching posts with each other, each is likely to have experienced considerably greater job satisfaction as a result of the change, since she would have achieved a closer match between her own ideologies and those permeating the climate of the school to which she had removed.

Moreover, teachers' strategies for coping with what they perceived to be unsatisfactory or undesirable situations were also determined by professionality orientation. Those whose professionality lay more towards the 'restricted' than the 'extended' extreme of the continuum and whose educational vision therefore tended to be relatively narrow were often able to cope by shutting out much of the view which a wider vision would have afforded them, and by focusing more narrowly on what they saw as their more immediate concern and one over which they were able to exercise control – their own classroom practice. Certainly, as a coping strategy, this was effective at Rockville and at Leyburn where the headteachers made relatively few demands of staff provided, in the case of Leyburn, the school appeared to be functioning well. At Sefton Road this was not an option, since the headteacher demanded more commitment to striving for excellence. At Rockville and Leyburn, however, 'extended' professionals found themselves unable to turn a blind eye and became increasing intolerant of, and unable to cope with, the widening gap between reality and their ideals.

Relative perspective

The relative perspectives afforded by teachers to their work concern how they view it in relation to other factors. Such perspectives incorporate prioritisation and comparison and are seldom static, but will tend to fluctuate in response to reprioritisation and re-evaluation which may result from changed, and changing, circumstances and experiences.

Factors which determine how teachers consider their work include comparative experiences, comparative insights, and the circumstances and events which make up the rest of their lives: their non-work selves. Teachers view and place their work as it relates to factors such as these. Comparative experiences, for example, could be previous jobs or having worked with different headteachers; comparative insights may include knowledge of how another school is run; and the relativity arising out of consideration of their non-teaching lives would involve the prioritisation which is a prerequisite of putting the job into perspective.

The outcome of having a relative perspective of their job is that teachers, having compared their current job-related circumstances favourably or unfavourably with the factors which constitute their evaluative yardstick, are able to rate these job-related circumstances as either relatively satisfactory or unsatisfactory.

At Rockville, teachers for whom the work context represented, for example, an improvement upon their previous work-related situations viewed it relatively favourably and were, predictably, less dissatisfied than were their colleagues who perceived Rockville to represent a deterioration of work-related conditions. In most cases, these less dissatisfied teachers also manifested higher levels of morale. Stephen, for example, had been recently appointed to Rockville and had been extremely unhappy in his previous post. His recent move to Rockville was considered relatively much more favourable. Barbara, too, was a new appointment – a recently qualified teacher who had held a series of supply posts before obtaining a permanent job at Rockville. This clearly influenced her outlook:

> *Interviewer: If you had to be redeployed from Rockville, to another school . . . would you be disappointed?*
> Er . . . yes, I think so . . . because I *do* see it as . . . sort of . . . well, they *wanted* me! . . . It's been my first permanent job, and it'll always be . . . special.
>
> *Interviewer: Er . . . on a scale of one to ten – where ten is high – what mark would you give your morale?*
> Er . . . I'd say, about eight and a half . . . I mean, I get down sometimes . . . and I get annoyed . . . but I really enjoyed last year . . . I don't know if it was because it was my first year in a permanent job . . . but, it was really nice to see something through to the end . . . you never get this on supply.

Barbara represented a noticeable contrast to other Rockville teachers, such as Susan, who described their morale levels as being very low and who were, to quote Susan, 'pretty desperate' to leave the school.

Comparative experiences and comparative insights are significantly influential on individuals' attitudinal responses to the situations in which they currently find themselves. In a work context, such relative perspectives on *current* situations influence job satisfaction levels, and those perspectives which incorporate anticipation of *continued*, *sustained* or *future* situations; anything whose temporal orientation is forward-looking, with some degree of expected permanence, influences morale levels.

Realistic expectations

Teachers' realistic expectations of their work contexts and situations do not necessarily reflect their 'ideals' but, rather, those expectations which they feel are realistically able to be fulfilled. Such expectations reflect values and ideologies, and will be partly influenced by professionality and comparative experiences and insights. In this way, the three factors I identify as underlying the diversity of attitudinal responses to the work context – professionality, relative perspective and realistic expectations – are clearly inter-related. Reflecting her 'extended' professionality, Amanda's realistic expectations of Rockville were that policy and decision-making would be based upon sound educational principles and pedagogical awareness, that a concern to accommodate children's diverse needs would be paramount, and that her teacher colleagues would be professionally competent. Her expectations were not met, however:

> I felt that I'd been very misled there . . . *very* misled . . . And there were so many other things happening . . . which, to me, were contrary to the stated ethos of the school – you know, if you can *state* what the ethos of a school is – well, it certainly . . . what was being stated didn't match what was happening. I

found . . . I mean . . . I didn't like the racist and socially divisive views that were being expressed . . . I'm not saying we've all to have the same political views – even the same . . . er . . . I don't think we all have to view society in the same way in a school . . . but a school states – Rockville made statements about . . . you know . . . it valued the child . . . it valued the home background . . . but the conversations I heard were entirely contrary to that. We talked about welcoming parents in, and people complained that parents *wouldn't* come in, and then spoke about parents in a derogatory way. There was no sympathy for the fact that the children were bridging a culture on behalf of the parents . . . so there was no real valuing of what the child was bringing in with them, there was no real valuing of the child.

Louise's expectations of working at Sefton Road were not met, particularly in relation to the workload that, as a class teacher, she would be required to take on, and the collegial support she would be offered. As a result, she was dissatisfied, demotivated and demoralised with her job.

Whilst in Amanda's case the disillusionment resulting from unfulfilled expectations gave rise to dissatisfaction and low morale, those teachers whose expectations were lower clearly had more chance of their expectations being met at Rockville, and fewer opportunities for disillusionment or frustration to create dissatisfaction of the intensity of that of Amanda.

Joanne was one of the Rockville teachers who manifested a professionality which lay very much towards the 'restricted' end of the continuum, as identified by Hoyle (1975). This was reflected in the much lower expectations she generally held when compared with Amanda and, particularly, in the nature of those expectations. She showed no concern for a rational basis to the teaching and policy-making at Rockville. In intellectual terms, and in relation to pedagogical awareness and educational ideologies and philosophy, Joanne and Amanda represented a polarisation of views and attitudes. Joanne's expectations were simply that the school would be well organised and run smoothly. They were at a superficial level, lacking the depth of analysis which underlay those of Amanda. Indeed, she seemed incapable of discussing educational issues and Rockville-specific circumstances with any depth at all. This is reflected in her assessment of Geoff Collins' leadership, which focused briefly upon how he handled and responded to staff. Her assessment, unlike Amanda's assessment of Geoff, did not include any reference to educational ideology and pedagogy. It was summed up, rather simplistically: 'I mean, he's . . . he's neither a good head nor a bad head . . . He's just . . . I think he's as good as you could get . . . or as bad as you could get! . . . you know . . . er . . . you're never going to get a perfect head, are you?' It is important to emphasise that professionality is only a partial influence on teachers' realistic expectations. Whilst at Rockville it was the case that there was a close correlation between 'restricted' professionality and higher levels of morale and job satisfaction, this should not be simply attributed to a good match between these 'restricted' professionals' professionality and that manifested by the headteacher and his deputy, and reflected in the school's prevailing climate. It is feasible to imagine another context wherein, despite such a close match of professionality, there may also be mismatch in relation to, for example, organisational and/or management issues. A less complacent and *laissez-faire* headteacher than Geoff Collins, though no less a 'restricted' professional may, for example, be more autocratic, dictatorial and interfering in his/her dealings with teachers. A strong professionality match would be unlikely to preclude this style of management being considered unwelcome or even unreasonable by some teachers whose realistic expectations may include their being given a large amount of autonomy within their own classrooms. Dissatisfaction and lowered morale would be likely to result from such a scenario.

Round pegs and square holes: teachers and their schools

An understanding of teacher morale, job satisfaction and motivation affords recognition of the importance that teachers attach to feeling a sense of achievement. This is the case with all teachers, no matter what their professionality orientation or their level of commitment to the job, because deriving satisfaction from feeling a sense of achievement is a basic human characteristic. Amongst teachers who afford it low priority in relation to the rest of their lives, though, there will be less reliance for experiencing a sense of achievement in their work rather than through other aspects of their lives than for teachers who manifest higher levels of job commitment.

The precise sources of teachers' sensations of achievement at work vary. For some, the source lies in feeling that they have contributed to children's learning; for others, it lies in feeling they have contributed towards formulating an effective school policy. Professionality orientation, as this chapter and others have illustrated, is an important factor that accounts for differences between teachers in relation to sources of sensations of achievement; but it is not the only factor. Realistic expectations and relative experiences also play a part, as I explain above.

The one factor that encompasses all these, though, is that to which I have referred in earlier chapters – that of the degree of compatibility between teachers and the contexts in which they work. It is to this that analysis of the research evidence presented in this book keeps bringing us. A good teacher–school match provides greater opportunities than does mismatch for experiencing high levels of job satisfaction, morale and motivation, through the greater opportunities it provides for feeling, and anticipating continuing to feel, a sense of achievement. A good match may be compared to the ease with which, in a child's shape-sorter, a square peg slots into a square hole and a round peg into a round hole. In relation to teachers and their schools, a good match involves shared ideologies, values and priorities which very often reflect shared or similar professionality orientations on the part of teacher and headteacher, and a shared vision of what the school should become and how it should develop. Where the teacher is mismatched, on the other hand, s/he is like a square peg being forced into the shape-sorter through a round hole. S/he does not fit in.

Achieving high levels of job satisfaction, morale and motivation involves matching square pegs with square holes, and round pegs with round holes. The next two chapters discuss ways in which this might be achieved.

A management perspective: issues for consideration

Key points
- School-specific rather than centrally imposed factors are the most significant determinants of teachers' attitudes to their work.
- Specific factors that affect levels of job satisfaction, morale and motivation vary from individual to individual.
- Professionality orientation is a key factor influencing levels of job satisfaction, morale and motivation amongst teachers.
- Teachers' relative perspectives influence their levels of job satisfaction, morale and motivation.
- Teachers' realistic expectations influence their levels of job satisfaction, morale and motivation.

Consider
- To what extent should headteachers try to manage their schools in ways that aim to accommodate teachers' diverse, and individual, job-related needs? With reference to any primary school staff with which you are familiar, imagine ways in which this might be attempted. How successful are these likely to be?
- What mechanisms for better matching teachers with schools could be introduced into the education system? How effective are such approaches likely to be?
- Is it desirable that a school staff should comprise entirely 'extended' professionals? What would be the advantages and disadvantages of this? Would you like to lead such a staff?
- To what extent may the principles underlying teachers' class management be applied to headteachers' staff management?

Part III

Policy implications

11

Getting the best out of teachers: implications for school-level management

Introduction

The Education Reform Act 1988 effected changes which have significantly altered the role of primary school headteachers in the UK. Not only did the implementation of the National Curriculum and the assessment procedures which accompanied it impose considerable administrative demands but the introduction of local management of schools (LMS) has also added an additional burden of financial management. Incorporating these and other changes, such as the increased power and responsibilities of school governors, teacher appraisal and school-based in-service training provision, and the general, increasingly prevalent, pressure to keep abreast of current educational issues, has meant that primary school headship has changed considerably since 1988.

Effective management has become a key component of primary headship, and the proliferation of primary school management courses aimed at meeting the needs of post-ERA school leadership has tended to focus on time and stress management strategies at the expense of sufficient emphasis on interpersonal skills and, in particular, individualism in headship (Coulson, 1988, p. 261).

The research that forms the basis of this book contributes much to the study of school organisation and management, not only because elements of it will undoubtedly ring true to many but also because, by focusing on a somewhat neglected component in this field of study, the perspective of the 'managed', it serves as an important reminder that there are, at the very least, two different perspectives whose consideration needs to be incorporated into examination and analyses of management and organisational issues, and into prescribed policy – those of the managers and those of the 'managed'. It is not essential that individual studies incorporate foci which allow for consideration of different perspectives. What is important is that, collectively, research in specific areas does this. This chapter presents an alternative view to complement work in the field which focuses mainly on managers' perspectives. It is a contribution to such a collective approach to developing a body of knowledge about primary school management, enhanced understanding of primary school management, and the formulation of prescribed policy. It makes management recommendations that incorporate consideration of what preceding chapters have revealed to be the key concerns of teachers who represent the 'managed'. It highlights what primary school managers need to take into account if they are to effect morale-, job satisfaction- and motivation-friendly management.

Managing to motivate: a teacher–class parallel

Imagine the following classroom scenario in a primary school:

> The pupils are all engaged on the same task: that of producing coloured patterns of tessellated shapes on squared paper. These are intended to be mounted as a wall display which, it is hoped, will impress parents and other visitors to the school at a forthcoming open day. The teacher has no clear idea of the full potential or the function of tessellation as a mathematical topic, but believes the patterns will look very attractive.
>
> The teacher spends most of the time sitting at her desk engaged on routine tasks, many of which are administrative, and children come out at intervals to show their work or ask questions. The teacher shows little interest in what the children are doing, and breaks off from what she is doing for just long enough to respond to queries about what to do next, or to give permission for children to sharpen pencils, get a second sheet of paper or to go to the toilet. So engrossed is she in her own work that she fails to notice several children who are not 'on task', who are spending long periods day dreaming, misbehaving or wandering around the room. The children have been given insufficient guidance on how to do the exercise and, as a result, many of them find the task hard and are making mistakes. Some, on the other hand, clearly have a good grasp of what is required and are creating accurate tessellated patterns which are much more complicated than the teacher would have thought them capable of, and more imaginative than she herself would have managed. When these are shown to her, however, the teacher remains relatively unimpressed. No praise is given in response to the children showing their efforts. Completed patterns are simply placed in a box on the teacher's desk. When she comes to mount the wall display, though, the teacher finds that several patterns are unfinished and many are incorrect, because there are spaces where the shapes actually failed to tessellate. The display is inadequate, unvaried, untidy and generally unimpressive. The teacher sighs, and blames the children.

To those whose educational ideologies veer towards child-centredness, the deficiencies in this hypothetical teaching situation are easily identifiable. The teacher failed to give adequate direction and guidance to the children before and throughout the lesson. Children's individual learning needs, ability levels and interests were insufficiently accommodated or even considered. Pupils were treated as a class rather than as individuals.

Their efforts went unrecognised, no interest was shown in what they were doing and the teacher lacked a general awareness of what was really going on in her classroom.

Most primary school headteachers would consider themselves very unfortunate to have amongst their colleagues a teacher like the one described, who clearly fails to get the best out of the pupils in her care. Yet on a different level but in precisely the same way, headteachers may be equally deficient in managing their teacher colleagues. Indeed, some of the chapters in this book have included illustrations of school management or, more precisely, of the management of primary school teaching staff, that are perceived by those who represent the 'managed' to be equally deficient as the class management described in the hypothetical case above. I have presented empirical research evidence of headteachers who have engendered resentment and frustration by what was perceived as their neglect of teachers' different professional developmental needs, arising out of differences in relation to professionality orientation and levels of commitment. This parallels the primary class teacher's failure to accommodate her pupils' different ability levels and interests. I have revealed examples of perceptions of headteachers' inadequate leadership and direction, which left teachers dissatisfied with working in schools that seemed to lack a sense of purpose. The class teaching parallel to this is the failure to give children proper guidance about what is expected of them and what, precisely, the task they have been given involves. Cases of headteachers' lack of appreciation of the need to motivate teachers through praise, and through showing an interest in their work, mirror the class teacher's failure to recognise the importance of praising children for their efforts and manifesting interest in what they are doing. I have included an example of a headteacher who was perceived to be so preoccupied with administrative affairs, organisational minutiae and operational efficiency that she provoked anger and dissatisfaction amongst her staff, who felt that her misplaced energies had the effect of diluting the quality of education the school provided. This equates to the class teacher's absorption in administrative tasks to the detriment of the pupils' learning.

If headteachers are to get the best out of teachers it is clear that much can be learned from examination of teacher–pupil relations. The relevance for staff management of class management techniques was highlighted by several of my interviewees, who commented on the similarity of their own motivational needs to those of children. As Kay (Sefton Road teacher) pointed out: 'Oh, I think teachers are just the same – they need just as much encouragement as children.' Applying the predominantly child-centred primary school class management approach, which is currently prevalent in the UK, to the context of staff management creates a parallel approach which I refer to as 'teacher-centred'.

A 'teacher-centred' approach to primary school staff management

If school leadership is to be enhanced by its adopting an existing model of people management, it must assimilate the principles and underlying philosophy, and incorporate the basic organisational structure, of the adopted model. To become 'teacher-centred' in their approach to staff management then, by applying a 'child-centred' parallel, primary school headteachers need to consider themselves as, effectively, class teachers on a larger scale, their schools as their classrooms writ large and their teacher colleagues as their classes of pupils in a more mature state. This involves adopting a 'teacher-centred' leadership philosophy and incorporating into their management an organisational structure that reflects this.

Adopting a 'teacher-centred' philosophy

Many of the headteachers identified and described in my study were evidently either unaware of the extent to which their leadership was capable of influencing teachers' attitudes, or they had neither the time nor the inclination to provide positive leadership. It is conceivable that some may either believe or feel that it should be the case that teachers, since they are responsible adults, should be self-motivated. A lot of teachers are, indeed, self-motivated, but there is no reason to avoid augmenting their motivation or boosting their morale by a few well chosen words.

Analysis of my research findings reveals five key features of motivational leadership: *individualism, recognition, awareness, interest* and *direction* – precisely the features of class management which were lacking in the hypothetical case presented above. Most headteachers will recognise this in relation to class teaching, but may not necessarily consider these features applicable to a headteacher–staff management parallel. Yet, as I have illustrated through the cases presented in earlier chapters, despite their greater maturity than that of children, teachers respond well to the kind of leadership which incorporates many of the features of effective class teaching and management. A 'teacher-centred' philosophy to primary school staff management acknowledges the importance of these five foci.

Individualism

Teachers are not all the same. They are, of course, different in temperament and aptitude, age, experience and subject interests, and in relation to ability, commitment and professionality. Each teacher will have individual needs which reflect his/her educational ideologies and values. Most teachers will lie somewhere between the two extremes of 'restricted' and 'extended' professionality, and a school staff will typically include a mixture of teachers, reflecting a wide range of different professionality orientations. The challenge for headteachers is to value this individuality by trying to accommodate these varied needs as far as it is possible, without compromising the needs of the school as a whole, just as a conscientious primary schoolteacher will offer a differentiated curriculum. 'Extended' professionals may need to be involved in decision-making, for example, or would appreciate being consulted about policy development. 'Restricted' professionals may be very effective classroom practitioners who need to feel valued in their role. To motivate staff on an individual level, headteachers need to see teachers as individuals rather than as a corporate whole. Some of the 'extended' professionals who were involved in my study were extremely frustrated by heads who were, themselves, of more 'restricted' professionality. These teachers were clearly not fulfilling their potential. Their talents and their value to the school went unrecognised. Headteachers do not necessarily need to be the most 'extended' professionals on the staff, nor the most intellectual. But they do need to recognise the value of such qualities in others and do their best to capitalise on these qualities rather than stifle them.

It is not only teachers' professionality that is reflected in their individual needs. Steers *et al.* (1996, p. 3) highlight the complex and multifaceted derivation of the individualism that members bring to an organisation:

> Individual organizational membership is segmented in nature in the sense that people belong to other groups (e.g. families) or organizations (e.g. churches), in addition to their work organizations. Furthermore, people have powerful experiences over the course of their lives (e.g. college education, raising children). The pattern and intensity of people's motives may change as they assimilate their continuing experiences. These changing needs and motives may result in behaviors, such as an expressed desire for greater independence and autonomy, that require some kind of response from the organization, a response that cannot always be handled by its existing structural features. Leadership, then, is proposed as a process to enable the organization to accommodate these kinds of individual predispositions and tendencies.

Applying a 'teacher-centred' approach to educational management involves incorporating consideration of competing pressures in teachers' lives and demands on their time and attention. The 'teacher-centred' headteacher recognises the advantages and rewards of enabling rather than constraining teachers by management that responds to their needs in much the same way as that of, and with much the same attitude as that underpinning, a child-centred teacher's responses to her/his pupils' needs. The 'teacher-centred' headteacher adopts a 'child-centred' frame of reference to her/his dealings with staff, asking her/himself at each appropriate opportunity 'How would I handle this person if s/he were a child in my class?'

Recognition
Teachers, like children, need recognition of their efforts. The positive effects of a leadership approach that incorporated recognition of teachers'

work are demonstrated in the context of my research by the case of Sefton Road Primary School. Leyburn County Primary School's case, in contrast, highlights the detrimental effects on teachers' attitudes towards working at the school of leadership that failed to incorporate recognition.

'Teacher-centred' management recognises teachers' efforts through positive feedback and, in particular, through praise. Recognition is a key motivator because of the important part it plays in the job fulfilment process, as illustrated in my model presented in Chapter 1. Recognition reinforces the individual's image of her/his 'self-at-work' and, in particular, of the effectiveness with which work-related tasks are carried out. It is a crucial influence on the extent to which the individual feels a sense of significant achievement which, in turn, leads to her/his experiencing job fulfilment. Without it, as the cases of some of my teacher interviewees illustrate (see, for example, Fiona's comments in Chapter 9 and Louise's case presented in Chapter 8), the path to job fulfilment is obstructed.

Recognition may take several forms. It may be applied collectively to the whole staff as a single unit by the headteacher's taking care, as did Nias *et al.*'s (1989, p. 105) headteachers (see Chapter 9), to thank teachers on every appropriate occasion for their efforts. This is certainly an effective form of recognition since it serves as a continued reminder to staff that their commitment and conscientiousness are appreciated. However, its effectiveness is considerably increased if it is supplemented with re-cognition that is applied to individuals and small staff units. This is the form of recognition that underpinned Phil's generally successful and motivational leadership of the Sefton Road teachers (see Chapter 7). It is particularly effective because it is highly personal and because it incorp-orates an element of exclusivity throughout the time it is conveyed. It singles out individuals for special attention at a particular point in time and, in doing so, gives them a psychological boost that emanates from their feeling that they have excelled.

It is important to emphasise, though, that as a component of a leader-ship approach, such a personalised, individualised form of recognition is highly susceptible to degeneration into favouritism. This would clearly reduce its effectiveness since it would engender resentment amongst those teachers who were generally excluded from it and, whilst those who were favoured would be likely to remain highly motivated, the overall effect would be a dilution of motivation levels amongst the staff as a whole. At Sefton Road Phil sometimes came perilously close to this disadvantageous form of leadership because he overlooked consideration of individualism, as I outline it above.

To achieve maximum effectiveness as a leadership tool, recognition must incorporate individualism. Applying consideration of the child-centred class management parallel highlights the importance of ensuring that personalised, individual recognition of efforts is fair and equitable. This does not mean that it should be applied in a systematic, sequential way to everyone in turn. This would render it practically useless by implicitly removing the meritocratic principles that underpin it. What it does mean, though, is that, just as a child-centred teacher would endeavour to try to find something praiseworthy about all her/his pupils' work and to guard against directing too frequent and repeated praise at some children whilst leaving others feeling comparatively deprived of praise so, too, should a 'teacher-centred' headteacher exercise similar care and solicitude for teachers' feelings in recognising their efforts. In this respect, though, an advantage afforded headteachers in their management of staff over teachers' management of a class is that much of the personalised, individual attention and, in particular, recognition s/he may want to direct at some teachers, may be obscured from others through careful management. Teachers are less likely to disclose to colleagues than are children to their classmates that they have been singled out for special recognition or praise.

Whether it is directed at the staff as a whole or at individuals, recognition may vary in the manner in which it is conveyed. It may be implicit, such as when a teacher's work is selected for more public display than is usual. Implicit recognition may be reflected in a headteacher's choices of classes in which to place, and of teachers to mentor, trainee teachers. It may be reflected similarly in choices of classes to include in visitors' selected tours of the school. It may also be reflected in the allocation of responsibilities, or in choices of classes in which to place problem pupils. Implicit recognition, however, is generally inadequate at motivating teachers and at enhancing their work-related self-esteem, since it is susceptible to misinterpretation.

Explicit recognition, on the other hand, leaves teachers in no doubt about how their work is rated by others. The 'teacher-centred' headteacher conveys positive feedback in many different ways and on various occasions; through supportive written comments in teachers' planning books; through a spontaneous congratulatory remark after witnessing a teacher's success with a child or after watching a well presented class assembly; through an exclamation of appreciation on noticing an attractive classroom display or a voluntary extra playground duty; or through a special personalised message of thanks in a Christmas card: 'Thank you for all your hard work this term – and particularly for the time you've spent reorganising the reading resources.'

Awareness

In order to recognise teachers' efforts, though, heads need to be aware of what is going on in their schools. This should not be a vague, general awareness. It involves having an overview of what is happening in every classroom. The 'aware' head will know, for example, what topic each class is doing and what work is being done in different subjects. This awareness needs to be conveyed to teachers if it is to be an effective motivator. Taking in weekly planning books and initialling them is not enough; the head needs to comment upon teachers' written plans, either orally or in written form and, ideally, also needs to be seen to be aware of what is going on when s/he moves around the school doing routine tasks. To demonstrate this 'awareness' explicit references need to be included in conversations. As I have illustrated in earlier chapters, heads who are 'unaware' of what is going on were heavily criticised by the teachers involved in my study, and much dissatisfaction and demotivation was attributed to them.

Awareness also involves knowing about significant events, situations and circumstances, both in school and out of school, that may affect teachers' and pupils' lives. The 'aware' primary school head knows the names of teachers' partners and children, for example, and, in the case of children, knows their approximate age, whether they are about to take A-levels, go to university, get married, divorced, start work or school. S/he knows, too, about arguments, disagreements or sources of conflict between staff, and s/he puts this knowledge to good effect by incorporating into her/his management consideration of the effects that such things may have upon teachers. The 'teacher-centred' head combines individualism with awareness in order to perceive and treat teachers as people, rather than as units of a whole staff.

Interest

An interest in individual teachers' work, as it translates into pupils' learning, goes hand in hand with awareness and is equally important for headteachers to demonstrate. My research shows teachers to be very sensitive to headteachers' apparent lack of interest in the children's education. This often occurred when heads were keen administrators and ran well organised schools, as was the case with Mrs Hillman at Leyburn. It also occurred when heads were perceived as generally inadequate for the role of headship, as was the case with Helen's headteacher at Woodleigh Lane.

Headteachers' interest in their work is a key influence on teachers' job fulfilment since it may contribute towards strengthening their perceptions of their work as valuable and worthwhile. The extent of its influence is affected by other factors, such as the headteacher's credibility and status as leading professional (Coulson, 1988, p. 258) and teachers' own self-esteem. Selective interest on the part of respected headteachers towards specific components of teachers' work may impede their deriving job fulfilment from them, particularly in the case of inexperienced teachers who may lack self-confidence. The headteacher who, for example, manifests a much keener interest in the academic progress of a group of very able children than in the less impressive targets reached by a child with special needs is conveying implicit values-laden messages to teachers.

Direction

Child-centred education has been criticised by its detractors on the grounds that, in its most extreme progressive form, it is characterised by chaotic organisation and unstructured classroom activities that produce superficial or insufficient learning. Certainly, if it lacks adequate teacher direction it can degenerate into chaos. But it need not be so. Child-centred education is, paradoxically, most successful when it is rigidly managed and skilfully co-ordinated and directed by the teacher.

By the same token, 'teacher-centred' primary school leadership is most effective when it incorporates clear direction towards the realisation of a shared vision of what the school should become. The leader's role in providing direction is emphasised by Steers *et al.* (1996, p. 3):

> the organization, as a formal and abstract blueprint (of sorts), is necessarily imperfect because actual human behavior is infinitely more complex and variable than any 'plan' could accommodate. An organizational design cannot possibly account for every member's activity at all times. Consequently, in addition to various structural features, organizations must possess a mechanism that can ensure human behavior is coordinated and directed toward task accomplishment. That mechanism is presumed to be leadership.

My research revealed much dissatisfaction on the part of teachers with heads who, by failing to provide adequate direction, left staff with a sense of lack of purpose. Where headteachers' failure to provide direction was interpreted as apathy and laziness, or as an abrogation of responsibilities for which they were being paid, teachers were particularly resentful. Helen, for example, spoke of her head at Woodleigh Lane:

> I mean . . . part of it is . . . I mean, this is the very, very lowest . . . level . . . but I do resent the fact that he draws that salary. . . . And, I mean, he draws £25,000 a year . . . for doing sod all . . . and I resent that. That offends my sense of justice . . . you know, when there are teachers who work a lot harder and get a lot less, and all that kind of issue.

In cases where 'extended' professionals were led by headteachers whose professionality was more 'restricted', these headteachers often lacked the professional credibility to be able to offer any kind of direction that would have been acceptable to many of their teacher colleagues. Geoff Collins of Rockville was such a head. Not only did his own reasoning lack depth and reflect limited insight but he was also unreceptive and impervious to the reasoned arguments of others. Geoff's personality, professionality and 'mission' combined to shape his management in such a way that his headship lacked the 'leading professional' dimension, which Coulson (1988, p. 257) identifies as a potential source of conflict with heads' role as 'chief executive'. I have already pointed out in Chapter 9 that he did not appear to operate at a high level of abstraction, but merely at a lower level of day-to-day actions. This was recognised by all the Rockville staff.

He was never credited with superiority in relation to knowledge and understanding of educational issues, pedagogy or curriculum development; indeed, Hilary, the ESL Language Centre teacher, described Geoff: 'It's the . . . it's the sensitivity to psychological development and child development that he doesn't seem to . . . understand, when applying . . . er, his philosophies . . . you know? To me, he just lacks a basic, fundamental understanding of child development.' His headship incorporated neither curriculum leadership nor monitoring, which Webb and Vulliamy (1996) identify as aspects of the role of primary headteachers, nor was he considered to be a transformational leader (Southworth, 1994, p. 18). In a sense, this probably occurred through an iterative process; Geoff did not offer any real direction to his colleagues and, mainly on account of his failure to do so, he was not respected as a headteacher. Yet because he was not respected professionally, had he bothered to offer direction it would almost certainly have been disregarded or circumvented by many of the staff since, being informed by his 'restricted' professionality, his direction would have been ideologically unacceptable to them.

If they are to earn the respect of their teacher colleagues, headteachers need to provide clear direction which is based on educational ideologies and values that are shared by, or at least acceptable to, the majority. Without this they will fail to motivate staff. However, if it is to reflect consideration of the other key features of motivational leadership examined above (individualism, recognition, awareness and interest), headteachers' direction must be provided within an organisational framework that incorporates mechanisms for ensuring that it is a direction teachers are happy to follow.

Adopting a 'teacher-centred' organisational structure

A particular post-ERA growing trend in primary school management seems to be the establishment in schools of senior management teams (SMTs). Recognition of the need for delegated responsibility, shared decision- and policy-making, and a general wider distribution of workload has prompted management course leaders to recommend management teams as an organisational strategy to help headteachers cope better with their jobs. As a result SMTs, which were before 1988 almost exclusively confined to the secondary sector, are now a widely accepted feature of primary schools, as Webb and Vulliamy (1996, p. 303) point out. Indeed, based upon the findings of their survey of 150 headteachers of large primary schools, Wallace and Huckman (1996, p. 312) suggest that 'the notion of team approaches to management has taken a firm hold in the primary sector, in large institutions at least'.

Of the three schools in which I carried out observation, only one, Rockville, had an SMT. My findings revealed the Rockville SMT to be a significant source of dissatisfaction with the teachers whom it managed. Its composition, its operation, its output and its repercussions were the sources of the general consensual, negative attitude towards it. In relation to its composition, the essential problem with the Rockville SMT was the general lack of professional respect for its members. Consensus amongst the Rockville staff was that the three colleagues who comprised the senior management team were, for the most part, the three who were the least qualified to do so. The way in which it operated did little to promote the SMT amongst the rest of the staff. The decision-making process not within, but in relation to its extension beyond the SMT, was widely criticised, and the way in which it operated in relation to the timing of its meetings and activities was also a source of dissatisfaction. The SMT meeting during school hours was greatly resented on the grounds that this tied up two members of staff who ought otherwise to be teaching and who, had they been doing so would, as support teachers, be helping to lighten the workloads of other teachers. It was not simply to a weekly meeting during school hours that the staff objected, but to what they perceived as the injustice of deploying the two senior members of staff as support rather than class teachers. Not only did this result in increased class sizes, which created dissatisfaction, but the general policy of undertaking non-teaching managerial-related activities during the school day was also greatly resented by most teachers, who advocated that senior colleagues ought to undertake management work after school to justify their higher salaries.

The policies and decisions which were the products or the output of the Rockville SMT were inevitably destined to unfavourable reception on the part of the staff, since the SMT's members lacked credibility as professionals and managers. Dissatisfaction with the SMT's output was both general and specific. At a general level, the management of the school, which was unquestioningly the main, overall function of the management team, was the object of severe criticism. The essential source of dissatisfaction seemed to be that decisions and policy were interpreted as having little or no evident rational basis but, rather, as reflecting the wishes of the management team. It was suggested by some teachers that decision-making was strategically- rather than ideologically-determined, and that the main underlying consideration was not how the school and its pupils might benefit but that dominant members of staff, particularly the deputy head, be upset as little as possible.

Specific policies initiated by the management team were identified as sources of dissatisfaction. There was some diversity in relation to which policies teachers disapproved of, and in the extent of their disapproval. This diversity reflected teachers' professionality orientations and/or the degree to which they, personally, were affected by the policies. Those whom I would categorise as broadly 'restricted' professionals were dissatisfied most by policies which were rather more organisational than pedagogical in orientation and which had an impact on their own class management. The more 'extended' the professionality manifested by the teacher, the more s/he tended to be critical of both organisational and pedagogical oriented policies and, therefore, to be overall more dissatisfied than her/his more 'restricted' colleagues.

The repercussions on the 'non-senior' staff of the establishment of an SMT at Rockville appear to have been entirely negative. The establishment of the SMT was very widely interpreted as the head's mechanism both for legitimising and implementing his hierachism, and it was clearly the catalyst for a chain reaction of detrimental repercussions which effected organisational deficiencies in the school and impoverished the quality of teachers' working lives in ways which are described throughout earlier chapters.

Whilst the Rockville SMT case seems atypical, representing what is perhaps an extreme example of an unhealthy school professional climate arising out of perceptions of managerial intransigence and insensitivity which probably do not reflect the norm, it nevertheless raises important issues about the appropriateness for fostering positive job-related attitudes amongst teachers, of primary school management that incorporates hierarchism.

The Rockville case highlights the importance in determining SMTs' success of shared values between managers and the rest of the staff and of the credibility and acceptability of SMT members. Underlying these is one key issue – the issue of who should be involved in schools' decision-making.

Traditionally, hierarchical decision-making structures have been applied to schools so that, however democratic in reality the decision-making process within the school may be, the authority of the head over her/his staff is, from the outside, recognised in so far as the head is held responsible for the outcome of decisions (a responsibility which is now, post-ERA, shared by the school's governing body). The extent of internal democratisation is at the discretion of the head but this is, itself, a feature of hierarchism. Moreover, even though wide consultation may occur, it is typically the most senior teachers who effectively have the greatest influence on decision-making, and whose opinions will hold sway in the event of disagreement. One of the implicit assumptions upon which this hierarchism is predicated is that those holding the most senior posts are the best qualified to make decisions; in other words, that seniority equates to decision-making competence. The Rockville case reflects an alternative perspective which challenges this assumption, and it is this challenge which has wider applicability.

Building on the Rockville research evidence, several interconnected and overlapping considerations emerge as constituents of the key issue of who should be involved in school decision-making. These considerations underpin the formulation of a 'teacher-centred' organisational management structure that has the potential to be a more morale-, job satisfaction- and motivation-friendly alternative to hierarchical management.

Hierarchically-based decision-making is exclusive. It respects seniority and status, affording them consideration over alternative, sometimes competing, claims of suitability for decisional participation. It overlooks recognition of the value and potential of those who are placed at the base of the hierarchy. It neglects consideration and utilisation of individuality and fitness for purpose. It is myopically selective, it wastes talent and, in doing so, is susceptible to the engenderment of unfulfilment and resentment.

Southworth (1994, p. 26) suggests a more evenly distributed form of school decision-making: 'All staff need to become leaders and visionaries. This will mean an end to deference towards and dependence upon the head.' What Southworth seems to be calling for is development of the teaching profession, making 'extended' professionality the norm rather than the exception. Flattening out the hierarchy, opening up real opportunities for teachers at any stages of their careers to contribute meaningfully to the decision-making process and fostering greater collegiality and collaborativeness and professional development are certainly very promising strategies for school improvement which have been put into practice with apparent success (Haigh, 1991). Yet ideas such as these are predicated upon an assumption that all teachers either want to play an active part in decision-making or that they can be persuaded, or coerced, into doing so. Reflecting their heterogeneity and, more specifically, differences in, amongst other factors, professionality orientation on the 'extended–restricted' continuum, teachers vary considerably in relation to their desire for decisional participation. Some teachers' vision does not extend beyond their classroom door, as is demonstrated by Hayes' (1996) ethnographic study of one primary headteacher's attempts to develop a collaborative approach to decision-making. Some teachers simply have little or no interest in being involved in many of the decisions which school managers must make, because these exceed the parameters of their very class teaching-focused job-related interests. In the context of my research, Brenda from Rockville and Louise from Sefton Road (see Chapter 8) fell into this category. Others may object to sharing what they perceive as the headteacher's responsibilities without sharing her/his higher salary. This expectation that senior teachers earn their money was manifested in my study by Helen's attitude to her Woodleigh Lane headteacher, and by many Rockville teachers' attitudes to their SMT and, in particular, to the deputy head. It is also identified by Coulson (1988, p. 258) as underlying the need for headteachers to be accountable and credible:

> The framework of teacher expectations, which is part of their occupational culture . . . puts pressure on heads to legitimate their promotion and status by equalling or exceeding their colleagues in the observance of teachers' cultural norms. By doing so they maintain and build their credibility as *leading* professionals and *head*teachers.

Greater democratisation in schools and more collaborative decision-making are clearly, then, as potentially problematic and fraught with difficulties as management through SMTs is. To put pressure on reluctant teachers to share decision-making is as likely to create dissatisfaction as does excluding those who want more involvement. This is not a 'teacher-centred' approach to staff management since it fails to incorporate individualism. What is needed is an approach to managing schools which acknowledges and respects the diversity of teachers' individual job-related needs, which allows those who want a share in the management to have it, and those who wish to to take a back seat.

Since the traditional hierarchical approach to primary school management – placing the burden of responsibility on the head's shoulders – is evidently becoming unworkable post-ERA (Wallace and Huckman, 1996; Webb and Vulliamy, 1996), it is perhaps time to address some of the emergent issues and problems through a radical rethink about how schools may best be managed to serve the dual purpose of easing head-teachers' workloads and endeavouring to foster positive job-related attitudes amongst teachers. Retaining the head's ultimate authoritative role but reducing the risk of this authority developing into autocracy, by flattening out the hierarchy, dispensing with the deputy headship role and putting into place in schools a committee structure for decision-making is one idea which could be pursued. The committee approach to management would be applied to all except day-to-day working decisions, which would be the responsibility of the head or his/her proxy, who may be nominated as such on a yearly, termly or even weekly basis. Committees would be specific to areas of school organisation and effectiveness such as teaching quality, curriculum development, finance and professional development. They could vary in their degree of specificity, or even incorporate more specific subcommittees. A curriculum development committee might, for example, incorporate curriculum subject-specific subcommittees. Teachers could select the extent and the level of their participation. Some may wish to sit on many, or even all, the committees. Some may wish to sit on none. This would be acceptable, but their subsequent criticism of decisions made would then be considered unreasonable. The level of teacher participation in their school's committee system of management would determine the extent and the nature of the hierarchism which evolved as a result. But this would be a self-imposed hierarchism which would be within teachers' powers to change, and they would therefore be unreasonable to resent it. This certainly represents a sweeping change to primary school management and would need to be piloted before widespread adoption. It is a management structure which is applied successfully to many university departments and, as a principle, seems potentially workable in schools. SMTs represent in some respects and, certainly, in theory, a step towards greater democratisation of schools' decision-making. A committee structure represents a few more steps nearer. Under the right conditions, SMTs may be successful in primary schools. There are undoubtedly examples of SMTs which are generally perceived positively by those whom they manage, but since a significant determinant of this is the headteacher and her/his attitude to management, much is left to chance. The notion of SMTs does not sit easy with that of a 'teacher-centred' approach to primary school management.

With the impetus to develop a new generation of higher-calibre primary head directing energy and attention towards the introduction of a mandatory headship qualification in the UK, it is perhaps an appropriate time to divert some of this attention towards reappraisal of the nature of the headship role and of the management strategies it requires. This book highlights the detrimental effects on teacher morale, motivation and job satisfaction of certain management approaches and leadership styles. It also illustrates the ways in which management can be effective in getting the best out of teachers through a more 'teacher-centred' approach. This is clearly the way at school level towards managing to motivate.

12

The wider picture: addressing key policy issues

Introduction

There is no rationale for researching teachers' attitudes to their work, uncovering the factors that influence what affects levels of morale, motivation and job satisfaction, identifying the lowest common factors and developing out of these findings models that incorporate generalisability and wider applicability, without then proceeding to address the broader issues of what can be done to make improvements to prevailing circumstances and conditions. There is limited value in understanding teacher morale, motivation and job satisfaction without applying that understanding to the associated practicalities and consideration of how they may be adapted to accommodate better the needs that have emerged.

This book has identified and illustrated these needs. It has revealed that how teachers feel about their jobs is predominantly affected by contextual factors. More specifically, it has shown levels of job satisfaction, morale and motivation to be determined by teachers' professionality-, relative experiences- and realistic expectations-influenced perceptions of how much, overall, their conceptions of their ideal 'selves-at-work' are realised within the work contexts in which they operate. It has identified the degree of match, in relation to these factors, between teachers and their work contexts to be the key determinant of job-related attitudes.

The preceding chapter presents ideas for school-level management initiatives that are informed by an understanding of teacher morale, motivation and job satisfaction. Since contextual factors have been revealed to be so influential, it clearly must be at this level that the most effective improvements will be made. Yet, relying on school-, or institution-level changes is optimistic and precarious. It leaves too much to chance. If they are dependent for their improvement upon a change process that is essentially unilateral, teachers' job-related attitudes are unlikely to be significantly affected. It is on a much wider scale that the key issues need to be addressed. A coherent, concerted attempt at tackling some of the main problems associated with teacher morale, job satisfaction and motivation is needed. This should be far-reaching, aiming to extend its influence beyond isolated pockets of enlightened school management and exemplary models of good leadership practice. It should influence the system as a whole by modifying the structure upon which it is based and its underlying principles. This final chapter addresses these wider issues of systemic improvement by identifying, and suggesting modifications to, some of the specific systemic features that create or exacerbate problems related to teacher morale, motivation and job satisfaction.

Problems and solutions

As I have illustrated throughout this book, the main underlying factor that gives rise to dissatisfaction, unfulfilment, demotivation and low morale amongst teachers is incompatibility with the specific institutional context in which they work. I emphasise that I consider this contextual factor to be the *main*, not the *only*, influence on job-related attitudes. I fully accept that centrally imposed reforms, initiatives and conditions may also be contributory to lowered levels of morale, motivation and job satisfaction, but I consider these influences to be comparatively transient and, partly as a result of this, subsidiary to the contextual factor.

Underpinning the contextual factor are specific inter-related, potentially problematic conditions and situations that are in place within the wider educational system. I identify the two main ones as *headteachers' authority and influence*, and *teachers' professional culture*. Below, I outline the nature of the problems that typically arise from these and suggest remedial changes.

Headteachers' authority and influence

This may best be illustrated by reference to some of the cases from the context of my own research. The issue is essentially that of headteachers' exercising too much power and authority within their schools. In all three of the schools in which I carried out observation there arose situations in which teachers, either individually or collectively, disapproved of a decision made or a policy imposed by the headteacher and felt that they had no real alternative to accepting it. The Rockville case, since it is described more fully in this book than that of any other school (see, in particular, Chapter 5), is perhaps the best illustration of the problematic outcomes that may arise out of this typical headteacher–staff power ratio situation.

In the Rockville case, there was very serious concern over and disapproval of specific prevailing circumstances for which the headteacher was considered responsible. The issue is not who was right, the head or his detractors but, rather, what teachers can do under such circumstances; what direct action options are available to them. I use the term *direct action*, in order to distinguish these options from palliative options or personal coping strategies, which are not aimed at changing situations but at changing attitudes and responses to situations.

The issue of teachers' direct action options concerns the mechanisms which are in place and the provision available within the system for teachers to instigate procedures for registering official complaints about policy and practice in their schools. It concerns managers' authority and accountability and the rights and, in many respects, the responsibilities, of subordinates in relation to their managers.

There are, of course, mechanisms in place within the state education system which allow teachers to register officially their complaints and concerns – to the headteacher, to the school governors and/or to the local education authority, in the case of LEA-controlled schools. However, these are generally considered to be drastic measures which are very seldom exercised and usually reserved for what are perceived to be extreme cases. In reality, most teachers adopt personal coping strategies which, in some cases, may include resigning, rather than invoke official complaints procedures.

The implications of this are that headteachers may often enjoy a greater degree of autonomy and are less accountable than should be – and is widely believed to be – the case and that individual schools may suffer as a result of deficiencies within them. Such deficiencies may impact upon, for example, the school's organisation, the teaching staff and the curriculum, any of which, in turn, is likely to have a detrimental effect upon pupils' education.

In the Rockville case, low morale resulted from teachers' sustained dissatisfaction and from their feeling powerless to exert any influence upon what they perceived to be an unsatisfactory situation. The case reflects quite clearly an establishment view and a tacit acceptance that managers are generally able to exercise a considerable degree of perceived poor management before they are seriously called to account, and that their views are generally likely to carry much more weight in any accountability process than those of their subordinates. The Rockville case reflects the unchallenged hierarchy which potentially underlies the organisation of most institutions and which is likely to be operational in all but the most enlightened. The case illustrates the disproportionately large amount of power and authority which, in reality, headteachers potentially enjoy. It also illustrates the inadequacy of the existing system in monitoring whether or not such power is ever misplaced. There is perhaps now a case for introducing into the state education system mechanisms for flattening out the underlying hierarchy.

There are, of course, many examples of extremely competent headship. There are also examples of measures which have been very successfully introduced in individual schools, aimed at greater democratisation and increased decisional participation (see, for example, Haigh, 1991). These, however, represent discretionary initiatives. The essential point is that headteachers have the power to exercise such discretion and, just as some choose to adopt more enlightened approaches to management, others may not. One option for a remedial strategy, therefore, would be imposing upon schools democratic, consultative models of management such as the 'teacher-centred' approach I suggest in Chapter 11.

On the other hand, not only may more consultative forms of management be unwelcome to some teachers, who have little desire for decisional participation and who are happy to be led or directed, but there is also an obvious contradiction embedded in the notion of a strategy for reducing autocratic management which, itself, involves imposing policy change. In the light of these considerations, mechanisms aimed at increasing the accountability of educational managers may seem more appropriate than imposing models of management upon schools.

Perhaps what is needed is the incorporation within the system of facilities aimed at providing teachers, possibly routinely, with initial, non-adversarial measures which allow them to raise serious concerns without going to the extreme of registering official complaints. This could be exercised at LEA level and one option may involve routine termly visits to schools by a designated school management and organisation officer, whose function would be to oversee management–staff relations in what, effectively, would be a kind of 'morale quality control' capacity. S/he would routinely interview every member of staff, precluding requests for interviews with her/him attracting attention and being construed as subversive. Emerging problems would be dealt with at her/his discretion, in consultation with all parties concerned. The 'teacher-centred' headteacher, characterised in Chapter 11, would consider this an acceptable, non-threatening procedure. The purpose of such an initiative would be to incorporate into the system an additional layer of mechanisms for checking headteachers' authority and for increasing their accountability. It may even incorporate procedures for raising levels of morale, job satisfaction and motivation amongst headteachers by commending exemplary leadership and publicly recognising schools that enjoy morale-, motivation- and job satisfaction-friendly working cultures.

Teachers' professional culture

My research findings have shown the teacher–institution compatibility problem to be particularly acute amongst 'extended' professionals. This highlights the problem of wasted talent and unfulfilled potential within the teaching profession, particularly in relation to those who, through their influence, may contribute towards raising the level of teachers' professional culture.

Hargreaves (1994) argues that educational reforms in England and Wales since 1988 are creating what he refers to as a 'new professionalism' amongst teachers. His 'new professional' is more client-focused, more predisposed towards collegiality and collaboration. Hargreaves (*ibid.*, p. 426) identifies changes to teacher culture reflecting teachers' acceptance of (even though this may emanate from resignation to), the recent re-forms: 'Older teachers who found the changes too stressful took early retirement; those remaining now divide into those who increase stress by trying to persist with the old structures and culture and those who are, sometimes reluctantly and painfully, generating a more collaborative cul-ture built on new social structures.' Elliott (1991, p. 311) also acknowl-edges a shift towards more client-focused professional images, which he does not confine to application to teachers.

  Professionalism and professionality are not, of course, synonyms and if, indeed, as Hargreaves (1994) argues, a new professionalism is emerging amongst English and Welsh teachers, it would serve as a useful ally to a 'new professionality'. This 'new professionality' would manifest itself as a shift of the prevailing level of teacher profession-ality along a continuum such as that identified by Hoyle (1975) to-wards the 'extended' extreme. Moreover, the features which Elliott (1991, p. 311) identifies as those of the new professional images reflect professionality at least as much as professionalism. They include, for example, 'a new emphasis on the holistic understanding of situations as the basis for a professional practice, rather than on understanding them exclusively in terms of a particular set of specialist categories' and 'self-reflection as a means of overcoming stereotypicial judge-ments and responses' (*ibid.*).

  The teaching profession will be seriously impoverished in terms of both quality and status if it loses significant numbers of its higher-calibre mem-bers, prompted to resign by continued dissatisfaction and demoralisation. Yet, unless teachers' professional culture accommodates the needs of 'ex-tended' professionals, it is likely to sustain such losses. Of the three 'extended' professionals profiled in Chapter 6, for example, one has now left teaching and another was, when I last contacted her, planning to leave the profession.

  There are two ways in which teachers' professional culture may be adapted to accommodate better the needs of 'extended' professionals. One is through promoting 'extended' professionality within teacher cul-ture, and the other is through stratification of the profession. I examine each of these options below.

Promoting 'extended' professionality within teacher culture
The headteacher of one of the schools involved in the 1993–4 piloting of a school-centred initial teacher training scheme (SCITT) is reported to have said: 'We wanted teachers to be trained within the craft and culture of the profession' (Pyke, 1993, p. 6).

  A particularly significant issue, however, in examining the extent to which 'extended' professionality is accepted amongst teachers is whether or not a single teacher culture exists. Sachs and Smith (1988, p. 425) summarise the debate:

> One strand of teacher culture theory has as its basis the proposition that be- cause teachers as an occupational category are not homogeneous, their cultures are not either. From this perspective the argument is made that teacher cultures are fluid, pluralistic and diverse, depending on the environmental, system-level and biographical characteristics of teachers. An alternative position is that teachers and schools are characterised by uniformity rather than pluralism.

Their view is that teacher culture is uniform, whereas Lortie (1975) sug- gests that there is no common teacher culture but that the profession would be better served if there were.

Acceptance of pluralistic and diverse teacher cultures clearly accommod- ates a continuum of professionality, such as that identified by Hoyle (1975). The notion of a uniform culture, however, effectively categorises as deviant any attitudes, ideologies and behaviour which fall outside the norm.

Grant and Zeichner (1984, p. 12) point out that most teachers, even those categorised as 'good', are intuitive rather than reflective or analyti- cal, and Sachs and Smith (1988, p. 433) refer to teachers' knowledge as generally 'practical in its orientation, largely uncritical and unreflective and . . . concerned more with means rather than ends'. These views im- plicitly recognise a single, predominant teacher culture which incorpor- ates a professionality lying closer to the 'restricted' than to the 'extended' end of Hoyle's continuum. Supporting them is Elliott's (1991, p. 315) view of what he refers to as 'a redundant occupational culture' within teaching, which 'embodies an "infallible expert" model of professionalism', which is 'the source of . . . crude stereotypes' and which predominates over 'reflective sub-cultures . . . found in pockets in many schools'.

Similarly, Hargreaves (1980, p. 132) refers to 'a widespread belief in the profession . . . that the pedagogical skills of teachers are essentially *intui- tive*, resting upon tacit knowledge'. His more recent work (Hargreaves, 1994) identifies the emergence of a new culture manifested by a shift towards a 'new professionalism', to which I have referred earlier. Nev- ertheless, his belief that the old, prevailing, culture is being replaced by a new one still implies acknowledgement of a single teacher culture (*ibid.*, p. 425): 'During the last 4 or 5 years there have been signs of erosion. The culture of individualism is beginning to crack. The way is prepared for transformation into a new culture in which individualism is being dis- placed by collaboration.' My findings revealed evidence of teachers' per- ceived awareness and acknowledgement of, for the most part, a loose duality rather than a diversity of teacher professionality-determined cul- ture. The evident perceived duality is based loosely upon many of the teacher characteristics suggested by Hoyle (1975) as those reflecting either 'extended' or 'restricted' professionality and which, fundamentally, con- cerns the extent to which teachers adopt intellectual, rational approaches to their work rather than intuitive ones. It is important to emphasise that the distinction was applied by teachers to specific colleagues. There were few cases of its being interpreted and discussed as a general trend; at least – and more precisely – there were few references to its having wider applicability than to specific school staff groups.

Since the duality of teachers' professionality was represented in this specific, personalised form, teachers placed themselves, as well as others, into either of two broad categories. The 'main' category was that of what was perceived as a predominant teacher culture reflecting a professionality which focused upon classroom competence and was concerned with practicalities. The second category seemed to be perceived as an extension of this – as a subculture shared by a few, rather more intellectual, reflective and analytical teachers who stood out from the crowd because they were concerned not only with carrying out their jobs competently but also with questioning the constituents of, and redefining, competence.

For the most part there was implicit consensus that 'extended' professionality, or those of its variants which teachers' different perceptions represented, was superior to the more practically oriented professionality which seemed to be perceived as the norm. As a result, since not all the teachers placed themselves in the 'superior' category, individuals' professional self-esteem differed.

Rosemary, a Rockville teacher, expressed concern over her own inadequacy when compared with other, better educated teachers:

> I have this feeling that because . . . when they changed the system to degree courses, and I think that there's all these young, more qualified teachers coming along, who are much brighter than I am and can cope far better, and, again, you know, you think, 'Oh, *am* I doing as good a job as they are? Can I do it any better?' You know, 'What else should I be doing?'

However, Rosemary was, amongst my sample, atypical with respect to the degree of self-depreciation to which she confessed. Most teachers gave the impression, despite implicit or explicit recognition of the professional superiority of those of their colleagues who exhibited characteristics of more 'extended' professionality, that although they themselves were perhaps less 'gifted' or less 'well read' or less 'intellectual' than these teachers, they were, nevertheless, adequately competent. Many gave the impression of being perfectly satisfied with their own level of professionality and of recognising a more 'extended' level as, although 'superior', unnecessary for the majority and, in their own cases, undesirable.

My research findings suggest that 'extended' professionality constitutes a teacher subculture which is treated with what ranges from tolerance to reverence within the predominant teacher culture of practicalities, rather than theory. Essentially, though, the influence which 'extended' professionals are able to have on reshaping the teaching profession, educational ideologies and practice, and even the ways in which their own schools are organised, seems minimal. Furthermore, this seems likely to remain the case unless 'extended' professionality is valued within the wider education system.

There are two complementary ways in which the mechanisms within the wider English and Welsh education system might promote and encourage 'extended' professionality amongst teachers. First, they may stimulate and, secondly, they may reward it. Both ways are applicable to both preservice and serving teachers.

Since 'extended' professionality essentially involves a competent, reflective, rational and, to some extent, intellectual approach to teaching, it may be best encouraged by teacher development programmes which include appropriate in-service courses, sabbaticals or secondments during which study and/or research may be undertaken, opportunities for teacher fellowships at higher education institutions, research partnerships between schools and universities, such as that identified by Pimenoff (1995), and opportunities for teachers to publish and to participate in seminars and conferences. Involvement in recently evolved partnership teacher training schemes, as school-based mentors, also provides opportunities for professional development (Zeichner, 1993, pp. 31–2; Hargreaves, 1994, p. 429; Evans *et al.*, 1995, pp. 102–27; Evans and Abbott, 1997).

Those involved in research and scholarship represent a minority of teachers but their evaluations illustrate the benefits for teacher development of such provision. Vulliamy and Webb (1991, pp. 225–6) report the effects on their teacher sample of research involvement required by award-bearing courses. They also highlight the 'knock-on' effect on teacher development when teacher-researchers involved their colleagues as research subjects: 'the research was also viewed as bringing about change in attitudes through questioning staff assumptions and raising their awareness through interviews and classroom observations' (*ibid.*, p. 230). There is very little published evidence of the extent to which 'extended' professionality is encouraged and promoted by the kind of provision for professional development I have outlined above. What little evidence there is, however, paints a pessimistic picture. Halpin *et al.* (1990) point out that 77% of their respondents reported their latest involvement in INSET to have been their own initiative, and only 14% reported pursuing the INSET as a result of advice from within their schools or from their local authority. Halpin *et al.*'s (1990) assumption that self-initiated participation in INSET is a characteristic of Hoyle's (1975, p. 166) 'extended' professionality is, however, misguided. Hoyle in fact makes the distinction that, whilst 'extended' professionals typically attend longer award-bearing in-service courses, 'restricted' professionals typically participate in courses of a practical nature, the latter of which constituted 77% of the INSET upon which Halpin *et al.*'s (1990, p. 165) study focused. Nevertheless, their data on who initiated involvement in

INSET provide evidence that there is room for much more encouragement from senior management in schools, from local education authorities and from the government. Indeed, Howard and Bradley's (1991) study of teacher development and employment after INSET courses revealed considerable ignorance on the part of many local education authorities of the qualifications held by their teachers. Eleven LEAs were approached before the researchers found three which were able to supply details of the highest in-service training award held by secondary and primary head-teachers (*ibid.*, p. 26). Howard and Bradley point out that neither LEAs nor the Department for Education (DfEE) (then the Department of Education and Science; DES) hold data in an accessible, usable form, or hold data on where the recipients of major INSET are, what posts they hold and what specific knowledge and skills they possess (*ibid.*, p. 31). Clearly, this ignorance reflects a lack of recognition in the UK of the value of this type of professional development for teachers, without which recognition of the encouragement and promotion of 'extended' professionality is unlikely to be realised. Similarly, Triggs and Francis's (1990) study of the value of long award-bearing, in-service courses revealed research degrees to be valued less than school-focused courses and diploma courses, particularly by LEA officers and headteachers. They also point out that higher education developments such as consultancy and fellowship schemes are underpublicised and are not sufficiently well known by headteachers.

At preservice level, 'extended' professionality may be promoted by the inclusion of appropriate content in initial teacher training courses. Typically, this would demonstrate the usefulness and value of applying educational theory and research findings to the practice of teaching. Students would undertake their own research. Analytical and reflective skills would be fostered, as would writing and oral presentation skills. The clear focus would be on developing potential 'extended' professionals rather than on training competent practitioners whose professionality is more 'restricted'. This could be achieved alongside the progression through a standards-focused ITE curriculum, which was introduced in the UK in September 1997. The key component would be an emphasis on the link between theory and practice and the relevance of the one to the other. Without this emphasis students may dismiss some course content as over-theoretical and irrelevant, and potential 'extended' professionals may be scared off.

Clearly, whilst remedial strategies which focus upon INSET provision and on initial teacher training will not *directly* affect individual schools' intellectual climates, they have the potential to do so indirectly, by raising the awareness and professionality levels of more teachers and, by doing so, expanding the size and the influence of the 'reflective subcultures' which Elliott (1991, p. 315) claims 'can be found in pockets in many schools'. Thus, the subculture may eventually become the predominant culture and would be one in which 'extended' professionals would thrive, and would be more likely to sustain higher levels of morale, motivation and job satisfaction.

Losses of 'extended' professionals to the teaching profession would be less likely to occur if there were more headteachers who were, themselves, 'extended' professionals. In the UK there have been recent initiatives to improve the quality of headteachers, but these have tended to focus upon training provision rather than upon recognition, and the development and promotion of personal and professional qualities and skills, such as reflectivity, rationality, intelligence and intellectual curiosity. One problem is that school governors, who select and appoint headteachers, do not always recognise the value of such qualities. Clearly, there is a case for arguing that measures aimed at improving the process of headteacher recruitment need to be adopted.

If 'extended' professionality is to be rewarded it needs to be incorporated within a career structure which recognises and values it. Such a career structure would recruit and promote 'extended' professionals in preference to more 'restricted' professionals. Information sought from job applicants, particularly to senior posts, would seek to reveal professionality, and teachers' qualifications and participation in long award-bearing courses would take on increased significance, which would be reflected in salary scales. Anecdotal evidence reveals the extent to which idiosyncratic and autonomous appointments procedures may fail to contribute towards promoting 'extended' professionality. Amanda, one of the Rockville interviewees, commented upon her perception of the precarious nature of headship appointments in her LEA:

> Well, if you know the way in which some appointments are made . . . I mean, I'm appalled . . . but, you know, the people with whom I have *most* contact . . . their short-listing is such that . . . er . . . generally speaking, the interviews that have been held in the last six months, that I know of, probably three out of four would've been good heads – it's been difficult. Having said that, often the fourth one has been the one chosen! Because, of course, the adviser has no vote . . . and, er . . . particularly in church schools . . . well, I mean, I know of one particular school whereby . . . when it came to the drawing up at the end of the interviews, the person who got the headship – who will be a very, very good head . . . I mean, I know him personally – would not have got it if it hadn't been for the skilful handling of the thing by the adviser and the chairman of governors . . . Otherwise, a bad appointment would've been made at that school.

Similarly, a headship candidate's personal experiences (Pepworth, 1991) illustrate the apparent disregard for professionality of some appointments committees: 'The letter of application had been restricted to two sides of A4 and 'CVs should not be included' . . . In deepest southern England, it would seem that some head-hunters are still in a fairly primitive state.' Clearly, one way to attempt to rectify the deficiencies of a system in which pluralistic methods and procedures are exacerbating a problem is to introduce greater cohesion and uniformity. In the specific case of teaching appointments, government or LEA guidelines (incorporating recognition of the importance of teacher professionality) would be a step in the direction of developing a career structure which values and rewards 'extended' professionality. However, in the light of those educational reforms of recent years in the UK, which have eroded away both central and LEA control and introduced greater autonomy for schools' governing bodies, uniformity of this kind seems an unlikely scenario.

One problem with initiatives that promote 'extended' professionality within teachers' professional culture, however, is their neglect of the role of 'restricted' professionals. Stratifying the teaching profession is an alternative that would ensure that the interests of, and the contribution to teaching made by, 'restricted' professionals is not overlooked.

Stratification of the profession
One of the key features of motivational school leadership I identify in Chapter 11 is individualism. Indeed, individualism in relation to teachers' job-related needs is a pervasive theme of this book. Individualism recognises that not everyone is the same and that, therefore, in relation to teachers, what suits one may not suit another, what fulfils or satisfies some may leave others unfulfilled or dissatisfied, and what motivates some may not motivate others.

Not all teachers, therefore, would want to be 'extended' professionals. Many may lack the levels of interest, commitment or intellectualism required for 'extended' professionality. Some may simply not be ready for it yet. Others will never attain it, but will be none the less happy, satisfied or motivated in their work for being so; indeed, as more 'restricted' professionals, their chances of sustaining positive job-related attitudes may even be better than they would be were their professionality more 'extended'. A teacher culture that promotes and favours 'extended' professionality would, therefore, not suit them. Such a culture would be more likely to alienate than to convert them, just as the Sefton Road climate alienated Louise (see Chapter 8). This would pose no problems for the profession and the education system as a whole if these 'less extended' or, in some cases, even 'restricted' professionals were poor teachers who would best serve the profession by leaving it; but they typically are not. They are much more likely to be very conscientious, highly motivated, extremely competent classroom practitioners who simply, for various reasons, do not want to attend long award-bearing courses of a theoretical nature, read educational theory, participate in research activities, contribute to curriculum development or be involved in policy- and decision-making.

Of course, the distinction I draw between 'extended' and 'less extended' professionals, on the basis of their interest in the activities listed above, is artificial and stereotypical and does not convey a sense of the greater complexity and subtlety in relation to attitudes towards specific work-related activities that location along the professionality continuum involves. The point I wish to make, though, is that a professional culture that is intended to foster high levels of morale, motivation and job satisfaction as widely as possible will be one that accommodates teacher diversity. Such a culture is one that reflects a stratified profession.

A stratified profession would be predicated on acceptance that there are different categories of professionals who each have important, but different, roles to perform. In the primary education sector in the UK, for example, reflecting teachers' different professionality orientations, qualifications and levels of commitment to the job, three professional strata could be introduced. The basic level would be that of competent classroom practitioner. At this level the emphasis would be on class teaching, with no extraclassroom responsibilities. This would be a level of professionality and practice typically sought by teachers like Brenda and Louise (whose cases I present in Chapter 8), who enjoy teaching, are competent and conscientious, but who have no wish to be take on responsibilities other than those which their class teaching demands. The second level would be that of more advanced teaching skills and wider responsibility. At this level teachers would typically hold responsibility for the co-ordination of an area of the curriculum, and their teaching would be rationally rather than entirely intuitively-based. Teachers at this level would be developing or developed 'extended' professionals. The third level would be that of analytical skills, which would be applied not only to classroom teaching but also to school-wide decision- and policy-making. Teachers at this level would be 'extended' professionals and would, in order to qualify for the status of the level, have had to undertake a designated course of advanced study. Teachers at this level would be entitled to participate in school decision-making.

A stratified profession along these lines would aim to offer something for everyone. I suggest it here as an idea in principle rather than as a carefully thought-out reform recommendation. To reach that latter status, the full practical implications would need to be afforded much greater consideration than I have applied to the general idea I present. As a principle, though, stratification would aim to enable rather than constrain teachers by meeting their different job-related needs and by allowing those who want to participate in decision- and policy-making do so, and those who wish to avoid such responsibilities to do so. Progression through the strata would have to be available as a right to those who wanted it but it would require designated courses of study, at appropriate levels, to be undertaken successfully. Promotion would be strata-linked so that, for example, certain promoted posts would only be available to level 3 qualified teachers, and some less senior posts to level 2 qualified teachers. This would help to ensure that schools were led by, and that their policies were decided by, 'extended' professionals. Stratification of the profession would therefore aim to inject a measure of quality control into school management and policy formulation. Pay would also be strata-linked.

Stratification of the profession is not a new idea. It has traditionally been incorporated into the French education system at secondary level, and it was particularly evident in the UK system for several years after the introduction of an all-graduate profession resulted in recently qualified graduates working alongside certificated teachers. It is also implicit in the government's plans to introduce a category of 'advanced skills' teacher into the profession (Carvel, 1998). It reflects recognition of a diversity in the teaching profession in relation to levels of commitment and professionality orientation, which will not disappear if it is not openly acknowledged. Provided that it incorporates facilities and resources for guaranteeing all teachers the opportunities to advance through the different levels if they wish to do so and when they wish to do so, it is perfectly equitable. Moreover, it has much to offer in relation to raising levels of morale, job satisfaction and motivation by aiming to provide teachers with the kinds of jobs they want, and to prevent their being constrained in these jobs by those who are doing the kinds of jobs for which they are ill-qualified. Stratification of the profession is essentially aimed at task–talents matching.

As a principle underpinning policy aimed at raising levels of morale, motivation and job satisfaction, task–talents matching has much to offer since it incorporates consideration of individualism, which is the key to understanding teachers' attitudes to their work. Throughout the chapters in this book evidence has been presented that demonstrates very clearly the detrimental effects on teachers' job-related attitudes of mismatch between individuals and the contexts in which they work; of trying to fit square pegs into round holes. If the teaching profession is to develop to its full potential, and if society is to get the best out of its teachers, attention now needs to be focused towards ways of incorporating into the education system mechanisms that aim to raise teaching standards by accommodating the rich diversity and individualism that underpin teachers' needs.

References

Andain, I. (1990) Protest of the undervalued, *Guardian*, 17 April.

Anon (1991) Which comes first, money or quality?, *The Times Educational Supplement*, 8 February, p. 23.

Argyle, M. (1972) *The Social Psychology of Work*, London, Allen Lane.

Atkins, M.J. (1984) Practitioner as researcher: some techniques for analysing semi-structured data in small-scale research, *British Journal of Educational Studies*, Vol. 32, no. 3, pp. 251–61.

Baehr, M.E. and Renck, R. (1959) The definition and measurement of employee morale, *Administrative Science Quarterly*, Vol. 3, pp. 157–84.

Ball, D. (1972), Self and identity in the context of deviance: the case of criminal abortion, in Scott, R. and Douglas, J. (eds) *Theoretical Perspectives on Deviance*, New York, Basic Books.

Ball, S.J. (1987) *The Micro-Politics of the School*, London, Routledge.

Ball, S.J. and Goodson, I.F. (1985) Understanding teachers: concepts and contexts, in Ball, S.J. and Goodson, I.F. (eds) *Teachers' Lives and Careers*, Lewes, Falmer Press.

Blackbourne, L. (1990) All's fair in the hunt for better jobs, *The Times Educational Supplement*, 11 May, p. A4.

Bredeson, P.V., Fruth, M.J. and Kasten, K.L. (1983) Organizational incentives and secondary school teaching, *Journal of Research and Development in Education*, Vol. 16, no. 4, pp. 52–8.

CACE (1967) *Children and Their Primary Schools*, (The Plowden Report), Vol. 1, London, HMSO.

Carvel, J. (1998) 'Super-teachers' to be paid up to £40,000: Blunkett unveils alternative for best classroom performers, *Guardian*, 3 March, p. 4.

Cattell, R.B. and Stice, G.F. (1960) *The Dimensions of Groups and their Relations to the Behavior of Members. Final Report on Research Project NR 172–369, Contract N80mm-79600, Human Relations, Branch, Office of Naval Research*, Champaign, IL, University of Illinois.

Chandler, B.J. (1959) Salary policies and teacher morale, *Educational Administration and Supervision*, Vol. 45, pp. 107–10.

Chapman, D.W. (1983). Career satisfaction of teachers, *Educational Research Quarterly*, Vol. 7, no. 3, pp. 40–50.

Chapman, D.W. and Hutcheson, S. (1982) Attrition from teaching careers: a discriminant analysis', *American Educational Research Journal*, Vol. 19, no. 1, pp. 93–105.

Child, I.L. (1941) Morale: a bibliographical review, *Journal of Educational Administration*, Vol. 38, pp. 393–420.

Coughlan, R.J. (1970) Dimensions of teacher morale, *American Educational Research Journal*, Vol. 7, pp. 221–34.

Coulson, A.A. (1988) An approach to headship development through personal and professional growth. In Clarkson, M. (ed) *Emerging Issues in Primary Education*, Lewes, Falmer Press.

Elliott, J. (1991) A model of professionalism and its implications for teacher education, *British Educational Research Journal*, Vol. 17, no. 4, pp. 309–18.

Evans, K. (1986) Creating a climate for school leadership, *School Organisation*, Vol. 6, pp. 61–9.

Evans, L. (1997) A voice crying in the wilderness? The problems and constraints facing 'extended' professionals in the English primary education sector, *Teachers and Teaching: Theory and Practice*, Vol. 3, no. 1, pp. 61–83.

Evans, L. and Abbott, I. (1997) Developing as mentors in school-based teacher training, *Teacher Development*, Vol. 1, no. 1, pp. 135–47,

Evans, L. and Abbott, I. (1998) *Teaching and Learning in Higher Education*, London, Cassell.

Evans, L., Abbott, I., Goodyear, R. and Pritchard, A. (1995) *Hammer and Tongue: The Training of Technology Teachers (interim report of the preliminary findings of the first year of a comparative study of school-administered and higher education-administered secondary PGCE initial teacher education)*, London, Association of Teachers and Lecturers.

Evans, L., Packwood, A., Neill, S. and Campbell, R.J. (1994), *The Meaning of Infant Teachers' Work*, London, Routledge.

Farrugia, C. (1986) Career-choice and sources of occupational satisfaction and frustration among teachers in Malta, *Comparative Education*, Vol. 22, no. 3, pp. 221–31.

Freeman, A. (1986) Management implications of teacher stress and coping, *Educational Change and Development*, Vol. 7, no. 7, pp. 10–12.

Fullan, M. and Hargreaves, A. (eds) (1992) *Teacher Development and Educational Change*, London, Falmer Press.

Galloway, D., Boswell, K., Panckhurst, F., Boswell, C. and Green, K. (1985) Sources of satisfaction and dissatisfaction for New Zealand primary school teachers, *Educational Research*, Vol. 27, no. 1, pp. 44–92.

Garner, R. (1985) Slump in morale affecting both staff and pupils, *The Times Educational Supplement*, 29 March, p. 10.

Gold, K. (1990) True confessions, *The Times Educational Supplement*, 4 May, p. C2.

Goodson, I.F. (1991), Sponsoring the teacher's voice: teachers' lives and teacher development, *Cambridge Journal of Education*, Vol. 21, no. 1, pp. 35–45.

Grant, C.A. and Zeichner, K.M. (1984) On becoming a reflective teacher, in Grant, C.A. and Zeichner, K.M. (eds) *Preparing for Reflective Teaching*, Allyn & Bacon.

Guba, E.G. (1958), Morale and satisfaction: a study in past-future time perspective, *Administrative Science Quarterly*, Vol. 3, pp. 195–209.

Guion, R.M. (1958) Industrial morale: the problem of terminology, *Personnel Psychology*, Vol. 11, no. 1, pp. 59–64.

Haigh, G. (1991) Flattening out the hierarchy, *The Times Educational Supplement*, 25 January, p. 15

Halpin, D., Croll, P. and Redman, K. (1990) Teachers' perceptions of the effects of in-service education, *British Educational Research Journal*, Vol. 16, no. 2, pp. 163–77.

Hargreaves, D.H. (1980) The occupational culture of teachers, in Woods, P. (ed) *Teacher Strategies: Explorations in the Sociology of the School*, London, Croom Helm.

Hargreaves, D.H. (1994) The new professionalism: the synthesis of professional and institutional development, *Teaching and Teacher Education*, Vol. 10, no. 4, pp. 423–38.

Hayes, D. (1996) Taking nothing for granted, *Educational Management and Administration*, Vol. 24, no. 3, pp. 291–300.

Hayes, L.F. and Ross, D.D. (1989) Trust versus control: the impact of school leadership on teacher reflection, *Qualitative Studies in Education*, Vol. 2, no. 4, pp. 335–50.

Herzberg, F. (1968) *Work and the Nature of Man*, London, Staples Press.

Hofkins, D. (1990) More staff exit early, *The Times Educational Supplement*, 16 November, p. 3.

Howard, J. and Bradley, H. (1991) *Patterns of Employment and Development of Teachers after INSET Courses*, Cambridge, Cambridge Institute of Education.

Hoyle, E. (1975), Professionality, professionalism and control in teaching, in Houghton, V. *et al.* (eds) *Management in Education: The Management of Organisations and Individuals*, London, Ward Lock Educational in association with the Open University Press.

ILEA (1986) *The Junior School Project*, London, ILEA Research and Statistics Branch.

Johnson, S.M. (1986) Incentives for teachers: what motivates, what matters, *Educational Administration Quarterly*, Vol. 22, no. 3, pp. 54–79.

Kalleberg, A.L. (1977) Work values and job rewards: a theory of job satisfaction, *American Sociological Review*, Vol. 42, pp. 124–43.

Kasten, K.L. (1984) The efficacy of institutionally dispensed rewards in elementary school teaching, *Journal of Research and Development in Education*, Vol. 17, no. 4, pp. 1–13.

Katzell, R.A. (1964) Personal values, job satisfaction, and job behavior, in Borrow, H. (ed) *Man in a World at Work*, Boston, MA, Houghton Mifflin.

Lawler, E.E. (1973) *Motivation in Work Organizations*, Monterey, CA, Brooks/Cole.

Leithwood, K.A. (1992) The principal's role in teacher development, Fullan, M. and Hargreaves, A. (eds) *Teacher Development and Educational Change*, London, Falmer Press.

Little, J.W. and McLaughlin, M.W. (1993) Perspectives on cultures and contexts of teaching, in Little, J.W. and McLaughlin, M.W. (eds) *Teachers' Work: Individuals, Colleagues, and Contexts*, New York, Teachers College Press.

Locke, E. (1969). What is job satisfaction?, *Organizational Behavior and Human Performance*, Vol. 4, pp. 309–36.

Lortie, D.C. (1975) *Schoolteacher: A Sociological Study*, Chicago, IL, University of Chicago Press.

Lowther, M.A., Gill, S.J. and Coppard, L.C. (1985) Age and the determinants of teacher job satisfaction, *The Gerontologist*, Vol. 25, no. 5, pp. 520–5.

Maslow, A.H. (1954). *Motivation and Personality*. New York, Harper & Row.

Maslow, A.H. (1970) A theory of human motivation, in Vroom, V.H. and Deci, E.L. (eds) *Management and Motivation: Selected Readings*, Harmondsworth, Penguin, pp. 27–41.

Mathis, C. (1959) The relationship between salary policies and teacher morale, *Journal of Educational Psychology*, Vol. 50, no. 6, pp. 275–9.

Mayston, D. (1992) *School Performance Indicators and Performance-Related Pay*, London, The Assistant Masters and Mistresses Association.

McLaughlin, M.W., Pfeifer, R.S., Swanson-Owens, D. and Yee, S. (1986) Why teachers won't teach, *Phi Delta Kappan*, February, pp. 420–6.

Mowday, R.T. (1996) Equity theory predictions of behavior in organizations, in Steers, R.M., Porter, L.W. and Bigley, G.A. (eds) *Motivation and Leadership at Work*, New York, McGraw-Hill.

Mumford, E. (1972) *Job Satisfaction: A Study of Computer Specialists*, London, Longman.

Nias, J. (1980) Leadership styles and job satisfaction in primary schools, in Bush, T., Glatter, R., Goodey, J. and Riches, C. (eds) *Approaches to School Management*, London, Harper & Row.

Nias, J. (1981) Teacher satisfaction and dissatisfaction: Herzberg's 'two-factor' hypothesis revisited, *British Journal of Sociology of Education*, Vol. 2, no. 3, pp. 235–46.

Nias, J. (1984) The definition and maintenance of self in primary teaching, *British Journal of Sociology of Education*, Vol. 5, no. 2, pp. 267–80.

Nias, J. (1989) *Primary Teachers Talking: A Study of Teaching as Work*, London, Routledge.

Nias, J., Southworth, G. and Yeomans, R. (1989) *Staff Relationships in the Primary School: A Study of Organisational Cultures*, London, Cassell.

Osborn, M. and Broadfoot, P. (1992) A lesson in progress? Primary classrooms observed in England and France, *Oxford Review of Education*, Vol. 18, no. 1, pp. 3–15.

Pepworth, R. (1991) Felled at the start, *The Times Educational Supplement*, 16 November.

Pimenoff, S. (1995) Seeking the truth? *Guardian Education*, 11 April, p. 6.

Pollard, A. (1980) Teacher interests and changing situations of survival threat in primary classrooms, in Woods, P. (ed) *Teacher Strategies: Explorations in the Sociology of the School*, London, Croom Helm.

Pollard, A. (1982) A model of classroom coping strategies, *British Journal of Sociology of Education*, Vol. 3, no. 1, pp. 19–37.

Poppleton, P. (1988) Teacher professional satisfaction: its implications for secondary education and teacher education, *Cambridge Journal of Education*, Vol. 18, no. 1, pp. 5–16.

Pyke, N. (1993) Heads take experimental aim, *The Times Educational Supplement*, 24 September, p. 6.

Rafferty, F. and Dore, A. (1993) 'Concerned' heads heckle Patten, *The Times Educational Supplement*, 4 June, p. 4.

Redefer, F.L., (1959a) Factors that affect teacher morale, *The Nation's Schools*, Vol. 63, no. 2, pp. 59–62.

Redefer, F.L. (1959b) Toward a theory of educational administration, *School and Society*, 28 March, pp. 235–7.

Richardson, R.C. and Blocker, C.E. (1963) Note on the application of factor analysis to the study of faculty morale, *Journal of Educational Psychology*, Vol. 54, pp. 208–12.

Rosen, R.A.M. and Rosen, R.A.A. (1955) A suggested modification in job satisfaction surveys, *Personnel Psychology*, Vol. 8, no. 3, pp. 303–14.

Rosenholtz, S. (1989) Workplace conditions that affect teacher quality and commitment: implications for teacher induction programs, *The Elementary School Journal*, Vol. 89, no. 4, pp. 421–39.

Sachs, J. and Smith, R. (1988) Constructing teacher culture, *British Journal of Sociology of Education*, Vol. 9, no. 6, pp. 423–36.

Schaffer, R.H. (1953) Job satisfaction as related to need satisfaction in work, *Psychological Monographs: General and Applied*, Vol. 67, no. 14, pp. 1–29.

Sergiovanni, T.J. (1968) New evidence on teacher morale: a proposal for staff differentiation, *North Central Association Quarterly*, Vol. 42, pp. 259–66.

Shreeve, W., Goetter, W.G.J., Norby, J.R., Griffith, G.R., Stueckle, A.F., de Michele, B. and Midgley, T.K. (1986) Job satisfaction: the role of staff recognition, *Early Child Development and Care*, Vol. 24, pp. 83–90.

Sikes, P. (1997) *Parents Who Teach*, London, Cassell.

Smith, K.R. (1966) A proposed model for the investigation of teacher morale, *Journal of Educational Administration*, Vol. 4, no. 2, pp. 143–8.

Smith, K.R., (1976) Morale: a refinement of Stogdill's model, *Journal of Educational Administration*, Vol. 14, no. 1, pp. 87–93.

Smith, K.R. (*c.* 1988) The structure of morale in organisations, unpublished transcript provided by the author.

Smith, L.M., (1978) An evolving pattern of logic of participant observation, educational ethnography and other case studies, in Shulman, L. (ed) *Review of Research in Education*.

Southworth, G. (1994) School leadership and school development: reflections from research, in Southworth, G. (ed) *Readings in Primary School Development*, London, Falmer.

Spencer, D.A. (1984) The home and school lives of women teachers, *The Elementary School Journal*, Vol. 84, no. 3, pp. 283–98.

Stagner, R. (1958) Motivational aspects of industrial morale, *Personnel Psychology*, Vol. 11, no. 1, pp. 64–70.

Steers, R.M., Porter, L.W. and Bigley, G.A. (1996) *Motivation and Leadership at Work*, New York, McGraw-Hill.

Sutcliffe, J. (1997) Enter the feel-bad factor, *The Times Educational Supplement*, 10 January, p. 1.

Tomlinson, H. (1990) Performance rights?, *The Times Educational Supplement*, 9 November, p. 11.

Triggs, E. and Francis, H. (1990) *The Value to Education of Long (Award Bearing) Courses for Serving Teachers*, London, Institute of Education, London University.

Vancouver, J.B. and Schmitt, N.W. (1991) An exploratory examination of person–organisation fit: organizational goal congruence, *Personnel Psychology*, Vol. 44, no. 2, pp. 333–52.

Veal, M.L., Clift, R. and Holland, P. (1989) School contexts that encourage reflection: teacher perceptions, *Qualitative Studies in Education*, Vol. 2, no. 4, pp. 315–33.

Vroom, V.H. (1964) *Work and Motivation*, New York, Wiley.

Vulliamy, G. and Webb, R. (1991) Teacher research and educational change: an empirical study, *British Educational Research Journal*, Vol. 17, no. 3, pp. 219–36.

Wall, T.D. and Stephenson, G.M. (1970) Herzberg's two-factor theory of job attitudes: a critical evaluation and some fresh evidence, *Industrial Relations Journal*, Vol. 1, no. 3, pp. 41–65.

Wallace, M. and Huckman, L. (1996) Senior management teams in large primary schools: a headteacher's solution to the complexities of post-reform management?, *School Organisation*, Vol. 16, no. 3, pp. 309–23.

Webb, R. and Vulliamy, G. (1996) The changing role of the primary-school head-teacher, *Educational Management and Administration*, Vol. 24, no. 3, pp. 301–15.

Williams, G. (1986) *Improving School Morale*, Sheffield, Sheffield City Polytechnic and PAVIC Publications.

Williams, K.W. and Lane, T.J. (1975) Construct validation of a staff morale questionnaire, *Journal of Educational Administration*, Vol. 13, no. 2, pp. 90–7.

Wilson, B.L. and Corcoran, T.B. (1988) *Successful Secondary Schools*, Lewes, Falmer.

Wolcott, H. (1973) *The Man in the Principal's Office: An Ethnography*, New York, Holt, Rinehart & Winston.

Young, I.P. and Davis, B. (1983) The applicability of Herzberg's dual factor theory(ies) for public school superintendants, *Journal of Research and Development in Education*, Vol. 16, no. 4, pp. 59–66.

Zeichner, K. (1993) Designing educative practicum experiences for prospective teachers, a keynote address presented at the International Conference on Teachers' Education: 'Teacher Education Toward the 21st Century', Tel-Aviv, 27 June–1 July.

Index